THE SUNDAY TIMES
TRAVEL BOOK

Edited by
RICHARD GIRLING

A GRAHAM TARRANT BOOK

DAVID & CHARLES
Newton Abbot   London   North Pomfret (Vt)

British Library Cataloguing in Publication Data

The New Sunday times travel book.——(A
    Graham Tarrant book)
    1. Voyages and travels——1951–
    I. Girling, Richard
    910.4   G465

ISBN 0-7153-8942-4

Typeset by ABM Typographics Limited, Hull
and printed in Great Britain
by Redwood Burn Ltd, Trowbridge, Wilts
for David & Charles (Publishers) plc
Brunel House   Newton Abbot   Devon

Published in the United States of America
by David & Charles Inc
North Pomfret   Vermont 05053   USA

CONTENTS

EDITOR'S NOTE

This was not an easy book to edit: there were more than 3,000 candidates for inclusion – all entries to the 1985/86 *Sunday Times* Travel Writing Competition – and space to include only fifty. Inevitably, many excellent writers failed to find a place – often for reasons of duplication rather than lack of individual merit. Simply to publish the fifty best entries would have meant overloading the collection with tales of Africa, India and the Greek Islands. On the positive side, the book has once again allowed me to console one or two talented but negligent entrants whose work had to be excluded from the competition proper because of their failure to observe the rules – most often by exceeding the maximum permitted length.

Thanks are due not only to the writers whose work appears here, but to all those who, simply by entering, ensured the competition's success. Particular thanks are due to *The Sunday Times's* co-sponsors, Speedbird Holidays, and to the judging panel, Tom Sharpe, Dame Naomi James and Jonathan Raban.

The three principal prizewinners were Stephen Lawson, for *Aboard the Trans-Siberian Express;* Janie Hampton for *River Journey up the Zaire;* and Niema Ash for *Sky Burial.* All the photographs in the book are the work of the writers themselves.

Richard Girling
The Sunday Times, London

DAVID GREEN

The Gulf of Finland on Ice

Perhaps they're penguins, I thought. But they were too far away for me to be certain, and the blinding light could have been playing tricks on the two of us. It doesn't help your orientation one bit when the land is indistinguishable from the sky, nor indeed when you're not quite sure whether you've left the land yet. Very soon we would not be able to see the line of tall evergreens that parted beach from cloud.

Our penguins remained elusively in the distance, though motionless. Underfoot the ice creaked and groaned dubiously: we were over the sea. An earlier wind had whipped up the surface snow into rivulets like tiny mountain ranges, and whirled spirals like ice cream from a machine. Beneath this the layer of ice was almost perfectly smooth, though occasionally an unseen force had pushed its plates together and upwards forming huge mountains amongst the hills and valleys. Every detail was spectacular, yet the whole formed a nothingness of intense light and cold (about twenty degrees below zero). We could only lock our vision onto those distant penguins and attempt to get that far.

In places the ice seemed to be frighteningly thin, and our boots turned it mushy as seeping salt water formed lakes in the snow-vales. The air, heavy with silent, still flakes, closed in behind us making our isolation almost absolute. The quietness seemed somehow to be incredibly loud, perhaps because wherever else I have been I could at the very least, listening hard, pick out some distant sounds of life, or even the wind in the trees. But here we were truly in a void; our footsteps had a booming, dull thud to them, and standing still with breath held left our ears desperately searching for something, anything, to catch hold of.

My senses were confused by this new experience, having previously associated sightseeing with sights to see, not to mention hear and smell. To keep my mind in check I decided to remember the journey here (a cavernous train with wooden seats) or the flight to Riga (alarmingly, the roof leaked), but I couldn't help falling into the mental free-form that this placed allowed. Here was somewhere in a meditative limbo between earthly chaos and spiritual ecstasy; we could have been on the crystal lake of the Apocalypse, half-way to paradise. . . If only it wasn't for the cold that nagged at us constantly. My feet had ceased diplomatic relations with the rest of me.

Our penguins held fishing rods and wore hats and coats of thick fur: they were humans – nay, Russians. I expect we were about three miles out to sea by now, though I could not smell any salt, hear any gulls or see any boats. The over-swaddled Russians had built curved walls of ice around themselves and drilled small holes through to the sea, over which they crouched with their fishing tackle, perfectly still. Some of them had faces: red-raw and wrinkled, with tiny eyes and pursed lips. Their breath hung about them indecisively. They looked – and there's no getting away from this – infinitely bored.

One of them gesticulated to us and, using harsh, staccato Russian (which neither of us understood) and rather violent stabs into the air, made it very clear that we had taken a dangerous route over the ice and that we were very stupid indeed. We noticed now a trail of well-trodden snow winding back towards the shore, obviously a route known to be safe by the experienced locals. We smiled feebly and re-frained from attempting any further communication with these intro-spective folk. They eyed us with vague curiosity and then returned to their (apparently fruitless) fishing. My friend and I settled ourselves onto the snow and uncorked a well-chilled bottle of wine in the hope of getting merry.

In a most oblique way this place was very exciting; the searing blanket whiteness was stunning and the sheer starkness ultimately beautiful. But it was not merry. We had to get up and gingerly stamp around to recirculate the blood. For an hour or two we trudged about trying to find something more (or something at all) to see, and even photograph. Finally, frozen stiff, we made our way back along the relative safety of the fisherman's path, with a cursory wave back to the huddled forms.

Ahead of us the tall pines that stretch out across the frozen plain of Estonia distinguished themselves from the snow-coated sky and earth. It seemed that the all-pervading light was weakening: it must have been late afternoon. This presented a thought that made me shudder with fright: this awesome, eerie world-apart in the dead of night, unbearably cold, no moon or stars, merely the moan of the mysterious gods beneath the ice . . . We hurried on.

What spirits lurked within the murkiness of the intertwined creepers of the forest? Such a dense blackness, and unreal noises . . . Oh, it wasn't like this at all, I'm sure, yet the shape silhouetted in the snow where the ice met the beach turned into our worst fears.

He was dead, there's no doubt about that. He was lying, clothed, on his back, legs apart, elbows resting in the snow with his arms inexplicably pointing straight upwards ending with contorted, blue fingers, like a pair of old, gnarled trees.

My heart gave me an unforgettable jolt when I thought him to be headless; yet there was no blood staining the fresh, even snow. Perhaps it was tucked under his collar. We were speechless, but we morbidly crept towards him when a sudden snap from the forest warned that someone was approaching and we ran along the beach then through the trees, hearts pounding, and gasping for breath. Never has fear gripped me so tightly, yet it was exhilarating, fantastic even. There was a schoolboy excitement about it, but weighed down by the heavy, weird atmosphere of the frozen Gulf. During the terrible siege of Leningrad in the last war supplies were eventually conveyed to the starving thousands on carts from Finland across the Baltic Sea and the Gulf of Finland (it was fortunately an exceptionally cold winter) – what must have been a fearsome journey. Now history is swathed in an inscrutable silence.

At the comparative safety of a deserted road we collected ourselves a little and then headed for the station, trying hard to chuckle about it all, though obviously we had both been deeply affected.

The final straw, as it were, came when we were back home: none of the photographs we had taken on that day came out.

R. T. DALY

ALL QUIET ON THE WESTERN FRONT

A hot June in the fields of northern France; and there is action all along the Western Front.

At Vimy Ridge, near Arras, the Canadian front line trenches are closed to visitors whilst workmen repair the concrete "sandbags"; and where the vast white monument thrusts two fingers out of the bald hilltop stonemasons chip painstakingly at the great walls, working to reinstate the names of the dead, crumbling through French frost or gales. A pretty student from Toronto takes us on a tour of the underground passages where troops came up to the line. We see the mess, hospital, kitchens, the endless dull tunnels, all hacked roughly from the chunky rock. Our girl guide shows us where an unexploded shell sticks out of a tunnel wall; and the main passage carries a groove created by the groping doomed fingers of troops advancing in the echoing darkness. It's chilly down there, but in the warm sunshine above tourists picnic in the vast grassy craters of No Man's Land. The tang of fir is on the warm air, the Canadian flag stirs. We buy an ice cream.

On the Somme, we ignore the English posters advertising tours of the battlefields; under a glaring sun we drive through villages provincial and obscure in all but their names to park at Crucifix Corner, and find our way up thick tangled tracks through cornfield and poppies to High Wood. Heat plasters the land and a lawnmower drones from the cemetery. Behind its modern barbed wire the wood is breathlessly quiet. The rides are soft, bare earth, rotovators having cleared away the sprawling brambles for the convenience of local huntsmen. Beyond the rides, shell holes are choked with undergrowth; the largest mine crater is a stagnant green pond. This ridiculous scruffy little thicket was the front line for two months, and eight thousand men died here. Here, in this unexceptional little wood. Is it possible?

Yet everywhere the woods are in the image of their ancestors, destroyed by the shellfire of seventy years ago; and new villages have sprung up on the sites of those obliterated by war. Only the graves are new, little corners of foreign fields.

At Delville Wood we eat cherry tarts sitting on the cemetery wall, and look across to where a crane towers incongruously above the trees. Here, in 1985, the South Africans are building a museum to commemorate their involvement in the Great War: a monument to idealism or to cynicism, we wonder?

The heat enervates: wandering amongst the graves seems suffocating, giddy work. Amongst the panoply of names and regiments, nothing sticks except the graves with no name: "A British Soldier of the Great War. Known unto God." I stare at this, trying to focus, trying to understand. Red roses sag wearily against the headstone.

Evening on the Chemin des Dames, that great Hog's Back ridge above the Aisne, scene of murderous futile French attacks in 1917, and of the last German breakthrough in 1918. This being France, a sign promising a war memorial and explanation of *La Bataille* leads to a monument to an obscure campaign of Napoleon in 1814. Malmaison is an enormous field of iron crosses under beautiful, noble oaks. The evening sunlight lies like a blessing on the manicured grass. Here another 40,000 dead men lay, victims of 1940. So all the pathetic, countless graves of only twenty years before were ignored; they were for nothing. How could it have come to this again?

A fine, free drive along the ridge, bound for Reims. On the way we pass a detachment of French soldiers camping at the edge of a wood. One levels his rifle, aims at us – and grins. We smile a little wanly. In Reims they sell picture postcards of the cathedral with flames billowing from its roof during the German bombardment of 1914. We eat cheaply, under the resentful eye of an Alsatian dog, which appears to feel we've appropriated its dinner. We agree, and give it some back: the dog seems pleased.

Verdun, July 10. We can wonder at, but not understand, the suffering of our grandparents' generation; the brutality and the pity of war.

We tour the town citadel with a party of Germans, who listen impassively to the martial music, and tales of French heroism. In the town, little sweetshops sell chocolate shells, and the Meuse lies flat and impassive. In the hills above are no rebuilt villages, only little roads through the forest, carrying coaches to the memorials and museums.

We visit the ossuary at Douaumont, where the bones of 130,000 unknown soldiers lie: everywhere the endless numbers. The place seems garish, the tragedy unmanageable. From the stark tower, the vast panorama is a sombre crumpled shroud of trees under a bruised sky; a view with no joy.

There is the fort, too: chill, damp, extensive. Always there are these cold places of war, where no sun shines. Forests of pencil-thin stalactites hang from the roofs of the deserted casemates, and in all the maze of passages, barracks, command posts, washrooms and ammunition stores there is only the steady drip of water, or perhaps the reverberant echo of a slammed door. The shells which fell on Douaumont like wild, random beats on a drum never quite burst through, leaving nothing but a fear on the air. Douaumont is one of the world's terrible places.

On the left bank of the Meuse there rises a ridge topped by the twin heights of Cote 304 and the Mort Homme. Under their forests, these hills lie quiet; a deserted little road leads to the top of the grimly-named Mort Homme, where a lonely crumbling memorial converts Nivelle's defiant battle-cry into the past tense with more resignation than triumph: *"Ils n'ont pas passé"*. The forest is quiet; we are alone.

Dull ranks of fir trees surround another memorial on the summit of Cote 304. The afternoon wears on, petrol is low; it is our last stop. We wander over the bare ground, below the gloomy trees, and gradually, from amongst the shell holes, there materialises a shallow ditch, deepening as it winds downhill amongst the gaunt pines. This twisted iron on the parapet is a barbed wire support; and here some rusty wire juts from the earth.

We ponder the find of a strange hollow cylinder, brown and crumbling with rust – is it a tin mug? As we debate, the trench leads to a concrete dug-out with half its roof smashed in. We become enthralled, amazed, and cross to another, deeper, trench. The flotsam of battle is everywhere now: an entrenching tool, the rotting remains of a boot. The old tin "mugs" are everywhere – they were stick bombs. Unexploded shells lie casually around, some tiny like toys, others the size of a man's torso. There are jagged lumps of shrapnel the size of dinner plates, heavy and cold. Here is a water bottle, a rarer and prized find. Mounting excitement: here are clips of bullets!

The late afternoon light is failing in the forest, and a little clearing attracts us. Here is a terrible, disturbing, pathetic scene: a jumbled collection of unmistakably human bones. Some are hollow like pipes, or end in the club of a joint. Two shells stand by, as though on guard, and someone has bound two sticks into a cross with string. German or French – no-one will ever know now, they are simply savage relics of a savage war.

We turn away; we are very quiet. Let the months and years come, we will not forget. Here lies our grandparents' generation: with pity and with some understanding we will remember them.

RUTH ANDERS

THE PHARAOH'S CURSE

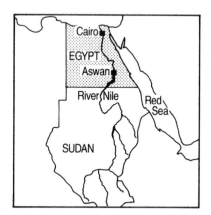

MONDAY

The blastfurnace heat at Aswan jumps off the tarmac and hits us like a blow as I lead my group towards the terminal building. "Keeping the rest to clean your teeth?" nudges Doctor Whistler, pointing to my depleted bottle of mineral water.

"Aha, that's right!" I smile, through gritted teeth. My head's pounding like a sledgehammer, and my stomach feels frail. I touch my pocket for the reassuring packet of Diocalm. Tour Directors aren't allowed the luxury of being ill. Away from Cairo HQ I'm in sole charge of ninety physicians and their wives on a pre-congress beano – four days of cruising the Nile and doing the sites.

A trio of rickety buses takes us to our floating hotel, the *Hatshepsut.* Once settled in gracious colonial-style comfort, I relax a little. The air of excited anticipation builds as doctors dive into their Welcome glasses of Ribena-like Karkade and their Baedekers with equal enthusiasm, like kids out of school.

At sunset our dining-room view of the shadowy river is spellbinding. Less prepossessing are the three bluebottles on the table decoration poised to divebomb my fried chicken.

Doctor Rawlings from Bradford, having warned me long and loud on the flight about the perils of raw food, cold food and ice, passes beaming, with a mountainous plate from the buffet. "Iris is having terrible trouble remembering the name of this ship!"

"Tell her to try thinking of a hat and a cheap suit!" I suggest, pleased with my ingenuity, and blissfully ignorant of how much I shall shortly be needing it.

During the night I wake to dash the two yards from bunk to bathroom. Taking one of every sort of pill I've brought with me, I convince myself I'm just overtired.

TUESDAY

Trouble strikes.

I'm sneaking a moment on deck before breakfast, feeling limp and watching a heron gliding around like a poker with a crick in its neck, when there's a Northcountry whisper behind me.

"Iris is very poorly this morning. I'm afraid she won't manage the temple."

Why does my heart sink? After all, one case of the trots hardly spells disaster. But I have this nagging suspicion that my luck as a first-timer tour group leader cannot hold. Sure enough, there is only forty per cent attendance at breakfast. One after another physician approaches my table conspiratorially, to complain of feeling unwell, or tell hair-raising tales of a companion's sleepless night. As the boat's engines thrum into startling life, mild apprehension gives way to serious foreboding. Doctor McRae bounces up like Tigger, smiling fit to bust. "Well, at least if we're catching Egyptian bugs, we can all treat each other!"

Quite.

Aswan town front, reminiscent of Worthing in terms of Thirties-style decay, slides slowly from view behind us. An hour later we tie up, and a small party departs stoically up the bank for Kom Ombo temple.

I remain nervously aboard, to hear doctors exchanging advice on every deck: Doctor McRae recommends a diet of rice and yoghurt. (He has been addressing the problem rather more seriously since his wife succumbed after breakfast on her way down the gangplank.) Doctor Turner swears by a universal prophylactic of gin and guava juice, offering me a swig from his thermos. Imodium changes hands like cocaine on Eighth Avenue.

Reeling somewhat from the gin concoction, and making for the captain's office, I console myself with the thought that if I need any-thing from an apendectomy to open heart surgery, there is no shortage of equipment or expertise to hand.

But Something must be Done, and I collar our captain, who is not in his office but enjoying a cigar on the pool deck with the purser. A pre-viously helpful fellow, he seems reluctant to discuss the matter, dis-missing the whole thing with a wave of his bejewelled hand as just the usual English gippy tummy. Neither his English nor my Arabic is good enough to argue, and anyway, perhaps I'm over-dramatising. Later, sitting weakly on a disquietingly depopulated sun deck as we drift downriver towards Edfu, I put the worries of tropical viruses aside and watch the river banks roll lazily by, parallel fringes of lush greenery backed abruptly by the yellow hills of the desert.

Donkeys graze by fields of breezy sugar cane, and minarets rise phoenix-like from seas of palm trees, their fronds swaying together like a corps-de-ballet. The river, serene and still for long dreamy stretches, bursts with occasional scenes of activity where bunches of noisy children play in the shallows alongside gleaming water buffalo, or groups of chattering women pound the weekly wash. A pair of feluccas drifts across our bows like lovebirds, their sails throwing long shadows across the tranquil water. Mesmerised by this biblical travelogue, and deliciously warmed by the late afternoon sun, I wonder if my lightheadedness is caused by the euphoric sensation of time-travelling or by imminent physical collapse.

Dinner is an even more depleted affair than breakfast.

WEDNESDAY

Kom Ombo and Edfu, like the fitness of my charges, have been and gone, and now at Esna a few determined explorers rattle by horse-drawn carriage towards the town centre at 6am. Esna, a series of dusty streets and alleys, is still asleep, apart from the odd scavenging tat-eared dog.

The temple sits some fifty feet down in its own huge sandpit, buried for centuries until someone tripped over what turned out to be the top of a pillar. High above, in abrupt contrast, sit the comparatively recent buildings of the town, their roofs and turrets catching the early morning sun.

Back on board, the senior consultants, having had a council of war, open up with a full frontal attack of heavy verbal artillery, ending with a chilling final volley:

"Most of us will be taking samples home for analysis."

And sending each other massive consultancy bills, I think to myself, while my well practised straight face almost lets me down with both this thought and that of the possible scenario in the Heathrow customs hall.

I assure the grim-faced surgeons in front of me that representations will be made to the shipping line on our return to Cairo, and that, meanwhile, the captain and I will, after appropriate consultation, revamp the menus.

"Revamp to rice and yoghurt!" trills Doctor McRae, *en passant*. "I'm still fine!"

I give him what I hope is a suitably withering look. Late that afternoon Plague Ship *Hatshepsut* reaches her final mooring in ancient Thebes, and there is a chorus of clicking camera shutters as we pass the unexpected splendour of a silhouetted Luxor temple.

Doctor Turner takes me aside to acquaint me in funereal tones with the details of a colleague's latest symptoms. I wish he hadn't.

THURSDAY

The decks are a little more lively, with the genuinely and partially re-covered sitting about in little groups, eyeing me accusingly whenever I pass. (I'm sure the Ancient Mariner had an easier time.) At least the numbers on the shore excursions are slowly swelling, although the collective preoccupation is not so much with details of what site we are about to visit, but how many "comfort stops" there will be.

Magnificent Karnak, with its corridors of stone rams, sky-embracing pillars and gigantic inscrutable statues, stretching apparently as far as the eye can see, is breathtaking. Ozymandias, whose famous admonishment has been haunting me from Day One, seems to lurk round every corner, laughing up his sleeve.

The captain, possibly in an effort to make some amends for our problems, offered today's trippers airline paper bags, just in case. Several who declined this gesture now regret it, and I'm thankful for the sandy ground which provides the perfect means literally to kick over the traces.

Back on board, the hoped-for but unexpected sight of a *deus-ex-machina* in the form of our travel agency chief is immensely reassuring. Gratefully, I enlist his help; he confers with the various spokesmen with charm, patience and a magic defusing device called being The Boss.

Relieved, I turn my exhausted attention to the details of tomorrow's expedition to the Valley of the Kings, and our return flight to Cairo.

FRIDAY
Finally back at base, it's amazing what a five-star hotel can do to revive the spirits.

The difficulties of the cruise are all but forgotten by most. "We've had a marvellous time," they beam, "really marvellous." Before I retire to bed, one small item appears for the stop press. Doctor McRae, the only one to have survived the cruise unscathed, has tripped on a kerbstone and broken his foot.

The gigantic carved pillars of the great temple of Karnak. (*The Pharaoh's Curse*)

Taking on coal and water at night at Ulan Udeh. Drawing by Sarah Wimperis, wife of the author. (*Aboard the Trans-Siberian Express*)

STEPHEN LAWSON

ABOARD THE TRANS-SIBERIAN EXPRESS

She started sobbing three hours before the border. The conductress tried to console her with a glass of sweet, strong tea but without much success. She remained in the long druggeted corridor, a crumpled figure in a pink dressing gown watching the forests spinning madly by. The tankard holding the glass depicted a Slavic swordsman defending a child and she held it tight as a keepsake.

It certainly was a crying matter. The birch forests of Siberia, so upright, so elegant in autumn, had been broken by this winter campaign. Brought into perfect arcs by wind and snow, the younger birches littered the track-side like ribs and tusks while the old and brittle, unable to bow before the onslaught, rose into the air like splintered spines. Even the express was beginning to show signs of vulnerability to the elements. The sinks and toilets were blocked with ice and the narrow cubicles connecting the carriages were thick with snow, their door handles stinging. Each cubicle was a treacherous no man's land, now braved by only a few passengers seeking out the dozing heat of the restaurant car which, nearing the end of its journey, had little to offer. She was, of course, crying for none of these reasons.

Her daughter loved the stations. She was usually dressed and waiting half-an-hour before the express pulled in. Arm-in-arm with the day-conductress, she would walk the length of the train, watching the ice being tapped off the water inlets and the track-hoppers getting a warning from the new MCK engine elbowing its way backwards. When the conductress and the girl turned and began their precarious stiff-armed run along the platform back to the wrought-iron steps of carriage No 3, it was the signal for a dozen others to do likewise. Feet were wiped, the steps were brought in, the samovar was stoked and nostrils which had stuck together like prickly gauze snuffled back to life.

At one station they had cut short their promenade and dived back to get a thermometer. A huddle of passengers gathered round the steps of the carriage to get a look at the reading and, lest their breathing distort the figure, Nadia held it aloft like a fish between finger and thumb. Thirty below. Several minutes before the express was due to pull out, the platform was empty. The station master was in retreat and only the ever-watchful V.I. Lenin peered down the track in the direction of the heroes who had to work on. They stood up from their points-cleaning to watch the express pass when, to the delight of her comrades, one of them bellowed "Mishka!" to the train driver through a rolled-up magazine. A brief and warming thigh-slapping routine ensued before headscarves bound tight as bandages were again bowed before the task in hand.

It was around Lake Baikal that the woman in pink had been able to share in her daughter's delight with the journey. She explained to us that she had spent her childhood in a village near Irkutsk. She pointed beyond a wooden pier to the place where she used to sit on a crate beside her father as he fished through the ice. At the age of ten, her talents had taken her away to Moscow where she had studied, married and made her home. As we watched the train's shadows turn and fold on the snowy shore, it became clear that she had not forgotten the stories which made this much more than a stark inland sea stretching as far as the eye can follow. Once, before she was born, her father had found a curious bloated and boggle-eyed fish on the shore. He had made a meticulous drawing of his find and had insisted that she take his handiwork with her to Moscow where it adorned, in turn, dormitory, flat and office. She was now taking it to Peking. She could imagine what was going on in the lugubrious depths of Baikal. These strange survivals from pre-history the *golomianka,* were no doubt nosing around the wreck of Old Prince Khilkov's locomotive which had plunged through the ice eighty years ago.

"Don't worry," she reassured us. "That was in the days when they were laying tracks on the ice; in the days, too, when you could get married out there." She swept her hand towards the endless expanse of ice and water. "And on a boat made in England." Her face became as bright as an icon as if she had momentarily glimpsed the old customs of Irkutsk: a bridal party bearing skates of bone and bodices of the finest needle-point standing on the southern shore and looking across Baikal; a sallow-faced groom from Chita smoothing his first moustache and pacing the deck of an ice-locked paddle-steamer.

By the time the express clattered into Zabajjkal'sk, on the Russian side of the border, the attentions of the conductress coupled with her own resolve had prepared the woman for the formalities. All that remained was paperwork and a passage to Peking. She had taken her last look at this obscure outpost of the Soviet Union and now stood with her back to the low sun.

"We will be here for some time. The wheels need to be changed for China and the officials . . ." – she indicated a rank of grey-coated youths further up the platform – "they will expect you to stand in the corridor while they search your room. So please," she started off towards her own compartment, "no reds under the bed."

It is indeed the room which interests them – the room, the space, into which a Trans-Siberian stowaway may be fitted. There is room for a couple: one here behind the luggage (hunched like a cosmonaut hurtling into the unknown) and another there beneath the bottom bunk (blankets burying a crouched figure waiting for rebirth). All the lights are up and cold air has come in with the officials. Young men with pale, waxy skins, they are straight out of some Moscow academy. Old hands wear leather gloves, old heads wear fur hats, as if they are badges of office: we hunt, we trap, we tame. These are reluctant hunters, ill at ease and inexperienced, wary lest a nervous glance could give flesh to fear – the fear of coming face to face with a cowering countryman, the fear of finding the loaded chamber in a game of Russian roulette. In this compartment, in this carriage, on this train, it does not happen and they move on to check the papers of the woman and her daughter.

Even as the guards are ushering them into the corridor, the carriage rolls into an immense echoing workshop. A tankard on the compartment table sits as a reminder of the glories of Soviet technology – sputniks and rockets spin out of a world inhabited by the Spassky Tower and an olive branch – and, as if to demonstrate that the mundane is as attainable as the sublime, not a spoon rattles, not a single drop of sweet Georgian tea is spilt, as the carriage is smoothly elevated and the task of fitting a Chinese-gauge undercarriage is taken in hand. The mechanics wink and whistle and smoke aromatic cigars. They look as though they should be on horseback flying towards the sun. Now they swing beneath the iron horse, a race apart from the officials pacing the corridor. Ruddy mortals, crouching and crawling around the undercarriage, they can look up for inspiration to the immaculate lives portrayed high on the walls of the workshop, to those models of determination and robust heroism familiar to all Soviet citizens: Riveters and Liberators, Welders and Flag-bearers, beaming Foundrywomen with goggles thrown back on their brows like aviators from the Great Patriotic War.

"We all have to do something for the good of our country." She had returned to the window and was watching me photograph the posters. "I will be spending three years in Peking, at our Embassy, so perhaps we will meet again when you collect your return visa."

One month later I did visit the Embassy, a little Russia behind a wrought-iron gate and walls once used to confine Cossack prisoners. There, in a small panelled office, was the drawing of a queer fish waiting like a fabulous train with headlamps ablaze in a Siberian night.

DAVID SHANAHAN

DOLMENS AND BLARNEY

It was a bright, clear spring morning when the boat docked in Rosslare and I disembarked in Eire.

Finding the roads almost traffic free, I decided to push on as quickly as possible towards the harsh and romantic west coast.

I was making good time when my eye was caught by a small, wooden sign, on which was written, "Harristown Dolmen". I pulled up opposite, wound down the window and stared. At this point I might as well confess to being what is called in the trade a "megalithomaniac". Any stone, no matter how small, if it has the tag "megalithic", then I'm hooked.

The sign pointed down a small lane running off the main road. Had I got time? It was still early, so why not?

Turning into the lane, I was overwhelmed by a feeling of plunging underwater. Dense masses of vivid green vegetation swayed and lapped in slow motion. The shifting surfaces scattered and diffused the light, so that it fell down, dappling the already dappled cattle browsing under the trees like schools of fish. The road became narrower and ran ahead of me like a twisting silver elver. I saw no signs and had gone a few miles before I saw my first human being.

A tall, thin man stood staring at a stone wall, as if waiting for an answer to a question he had put to it. I wound down the window and asked him if he knew where the dolmen was.

"The dolmen? Sure, of course I know where the dolmen is. Isn't it just over dere, behind dem hills?"

He gave me an armful of left and rights, and off I went.

Half an hour later I stopped the car, got out, sat down on a bank in an empty green world and admitted to myself that I was lost. After a while, the feeling that I was completely alone in the world became less frightening. I sat watching with passive pleasure an unending variety of greens weave and dance in the breeze. Above the shuddering tree-tops, swallows darted like pond skaters across a thin, blue film of sky.

The approach of an old woman disturbed my nature watch. As she came level, I got to my feet and said hello.

She gave me a great, gummy grin which almost split her face in two. She was small with coarse, wire-wool hair and bright bird's eyes that missed nothing. Her hands, resting on the pram she was pushing, were those of a giant. The pram was full of what appeared to be nettles. In the middle of these, nestling like an egg, was a bottle of milk.

Nervously, I asked her if she knew of Barney's Dolmen. As I heard the words I knew they were wrong, but couldn't for the life of me remember the dolmen's proper name.

She gave me another cavernous smile and said: "Barry's Dolmen? Sure, of course I know it. Follow me an' I'll lead yeh right to it."

The thought of creeping along in a car behind an old woman pushing a pram full of nettles didn't appeal so, mentioning a pressing engagement, I got a garbled set of directions and bade her good day.

I must have passed in and out of several counties that morning, looking for that dolmen. People cheerfully pointed me in the direction of Barry's, Harry's, Carry's and, in one case, even the Black Dolmen. Sometimes, if they didn't know the one I was after, they sent me off in search of one or two they had of their own.

So, when at last I came to a small village with a large church, I decided that perhaps the priest might be the best person to tell me where these prehistoric pagans buried their dead. A woman arranging flowers around an anaemic statue told me that Father Burne was, "even now, in the sacristy".

I passed an old man cutting back the undergrowth with a rusty scythe. He said hello, so I thought I'd give him a try first. He was the first person I'd met that day who didn't know what a dolmen was. When in the course of my explanation I mentioned the word pagan, he jerked as if he were on the end of a wire.

Looking nervously over his shoulder in case the priest should hear, he scratched his head and rolled his eyes, all the time muttering that terrible word. Then suddenly he clicked his fingers and spat the word out.

"Pagans! Dere's an old Protestant graveyard, overgrown now, you understand, up dere, by de old crossroads, as used to be dere."

I waited patiently while he told me forty different ways to get there. Then, thanking him, I beat a hasty retreat to the sacristy door and knocked.

The door was opened by a tall, bulky man in his late sixties. His stern, bloated red face overflowed the shining white barricade of his dog collar. Profuse amounts of grey and ginger hair sprouted from nose and ears. Above his eyes a thick, prickly hedgerow jutted at right-angles to the bone. He listened with a terrible look of disdain on his face. Then he thundered:

"What in God's name do ye wantta be looking at tings like that for? Are ye a Catholic?"

I shifted uncomfortably and confessed that I was.

"A lapsed one, I suppose." He sniffed, and oceans of hair swayed in his nose. Ignoring my mumbled apologies, he turned and conversed with a shadowy figure which had spread like a silent stain over the carpet as we talked.

The shadow appeared to have an extensive knowledge of dolmens and their whereabouts. It passed this information on in a terrible hushed whine that seemed to creep in and fill the head.

The priest relayed the directions, spitting out the words as if they were poison. I thanked him and his shadow, and hurried back to the car. The shadow's information proved to be correct; fifteen minutes later, I found my dolmen.

It stood in the corner of a small field, larger and more impressive than any I'd yet seen. The great, grey stones seemed to be heaving themselves up out of the earth like pieces of ancient bone, to squat in the alien flesh of the present.

These majestic stones, flecked with orange and white lichen, are the last of thousands that once littered the prehistoric landscape. Most have long disappeared; many of those left have been pressed into service as gateposts on farms, or blacken slowly as lintels over fireplaces.

Late bluebells grew in profusion on the tumbled remains of the great mound. In a stream nearby, two stones from the cairn circles still stood upright. Over a hedge I could see a large stone sitting in the middle of the field, basking in the sun like a great toad.

I took some photographs; then, tired and happy, lay on the mound and watched some large, white clouds with grey bellies drift like giant manta rays through the swirling air. High above them, thin wispy cloud lay like plankton on the endless surface of the sky. The search had taken it out of me and I must have dozed off. I was woken by voices and saw two elderly ladies seated at a nearby bench, which had almost disappeared in the undergrowth. Feeling curious, I went over to say hello.

They were an odd couple; dressed in old-fashioned summer frocks, blue with white spots, their hair cut level with their chins, pudding-bowl style. Odd hairs straggled out of various warts, and the brown freckles of age gave them a strange resemblance to the stones.

"We're sisters and spinsters," they told me with a laugh; but, more importantly, members of The Waterford and District Friends of Ancient Monuments Society. This august body had been responsible for placing the bench we were now sitting on. It was there in order that people might have a picnic by a monument, on just such a day as this.

We talked of dolmens and stone circles. They shared their tea and sandwiches with me as the day slid away behind us. They laughed like a couple of schoolgirls, hands fluttering to their mouths like butterflies when I told them of my encounter with the priest.

"We're Quakers, you know," one told me, and, "Oh, we do find the antics of the natives so terribly funny!"

This statement, from two ladies as eccentric and charmingly Irish as anyone I'd met that day, just about summed up my own feelings. Towards evening I went in search of bed and breakfast; the mad rush to the west could wait.

THE SKY BURIAL

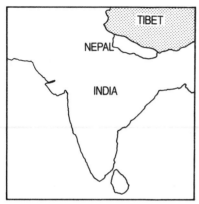

Six AM. I wake before the alarm, filled with apprehension. I had resisted attending the sky burial. However, I know that experiencing such a unique, ancient ritual is the essence of travelling. If I avoid it, I might as well be on a tourist bus, shielded from Tibet and from myself.

Pascal, Doune and I begin the hour-long walk out of L'hassa. We pick our way through a rubbish dump and climb to the burial site, a stubbly patch on top of a rocky hill, surrounded by desolate bare mountains, looking like wrinkled old elephants' hide. Five Tibetan men and a boy of about ten, dressed in worn jackets and trousers, are seated around a fire, drinking tea, talking and laughing. They smile welcome. Nearby is the altar rock where the burial is to take place, a large flat rock with bowl-like depressions, separated by a gully which is strewn with discarded clothing and hanks of hair. We sit by the edge of the gully facing the altar rock. Pascal gestures toward the mountains. I look up. Rows of large silent birds are perched on the mountain ledges – vultures. Their colours blend with the mountains. Ravens swoop in the gully and gather nervously in black clumps on the altar rock. A white square bundle, tied with rope, sits among the ravens. A small dog struggles up the rock and chases them. The rising sun slowly turns the drab greys and dull browns of the mountains to patches of pale gold and dusty pinks. It becomes warmer. About fifteen Westerners trickle in. No Chinese. In the past some have jeered at the burial procedure. Now Tibetans stone them. Westerners still seem welcome, though they too have created "incidents". Several days ago an Australian, desperate to capture the sky burial on film, although Tibetans forbid photographing, hid behind some rocks. He was discovered and chased. Next day Westerners were stoned. Yesterday several filtered back. Today we are greeted with smiles. Tibetans are wonderfully tolerant and forgiving. Still, I feel certain our days at the burial site are numbered.

A little after eight o'clock the sun touches the altar rock, the signal for the burial to begin. One of the men dons a grubby white coat and a surgical-type cap. He says something in Tibetan. Someone translates:

"While we work, no pictures." The man in white, two other men and the boy, climb onto the rock. The remaining two Tibetans, relatives of the deceased, sit by the fire. The man in white is thin and wiry with flashing black eyes and black hair sticking out from under the cap, wild looking. He unties the bundle. A woman, naked except for an unbuttoned faded red blouse, tumbles out. She looks pregnant, young-ish, with long black hair. (Later we learn that her body was carried a long distance on someone's back, for there are only a few places in Tibet where sky burials are performed.) The man in white drags her body over the rock and lays it face down in the centre. He begins with-out ceremony by pulling off the blouse and flinging it in the gully. He pulls a large knife from his belt, and with surgical precision cuts a slit down her spine. Starting from the shoulder blade he strips the flesh down the left side of her back, using swastika-patterned cuts. (For Tibetans the swastika is the symbol of the wheel of life.) This done, he neatly hacks off her left arm and tosses it to the young boy, who, squatting on his haunches, pounds it to a pulp with the back of an axe. He grunts and groans with the effort. The man in white continues to hack the left side of the body, panting loudly like someone chopping wood. The two men, also squatting, are thrown flesh and bones which they pound in the bowl-like depressions. The sounds of panting and puffing combine with those of flesh being pulverised and bones being smashed. *Tzampa,* a mixture of barley flour, tea and yak butter, is added to the flesh and bones to make a paste. Everything happens quickly. The men work with practised skill, pausing only to sharpen their axes or for a short cigarette break.

The woman's right side is begun, the flesh sliced expertly from the ribs. The man's white coat becomes splattered with blood. By now the rock looks like a butcher's shop, bloody with tattered flesh and strewn limbs, and the woman like a butchered carcass. I turn away many times, unable to watch, then am drawn back, unable not to watch. The butcher flips over what remains of the body, a torso with no back or limbs. He chops hard through the chest cavity and reaches inside to pull out the heart. Holding it up, he shouts something to the two Tibetans by the fire. They nod. He chops the heart to bits. Then the stomach is slit open and the organs removed. These are cut up and kept separately. The work is easier now. While they work, the men talk and joke. The Westerners are silent. Lastly, the head is separated from the neck with one precise blow. The butcher holds the head by the hair and deftly scalps it, then, tying the long black hair into a knot, he tosses it into the gully. Next he picks up a large flat stone and, hold-ing it overhead, mutters a prayer and smashes the skull, twice. One of the seated men brings tea to the rock. An old man dressed in traditional clothes appears and, facing the rock, says a prayer and prostrates him-self.

At this point the butcher, turning to the vultures, calls: "*Shoo* . . . *Tzshoo* . . ." At the signal about a dozen vultures, the vanguard, leave the mountains and swoop onto the rock. The butcher throws them bits of flesh as they gather around him. They are huge beautiful birds with white necks and legs, and speckled tan and white bodies. Their wings flutter and spread to reveal white undersides and dark brown tips. Some are so close that we can see their bright blue eyes. The boy bundles the chopped organs into a cloth. Several vultures try to steal bits of flesh from the boy. The butcher chases them off the rock with kicks and abusive shouts, as though punishing them for bad behaviour. The boy carries the bundle off the rock, the two men accompany him. Then the butcher, facing the mountains, addresses the vultures in a shrill sing-song voice, calling, "*Tria* . . . *soya* . . . *tria* . . ." Suddenly hundreds of birds fill the sky, hover in a quivering cloud above our heads, their wings beating a nervous fluttering sound, and descend on the rock, completely covering it. As the vultures vie for space, the ravens cling to the edges. The butcher serves the preparation of flesh, bones and *tzampa*. The *tzampa* has been added to make the mixture more palatable, for it is a bad omen if anything is left uneaten. The vultures eat greedily, fighting over scraps, slipping off the rock in their haste to consume. The ravens, uninvited guests, must be content to scramble at the outer edges, snapping up any morsels the vultures accidentally drop.

At this point several Westerners attempt to photograph the vultures. The butcher becomes incensed. Leaping off the rock, he rushes at two German girls, brandishing his knife and shouting. He points the knife at the heart of one of the girls. Livid with rage, he grabs their cameras and rips the film from them, tearing it to shreds and throwing it in the fire. The other cameras are quickly hidden.

The birds finish eating but do not leave the rock. They flutter about nervously in staccato hops. I wonder why they linger. The answer comes quickly. The bundle of organs is returned to the rock. They have been waiting for these choice morsels – dessert. They voraciously consume every last bit. Finally the feast is over. The vultures take to the sky bearing the deceased with them, upwards to the heavens. The rock is empty. An hour ago there was a body on the rock; now there is nothing. The butcher sits with the other Tibetans around the fire in animated discussion. There is no sign of mourning, no tears, no wailing, no prayers. Except for the two men, there are no family or friends present. Attending a sky burial for a Tibetan must be the equivalent of going to the morgue for a Westerner.

Two men climb the rock to check that all has been eaten and to clean it for the next burial. I sit too stunned to move. This has been the strangest, the most bizarre thing I have ever witnessed. Powerful images rage through my brain. What amazes me is that, in spite of the horrific nature of what I have seen, I feel neither repulsion nor revulsion. One reason must be the inevitable distancing of oneself from the intensity and nearness of the experience. But more important is a feeling that the sky burial fits in with the isolation and strangeness of the setting. In that alien environment, somehow it all makes sense. I am the last one to leave.

A. H. COOPER

PLEASE TO MAKE A RESERVATION

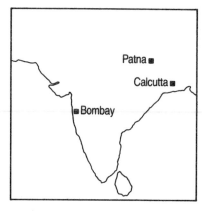

"Excuse me, do you speak English?"

"Oh yes, certainly."

"I want to reserve three seats on a train from Calcutta to Patna."

"Please?"

"I want to reserve . . ."

"Where are you wanting to go?"

"Patna."

"Have you a reservation?"

"No. That is what I want."

"Please you wait over there."

"I want to go during the day so that we can all see the countryside."

"Certainly. Over there."

A long queue shaped like a cobra waits "over there". Everybody pushes in front. The clerk behind the screen works with only half a mind functioning. From time to time he wanders off and chats to someone. At every transaction he writes copiously and painstakingly slowly in a book. The lazy punkas overhead do little to ease the discomfort of the temperature and humidity. I count fifteen frustrating moments before I reach the counter.

"I want three tickets for the train to Patna – on Friday – the day train."

"Where do you want to go?"

"Patna." I speak as if to a child, and add, "On Friday."

"No train Friday."

"Is there a train on Thursday?"

"Of course."

"At what time?"

"It leaves Howrah station at seven o'clock."

"Good. Can I reserve three tickets?"

"Where is your reservation form?"

"I was sent here to get it."

"Oh no. You must get it at the end counter."

I can feel the perspiration trickling down my back. I must keep my temper under control. Remember you are in India. Don't get impatient.

I wait yet again. A white form is handed to me.

"Please fill it in and come back here."

"Can't I do it here and now?"

"No, sir. Please to come back."

The form seems as complicated as a tax return. Date, time, destination all seem obvious. Age?

Here we go again. Yet again I have to write down passport numbers, visa numbers, when and where issued. Just my luck to have left the passports in the hotel.

Back to the hotel, fill in the details, another fifteen more minutes (seems like an hour) in the queue.

"Ah but you are British tourist."

"So?"

"There is special allocation of places for tourists."

"Splendid."

"You must take this form to the office round the corner."

"Not here?"

"Not here. Round the corner."

My knees are sagging. This wretched heat and humidity. Out into the sun yet again, into the noise, the crowd. Two beggars hold out their hands. I am too hot to bother with them. Round the corner. In here? A dingy doorway. No, try the next one. Yes, this must be it. Eastern Railway. I queue.

"Not here. Round the corner."

"Round the corner?"

"Yes, sir. This for second class only."

"But I want second-class tickets."

"Tourists in first-class office."

The logic of all this is beyond me. Temper is beyond me. I stumble out again. Another entrance to Eastern Railway. Another queue.

"Can I buy my tickets here?" I plead. I produce my reservation form.

"Where are you wanting to go?"

"Patna." I point to the form, then add, "What time does the day train go on Thursday?"

"Ten to nine."

"But the man in the other office said seven o'clock."

"No, sir. Ten to nine."

I wonder if anyone knows what is going on. I get my money out ready to pay. The reservation form comes back across the counter.

"Please to take this upstairs."

I look through the crowd at the steep stairs to the upper office. Will I get these tickets in time for Thursday?

Up and into a small office. At least it is quiet here. Four clerks sit at a long desk, chatting. Another lies peacefully asleep in the corner. I approach. I am directed to the man at the end. He is a polite little man with a worried expression. He collects the reservation form, writes something on it, the third person to do so. Words and figures seem to cover it.

"Please to sit down."

After ten minutes, I get up.

"Please. Just one moment."

Patience. Just remember. The other clerks chat. The sleeper sleeps. I am beckoned.

"You must take this down to desk number twenty-three. They will give you your tickets."

I am beyond thought. My shirt is soaked through, my head is spinning. I am back in the hubbub, back in the queue.

At last I am holding six beautiful tickets, three for reservations, all meticulously written on. I turn to walk out.

"Please take this with the tickets upstairs."

I thought I'd got rid of that wretched reservation form.

The stairs seem like the north face of the Eiger, the temperature sheer hell. I sit while the worried little man examines the tickets. He writes in a book. He talks over a telephone.

With a broad smile he comes over.

"Here are your tickets."

"Good." I refrain from sarcasm.

"The train leaves Howrah station at nine-thirty . . ." he pauses. I hold out my hand. ". . . PM."

"Night, but . . ."

"Certainly. Very good train. Sleeper reserved too. You like it."

JANIE HAMPTON

RIVER JOURNEY UP THE ZAIRE

"Into the eighth day and I really feel I've had enough. I'd like to be transported to a bathroom in the Ritz and then to a dry Martini in the bar." Graham Green, *Congo Journal, 1959.*

Eighth day, Zaire River, 1985. We often lost each other on the seven barges being pushed a thousand miles up the Zaire River, once Conrad's Congo.

I found my son Joseph, aged seven, in one of the five bars with Sammy, a young soldier. Sammy was concentrating on Joseph's dot-to-dot puzzle.

"He's very good at them," said Joseph. "He never misses a dot."

"Where's Daddy?"

"Gone for a pee at the back."

It was all right for men, they could go over the side. Women had to cope with the dark, smelly "cabinets" and first invite the rats to leave through the crumbling rusty holes. These were the boats left at the Belgian Congo's independence in 1960.

The bar is a scattering of upturned beer crates around a fridge with music pounding out of an oil drum. Only two feet above the glassy water a dozen dug-out canoes are lashed to the side and more join us all the time.

A man leaps from his canoe as it hurtles towards us. His chest reads, "My Mom and Dad went to Canada and all they brought me was this lousy T-shirt". He hangs onto the bark rope as his wives clamber out carrying flat baskets of headless smoked monkeys. Their faces are split by blue scars down the forehead and nose.

The man has come to barter hippo ivory earrings for cigarettes and a Chinese fishing net. In the flat bottom of his canoe a fire smoulders under a clay pot full of red palm oil.

Orlando appears on the next barge and leaps the gap, plugged with water hyacinth, refuse and a dead pig.

"What's the joke, Joe?"

"Smiling keeps me cool," says Joseph nonchalantly, sweat dripping from his chin.

"I've given Oscar a nice wash and mended his tail with Elastoplast."
Oscar was Orlando's tenth birthday present, a crocodile bought for
£3. He died the next day and became stew.

"As it's Orlando's birthday, I need another beer," exclaims André,
the resident nurse. Any excuse to cadge a drink. The barman tosses the
notes into a pile in his fridge. Inflation has made them worth as little
as ½p.

André has just delivered the third baby this week. He says he loves
me. Well, not just me: he loves all white women. If I won't divorce
Charlie, can he marry Daisy?

"But she is only eleven years old."

"Never mind. How much is she?"

To emphasise her beauty and intelligence, I quote a ridiculous price.

"O, she is expensive, but I will pay in instalments."

"She won't be ready for ten years."

"I can wait. But she must be a virgin. Is she?"

Charlie rejoins the shouted conversation in pidgin French and
Lingala.

We glide past islands with huts on stilts and waving people. Each
island bears a white arrow to show the way, but the riverbed changes
continuously and new channels have to be navigated each trip.

Talk turns to the night before when we were woken as the convoy
hit a sandbank with such force that the steel cables holding it together
were torn loose. The leading barge was tilted at right angles and the
rest floated gently apart. Bollards, decks and railings were ripped up.
By morning we were on our way again.

"C'mon, let's get food," says Orlando.

In single file we push past traders ranged along the narrow decks.
They sell everything from expired penicillin injections, pirated cas-
settes and old clothes to skin lightening creams – "As Used by Top
American Society". It had taken three days for the anarchy of two
thousand Zaïrois to transform themselves into an organised travelling
market.

Eliki, a disabled dwarf, sells old copies of *Jane's Defense Weekly* and
Merseyside Trade Annual. His wide chest tapers to a minuscule waist
and spindly useless legs. Every morning he runs along the deck upside
down on his hands.

We climb the slippery metal stairs to our cabin on the upper deck.
On the roof of the next barge is a group huddled round a radio, cheer-
ing a football match in Kinshasa, five hundred miles downstream. It
reminds us that today is a Sunday.

Daisy is having her long golden hair plaited by giggling young
women. They are fascinated by it and she is picking up French fast,
compensating for five months out of school.

I step over tiny children drawing with their fingers in spit on the

Dug-out canoes being towed upstream by the barges, while their owners barter goods on board. (*River Journey up the Zaire*)

The men set out their second-hand clothes stalls while the women do the washing-up. (*River Journey up the Zaire*)

rusty floor outside our cabin. They are not allowed out of this dark passage, in case they fall overboard.

No light and little ventilation penetrate our tiny cabin. The aroma of drying fish hangs heavily and it is stifling. Cockroaches scuttle under the narrow bunks. I grope for the saucepans and our meal tickets. The £40 fare includes one meal a day for fourteen days, regardless of when we arrive at Kisangani. The last trip took forty days, by which time a dozen people had died of hunger.

Across the passage Titi is cooking sliced green lizard with chillies. It tastes like chicken. Her fine features recall the Arab slave trade, long before the Belgians came. President Mobutu's face nods on her behind as she pounds plantain in an ebony mortar and then slices the yellow dough with cotton thread.

Kofi, her husband, has done well in four years of selling plastic shoes on the river. Their cabin is a shining example of conspicuous consumption – fridge, light, fans and two ghetto-blasters. Beautiful Titi is his prize possession. In the next candlelit cabin four men sit round a trunk of loose pills, carefully arranging coloured antibiotics in tubes of cellophane. One has a withered leg from polio.

The meal queue winds its way around the upper deck between trunks, sacks of salt and dozing traders. Many people have succumbed to torpor after a week's heavy drinking. They sit staring at the sunlight reflected off the monotonous river.

Pinching our children gives rise to brief entertainment, especially when the children yell abuse in retaliation.

An enormous old woman spills over a fold-up chair. Her water-melon breasts rest heavily on her lap and her cleavage starts where other women have a navel.

"Do you think the crane lifted her on at Kinshasa?" whispers Joseph. She returns his toothless smile and waves as graciously as the Queen.

Four boys pose for a polaroid wearing eye-shades advertising Mercedes-Benz. One enhances his image with the photographer's watch. A fisherman passes, dragging a child-sized fish. Its blue eyes swivel sadly and its red gills flap in terminal gasps. Rust, mud and bottle-tops cling to its gleaming grey scales. It, too, is hauled into the picture while the fisherman is bargaining with the *"chef du barge"*. The camera flashes and everyone applauds. A price is settled and the fish is pushed back down the stairs, flumpity, flump, bump. The photo appears, the boys standing drunkenly at an angle, inert and bleached, the fish in darkness. ·

I hand our saucepans and tickets through a hatch and shout *"Cinq!"* into the cavernous kitchen, manned by ten Brueghel-fat women. The

ABOVE: Home for the next 400 miles. (*Overland to Kinshasa*)
BELOW: Skinning a grizzly in the wilds of British Columbia. (*The Land God Forgot*)

giant pots rest on wheel-rims glowing with charcoal.

At another hatch an arm appears holding up bright enamel bowls and someone dashes forward to claim the grey cassava and fishheads. We can afford to supplement our diet with pineapples and crunchy caterpillar kebabs from the fishermen, tinned milk and plenty of beer–cheap and cold. The bread on sale is hard and green, though the same price as a week ago.

Tied to the railings are crocodiles of all lengths, turtles craning their long necks towards the water and two thieves – their heads shaved in asymmetrical patterns. They will be handed over at the next town in two days.

We eat our meal watching a hundred canoes drift downstream into a blue and gold sunset, to their villages five miles across the river. Young men leap past us from the roof above, splashing into the water to catch up with their canoes, beer bottles held aloft. Standing to paddle, the fishermen are extended by their reflections and appear to be walking on the water on wavering stilts, their long paddles a second leg.

Strings of paraffin lamps gleam along the upper decks and dance in the inky water. Ahead of us lightning flashes in the navy clouds.

Yes, you were right, Mr Greene, and there are another eight days until we reach the "Bend in the River" and the centre of the African equatorial rain forest.

On the next page Jamie Hampton's husband, Charles, takes up the story with an account of an overland part of the same journey.

CHARLES HAMPTON

OVERLAND TO KINSHASA

The truck was a Mercedes 930 – the smaller end of their tough, go-anywhere, carry-anything range that have conquered some of the worst roads in Africa. We boarded it, after a long argument over the fare and an even longer wait for the ferry, at 4.30pm on March 3. We were at Ilebo, the railhead of the Katanga railway in southern Zaire, on the Kasai river. Ahead lay a 400-mile journey to Kinshasa, the capital, at a cost of 900 Z (£18) per head and half-price for the children. We have three, Daisy (twelve), Orlando (ten) and Joseph (seven), but when Janie and I lifted them up to grasp the iron cage and climb onto the sacks and crates inside, we little realised that the "fun-ride" would last, not the scheduled three days, but six, and that we would be sharing the cramped space with twenty-nine other passengers.

Road travel in Zaire is an open-ended adventure that recalls a stage-coach ride in the Wild West, or crashing through jungle atop an elephant. On the first stage to Kikwit the road descended five times from baking empty savannah into dense forest where the soft sand turned to mud and rusty ferries carried us across swollen, brown tributaries of the distant Congo. The lorry lurched at a snail's pace up and down the hills, avoiding boulders and crevasses, splashing through axle-deep pools and swaying precariously from side to side. When a better stretch appeared ahead, seldom more than a few hundred yards long, we would accelerate up to fifteen or twenty miles per hour. Then it was the low-hanging branches which brought cries of *"Attention!"* from those passengers who perched on top of the driver's cab at the front. We were thwacked by palms, scratched by trailing, thorny creepers and menaced by lichen-smothered boughs, five inches in diameter. It was great fun at first: everyone screamed with laughter when Janie got a clunk on the back of her head and swore like a trooper.

The first day, we stopped twice to buy sacks of cassava – a white, stick-like root whose sweetly vile smell hung in the air and attracted flies whenever we were at a standstill. The "patron" of the Mercedes was riding in the cab along with two girlfriends and the driver. His existence must surely rank among the heroic legends of market economics. Every week or two he takes his battered truck out of Kinshasa loaded with 5,000 litres of Belgian lager, the life-blood of this benighted country. The fuel for the trip must be obtained through endless patience and bureaucratic chicanery, and carried in drums on the back. He has two ragged stevedores, riding up top, to hump the crates and dig the lorry out. The profit from the beer, sold at a gently escalating price as Kinshasa becomes more distant, is healthy enough; but there are unseen overheads such as hungry soldiers demanding protection money, and of course many running repairs. The home-ward journey, with tiresome but obligatory empty bottles, poses the real challenge to his entrepreneurial skills. Cassava is bought from peasants along the road for £7 a sack and resold in the capital for £12; but it is very heavy and bulky – an added threat to his precious fixed asset on these truly appalling roads. Passengers are the best bet. Their need must be great, for the fare is the equivalent of a month's pay for a secondary school teacher. Most are scared at the prospect of travelling so far from home, and reasonably docile when required to sit, tightly packed, on hard, bony sacks, under the tropical sun for nine hours at a time. Of one thing Monsieur Le Patron has assured himself, many such journeys ago. No passenger will be permitted to come bet-ween himself and a little extra profit, however loudly they may com-plain. After all, their money is already safely inside his initialled leather attaché case – the cause of a rather acrimonious exchange with the crazy M'zungu travelling with his children.

That first evening, the lorry's headlights failed and the forest too often obscured the full moon to make further progress possible. Dazed by the sun and unseen dangers, we went early to bed in a rattan "hotel" at thirty pence a room. The next morning we left at dawn – 6.30am – and stopped twice more to load up with cassava and grab a plastic beaker of coffee at a ferry stage. Then, some five minutes ride into the forest, there was a loud crack and we came to an abrupt halt. The rear leaf-spring retaining flange had sheared off at the chassis. The patron and his driver got out and stood scratching their heads. No-one found lateral thinking easy in that sweaty, mid-morning heat. We had passed at least one wreck in the last mile or two and a party was de-spatched to cannibalise it. The stevedores began the hopeless task of attempting to jack up the overloaded truck in the soft, sticky sand. The rest of us walked to the next little settlement and collapsed in the shade. The repair took all day – an idyllic day as it oddly turned out, for Janie asked directions to the source of water, which led us down into a deep, darkly shaded jungle paradise where a cool, clear stream, laced with intricate, basketwork fish traps, soothed away our fears and headaches and kept the children engrossed for hours. I killed a chicken and we had just brought it to the boil back at the roadside when, to our astonishment, there was a shout from the patron and the lorry lurched off up the road. Gathering our scattered possessions, we dashed off in pursuit amid howls of laughter. The spring was lashed in place with rope and wood and the lorry's progress became slower than ever. We crawled by moonlight into a large, clean-swept village, where children were pounding drums and singing with shrill energy. I realised with a sickening sense of dread that I had not eaten all day, that I was hungry, tired and angry beyond all reasonableness, and that I was thus incapable of protecting my family. Above all else, in Africa, one must hold on to one's patience.

I learnt a valuable lesson that evening when Janie finally served us our soggy rice and stringy chicken: eat whenever you can. On the lorry it was not easy. Food is short in Zaire and we found the slimy grey cassava porridge, bought cold in a sausage shape, wrapped in leaves, hard to swallow and digest. Apart from the occasional pineapple seller, fresh fruit was surprisingly scarce and meat – mostly chilled monkey – too spicy for the children, especially after Orlando contrived to get a speck of chilli in his eye: judging by his screams, it was sheer agony. This left tins. In that extraordinary market economy one encountered Spanish sardines and Dutch condensed milk at a tiny, wayside stall, just when all hope seemed gone.

The problem was that one never knew when the lorry would stop. The third day was our first taste of scheduled travel. Apart from an hour's halt when the spring slipped again, we progressed at an average of 8mph from dawn to sunset. The stevedores would leap down into the road and buy a sour, pithy orange; then jump back aboard and tear into it with their teeth, while we watched longingly with dry tongues and salty lips. When finally we ground our way into the hilltop town of Idiofa, we were too stiff to move. Never has a beer tasted better than that night, in a little thatched bar by the light of flickering paraffin wicks, where Orlando showed the drunken soldiery how to breakdance and Daisy chatted demurely with the prostitutes.

The fourth day was spent in idleness while the lorry was repaired and reloaded. Zairois towns are eerie places by daylight, there being no traffic and few people about. I went to the large Catholic mission, where schoolchildren ran out shouting: presumably their teachers were away somewhere, supplementing their meagre salary. The church was cool and beautifully decorated, with a slender crucifix, fifteen feet tall, carved out of mahogany, its expression abstract and stern. One is drawn to such things in a world so dominated by the economics of survival. As dusk fell we rejoined the lorry, momentarily cheered by an apparent reduction in the number of passengers. But round a corner we stopped at a bar and out they all came – the bossy matron with her china teapot and blue plastic bucket, the smart married couple, the mother with a baby and two toddlers who prayed and sang. Move up! "It's disgusting," said Joseph, with all the disgust at his command. A few extra sacks of manioc were tossed, none too carefully, into our midst. The mother screamed. Janie burst into tears, the patron bellowed at all of us. At length we moved off. That night we drove non-stop through heavy rain. In the brilliant moonlight the palms possessed an awesome magic as their storm-tossed silhouettes passed by overhead. The flapping tarpaulin soon tore down its entire length and Janie, lying in a narrow berth between sack and iron bar, was soaked to the skin. There was a moment of high drama before the storm broke when our lorry confronted another on a narrow strip of road where neither dared trust the sandy verge. A loud argument passed from cab to cab until a massive Australian, travelling with us, was urged to display himself in the opposing headlights: this speedily decided matters in our favour. By dawn we were all watching out anxiously for signs of Kikwit, a large town where we could obtain a square meal and a hot bath. The tarred highway, built by the Americans, began here: there were still 250 miles to go, but it would be worth the sacrifice to quit the lorry and take an express bus.

As if sensing our treacherous intentions, the patron and his exhausted driver continued on past the town and down the road for a further thirty minutes before halting. By then, our sense of outrage had subsided into dumb resignation. Wearily we pursued the routine of survival. Eat what you can, when you can. Conserve your water. Make sure the children wear their hats and stay away from the edge. All that day we staggered from side to side down the endless highway; 20mph was all the driver dared to go, and by nightfall we were still ten hours away from Kinshasa. Another night of rain: would he fall asleep at the wheel and kill us all? The children were complaining constantly now. I was perched on the very back, fighting for air under the suffocating tarpaulin, fighting to stay awake, staring at the road blurring between my feet. At 3am we came to a damp standstill in a crowded lay-by. Kinshasa was in view: the enormous Congo flood-plain was a mass of lights. At dawn we made our slow, heart-breaking way through the rapacious roadblocks: all that hard-earned profit draining away. The patron was anxious to be rid of us and called a taxi-driver over at the first township. There was just time to recover the clothes we'd lent and rescue our remaining chicken from inside the spare tyre. Then the lorry was lurching away from us down the dirty street. A lump in the throat? Enough to say that we'd done it the way "they" *have* to do it – and survived.

REVEREND PETER BIRKETT

THE LAND GOD FORGOT

"Waal, genlmen, I guess we have to get out of here real quick."

So said Mike our guide.

It was September 1985. We had been caught by early snow 9,500 feet up on a glacier in the coastal range of mountains in Northern British Columbia. It was as cold as a witch's tit and we were not equipped for snow.

We got back to our base camp at Haketty Creek 1,000 feet lower down, and there we spent an uncomfortable night under a tarp strung between four jack pines. The tarp sinking ever lower to the fire necessitating constant alerts to get the snow off it. Providentially we had taken some bottles of rye whiskey, sometimes known in that country as "Road Straightener". It kept some warmth in and some of the cold out.

We tied the horses to jack pines in some sort of cover that night, ploughing through a foot of snow with feet frozen in wet cowboy boots.

The next morning it took over two-and-a-half hours to pack loads and get them aboard some miserable hump-backed, shivering, ice-encrusted pack beasts, using ropes that were stiff and frozen.

The first day of our return was pure misery. A pack horse went berserk and shed its load, which took ages to sort and cinch down again. Floundering about in the snow and with a good deal of "you bloody cayuse! Stand! You son of a bitch."

All feeling went out of hands and feet, and when we hit dense forest every lodge pole pine we brushed against shed its load of snow down our necks and into our saddles. We cascaded down hillsides where a horse's hind feet were higher than its head and the snow balled in the hoofs. We scrambled in steaming clouds of breath and perspiration up mountain passes and down the other side, until we made a deserted log, cabin by Miners Lake.

Built long since, it had become a desirable dwelling place for myriads of bats. We found one candle. Evicted as many bats as we could. Gave it a rudimentary sweep out with pine branches. Fixed a kind of meal. And after drinking the last of the rye, crawled into our sleeping bags and passed into oblivion on the plank floor.

As we got lower the snow gradually died out and, hitting a logging trail, we made Kleena Kleene and One Eye Outfit, the log cabin of our guide.

On my retirement after forty-three years as a parish priest in England I went out to British Columbia to learn how to be a cowboy and to work for my keep as a ranch hand. It had been a pioneer existence of log cabins. Fetch your water in buckets from the creek. A diet of moose meat. Candles. And a two-hundred-mile drive along a terrible dirt road for the nearest bath, bank or bottle of gin. I fell in love with it all and go back as often as I can.

Last September I took Christopher, a friend, and got Mike, whom I had known when cowboying, to equip and guide us up into the unnamed, unmapped and unvisited mountains.

It is a hard land from which to wrest any kind of living. It has been called "The land God forgot". Though someone once said, "Nope, He did not forget this country. He remembers it well. He hates it."

It is the land of the grizzly, the moose and the wolf. The human, if he goes into it, intrudes on their domain and in a sense pollutes it. The sublimity of the mountains and eternal snows. The silence which one feels could be cut into great chunks. The knowledge that no other human breathes between you and the Pacific Ocean miles and miles away. The great skyscapes. The sheer vastness of it all fascinates and thrills me.

We had started our expedition in wonderful Fall weather. The aspens hanging their leaves like golden guineas. And our going out like our coming in was not without adventure.

The terrain, although normal for British Columbia, was not the sort that one would dream of asking an English horse to negotiate. Musky swamps, rock slides and screes, glacial rivers, thick forest full of dead falls, not to mention grizzlies.

To begin with there were blazes on pine trees to mark a trail, but they soon faded out. Often we had to axe our way, and one day we came to a lake which faded into the distance in both directions. A rocky promontory stuck out into it. The question was, did we backtrack or risk getting round in the hope that the lake was shallow?

We decided to risk the latter. The lake was not shallow. When my boots filled with water, I realised my horse was swimming. There was nothing to be done about it. I sat there feeling pompous and rather foolish and praying he would hold out and make dry land. He did. So did we all. But the pack boxes that held the food were squirting water like colanders, and inside was a sticky mixture of flour, beans, eggs and chocolate. We lived largely on trout we caught and tinned Danish herrings for the rest of the trip.

Bogs were another hazard. If your horse came down in one it was a soft fall. But rolling about trying to get your footing when wearing heavy leather chaps and watching your horse sinking deeper at each heaving struggle is a panic-making experience. Yet it was all idyllic. We were in an environment straight from the hands of the creator. The very animals were tame, with no fear of man. They had never seen him and did not realise he was not to be trusted. The mule deer with twitching ears came within arm's length to see what this extraordinary two-legged man-animal was.

Christopher one day was fishing for Dolly Varden in the creek. Some deer came right up to Mike, and I wished so much Christopher had been there to see. When he returned with our supper of trout he said, "I heard a noise behind me and there was a mule deer breathing down my neck."

The grizzlies we saw fortunately were not so inquisitive.

There were times when I realised I was getting a bit old for these frolics, but I remembered the words of a cowboy eight years before, and gritted my teeth and pressed on.

We had been rounding up cattle and cutting out bulls on a very hot dusty day. At the end of it all he had ridden up to me and said, "Waal, Pete, one thing's for sure. Preaching hasn't turned you into a lily."

Ever since then, in moments of stress I have said to myself, "Now don't be a lily."

I said it quite often on this journey.

We all have our dreams. They can remain just dreams.

But as Thoreau once said on his escape from the city to the woods, "I learned this at least by my experiment; that if one advances confidently in the direction of his dreams and endeavours to live the life he has imagined, he will meet with a success unexpected in common hours."

I am one of the lucky ones. I have met with success unexpected. And when I go on my last journey across the great divide, if anyone is foolish enough to waste money on a tombstone, they can inscribe upon it:

"Pete. Not a Lily."

TIM PEARS

STEAMING IN MANHATTAN

We shot over Third Avenue Bridge and landed with a bump on Manhattan. It seemed appropriate. "Don't be intimidated," we'd been warned. Unfortunately we were then caught in the wrong trade-wind of traffic and were blown inexorably back onto the Bronx, having to re-enter, less dramatically but in the flow.

They say everyone has a distinct feeling of *déjà vu* the first time they visit New York and see steam rising from the streets and skyscrapers poking the sky, a specious phenomenon caused by the movies. But I didn't feel it; I just wanted to know where the steam was coming from.

At the car-hire dropping off point we were charged by miles on the clock, though our Canadian Oldsmobile was calibrated for kilometres. Being unpractised at the art we were soon left out of the ensuing argument, clerks gathering to remonstrate with one another. Our role was reduced to intermittently demonstrating English resolution by refusing to pay the difference, and the disputation got under way again, garrulous and relaxed, the typist taking time out to explain to me that "the steam come out of the soowers. It don't smell 'cos it's nootralised, see".

We strolled down the Bowery, towards our hosts, in good humour. Bums of every age and race lay above the warm air vents or sat drinking on the wide sidewalk – destitution, like soccer hooliganism, drawing them together.

Sam and Sue live in a converted warehouse loft, shaped like an angular hoop and vast, like two connected bowling alleys; one for living in, the other Sam's studio. Sue descends to work leaving Sam high up in his loft with his enormous and coolly beautiful paintings of trees and icebergs.

After dinner I took a beer and cigarette up to the roof. Aeroplanes circled the lit-up antennae of the skyscrapers like lazy, luminous bees, while below I tracked the whooping sirens of police cars swooping through the city streets after their prey. In an emptied parking lot kids played touch football, the game revealed from above as a violent dance, a complex pattern of opposing movements, each player intent upon his often minor role in the overall choreography, the pattern repeatedly stopped, shifted around and restarted, as if the choreographer in his pursuit of perfection were constantly repenting and starting anew.

The next day we walked with Sam over to the East Village; the subway rumbled beneath us. "That's where the steam comes from," he said, "where else?" Galleries have mushroomed in the hispanic ghetto, and we stumbled from one raucous exhibition to another.

I returned the following morning for Mass in a Catholic church. The congregation consisted of half-a-dozen derelicts who shuffled in and were lost in the ranks of pews, and one multitudinous family in black who squashed themselves into the very back pew. Arranging chalice and paten at the altar was an informally attired priest, who then peered at us from the vestry doorway until ten past eight, when he stepped forward to announce that the clocks went back the night before and the service would start in fifty minutes. So I strolled home by the river park, overtaken by an endless procession of joggers.

The next day Sam took us to SoHo, where the first opening of the season was underway in a gallery owned by the same Iranian who spray-painted Guernica. The celebrity himself was a subway graffiti artist; we mixed with beautiful people and dowager patronesses, as Keith Haring climbed over his doodle sculptures for the endless popping of flashbulbs. A young man told us: "You know what this is all about? One thing – money." But he'd seen the Giacometti exhibition.

We caught the subway home; doodles similar to those selling for thousands of dollars still brightened the walls, and were themselves vandalised in their turn. Few of the commuters noticed; most slumbered in the warmth rising from others' bodies and the soporific rhythm of the carriage. But my neighbour was wide awake. "How could steam come from da subway? *You* still got steam trains may*be*, but dis is Noo York. We're electric. No-one knows where da steam comes from."

Sam had warned us about the subways. "Really, take care. Bad things happen." So, waiting for a connection, we stood in the safe area in the middle of the platform. A cellist played the Catalan *Song of the Birds,* while in the gunnel between the tracks tiny, furry mice scavenged for some oily sustenance.

While the commuters go home to Brooklyn and Queens, office cleaners pass in the opposite direction. You can trace them working, cubed blocks of light rising up the skyscrapers.

Jed, photographer and master printer, took us up to the top of the World Trade Centre, where we tried out his new wide-angle lens and swayed in the wind. Far below, too far for vertigo, ships chugged diagonal paths between Staten, Liberty and Manhattan Islands, their wakes the slow, lazy brush-strokes of a Japanese master. We looked

across the Hudson to New Jersey, acres of industrial plant on reclaimed marshes, beneath which sulphurous fires had been smouldering for years.

"Maybe that's where the steam comes from?" I ventured.

"No," said Jed. "It comes from the Chinese gambling dens, spreading across the city under ground. Prob'ly opium; you might get a contact high."

The buildings of Manhattan leaned away from us to the horizon,
and Chinatown swelled imperceptibly, squeezing the Jewish garment
district in upon Hester Street and making Little Italy ever smaller. The
following morning we had breakfast of soy bean milk and twisters in
The Dumpling House, served by waitresses who needed to learn the
English words only for the dishes they served – though official city
posters were not yet trilingual, printed only in English and Spanish.

Sam adjudged us ready for the uptown galleries, on 57th and Madi-
son. An exhibition of Schiele paintings had just closed, but they still
hung on the wall. "Yeh, well I guess you can come stand in the doorway, but no foither. They're not insured." Delighted by the work of
Rafael Soyar I pretended to be rich (rank and threadbare plimsolls a
sure sign of aristocratic eccentricity) and was indulged by the assistant
in an acquisitive fantasy: "The nude at forty thousand dollars or the
self-portrait for fifty? Hard to decide." And finally we saw a hundred
Giacomettis in a private gallery, like orchids in a window-box.

Over in Greenwich I met Lewis. "Steam? I call it hell-smoke. It rises
from the infernal fires." He had an old black and white television, and
all he watched was the 24-hour weather station. His passion was to go
to the top of the Empire State Building during an electrical storm and
watch the lightning sheeting across his city. "The first skyscraper,
around 1900, was only eight storeys high, but no-one believed it was
possible," he told me. "They'd erected the skeleton of the building
when a big storm brewed up. People came in from all the boroughs to
watch it fall. The architect, he climbed it and stood on the top. After
that, they believed."

Fernanda met me at the Museum of Modern Art, but it was closed
on a Wednesday, so we went to find lunch. "The steam? Pierre was
here last week, he asked the same question. I just don't know."

"That's okay," I said. She took me to the Frick Museum, erstwhile
home of a millionaire art lover who bequeathed it to the city. In rooms
set around a fountain garden we walked along walls blessed with
Vermeer's divine light, the self-scrutiny of Rembrandt, El Greco's
quivering faith and the humanity of Holbein's meticulous portraits of
Cromwell and More.

Our last day I walked onto Brooklyn Bridge, intending to cross the
East River and look back. But I only got halfway, unwilling to leave
Manhattan before I had to. So I returned, and wandered past City Hall

and back along the Bowery. A blur stumbled from a doorway. "Ya gotta quarter mister, for da subway?"

"I've got a dollar if you can tell me where that steam comes from."

"Hell, dey was dere befaw da city, long befaw. Dey was dere when Giovanni da Verrazano discovered Noo York in 1524. He told da Florentine Court dere was an active volcano. In sixteen hundred an' nine Henry Hudson tought dey was springs. He didn't trust 'em, he kept to da river. You know what da Iriquois Indians say? Ya can put up buildings, roads, railyards, tanks, it don't matter. Da steam'll still rise through 'em, and one day it'll lift the city clean off Manhattan Island, and carry it out to sea. Forever, ya hear?"

I gave him two dollars and was soon on the special subway train to JFK Airport, leaving Manhattan under the river. I hope it'll be there when I go back.

CORAL BEADLE

AMONG THE HILLTRIBES
OF NORTHERN THAILAND

In that universal hour of freedom between school and bed, children gathered in the space that passed for the village green and found more joy in sticks and sand than in all the toys money could buy.

Only here there were no expensive toys for them to choose instead. The only real toy was an unbelievable bicycle carved out of wood by some elder craftsmen and shared, like everything else in this village, as if the children were already members of the co-operative their parents ran.

When the ice cream man pedalled into the evening playground he was stopping on a round that covered twenty miles, and looked out of place among the colourful youngsters delving into the ice-box mounted on his handlebars.

But then so did I. Me – the white one with the broken leg, sitting on a log among the opium-growing hilltribes of Northern Thailand, complete with crutches. Recent victim of attempted rape, gory road accident and desertion by travelling companion – a wise woman to forsake her share of my ill-luck.

Only now I'd achieved something positive. For like the ice cream man, I was accepted.

When I'd arrived, the whole village had turned out calling *"Farang, Farang!"* Someone had asked was the *Farang* with the CIA, checking on the opium growing.

No, I'd simply avoided the organised tourists treks, regularly robbed because they camera-clicked their way through invaded villages like locusts. Me, I thought, I'm different. I found myself a personal guide, made repeated trips to the same village until I was accepted – caked with their dirt, but entertained to tea by the headman like a VIP.

Soon I'd be able to bring out my camera without fear of giving offence. In the evening playground the children came close enough to kiss, chattering at me in the mistaken belief that I could speak the Thai they were learning at school from squads of teachers sent into the hills as part of a government-backed programme of integration. The aim was to reduce political infiltration through the tribes by Thailand's Communist neighbours.

The girls, junior embroiderers, came to touch the man-made fabrics I wore – beautiful eyes looking out above their high cheekbones, and small dark frames weighed down by pleated skirts heavy with exquisite, filthy embroidery. Below their black cotton leggings were feet caked with the red clay of the playground and the hut floors where they lived.

The boys with equally angular good looks ran about in loose black trousers which hung like skirts, huge red pom-poms bobbing on their hats, bell buttons jingling on their embroidered jackets. The little ones went naked, big bellies smeared with dirt, cropped hair matted with mud, and streaks of dirt tracing today's tears down chubby cheeks as they frolicked among puppies and pigs. Puppies that I had to assume they were going to eat because I never saw a full-grown dog.

But that didn't worry me – not as much as the fear that I might, after all, be a tourist, a traveller from the future come to erode the quality of hilltribe life, another incitement to adopt modern, Western ways.

By moonlight I had trekked with villagers to the old school hut – a shack with a thatched roof and walls of bamboo slats around an earth floor. Inside, twenty young girls ranged in four rows had danced in perfect time to a crackling, battery-driven cassette-player. Silver had chinked and flashed in flickering candlelight; torches hanging from their waists banged against their buttocks as they shuffled through the steps of a tribal dance, rubbing hands over swivelling hips like women luring lovers.

In fact, I was told, they were twelve-year-olds, still two years or more away from marriage, and practising for a Christian festival. When they grew bored they chattered as they circled in the dance, and giggled when they had to sing a love song.

I had sat silently by in the headman's hut as he played host to visiting tribesmen who, over three bottles of whisky, discussed the plight of a man caught transporting opium into town and now languishing in Chiang Mai jail. I learned that 15,000 baht – five hundred pounds – was needed to avert a court case and secure his release. Every member of the co-operative was bound to contribute to meet the payment they would never describe as a bribe.

In the cool of a dawn over blue hills, I had seen the village gather for a trip to the Burmese border that could be a cover for an opium shipment, though outwardly an outing to see relatives.

I had watched from the sidelines as the headman climbed into the back of a village pick-up truck with an entourage of men, women and children hoisting themselves up after him, husbands grabbing the family wealth – huge necklaces hewn out of silver – from their wives' necks, to wear themselves during the trip.

As the over-burdened vehicle pulled off, wheels spinning in the dust, people standing packed like sardines in the back, a mother sat down on a log embroidering, watching her toddlers grubbing in the dirt, barely more than a girl herself. Bits of discarded pink and orange thread gathered round her feet as the older children set off over the hill to school in the next village, modern exercise books and plastic satchels hugged against their hilltribe costumes.

At the water pump young girls had gathered to wash clothes, pummelling embroidered skirts with their feet, reluctantly making way for the tourist who went to the pump with a toothbrush.

But now they were used to me – and all I needed was an excuse to pull my camera out. I got it in the evening playground as all hell broke loose. Two hundred people emerged as if from nowhere to join a crowd gathering around a pick-up truck, and I prayed it wasn't for the arrival of another *Farang* because I didn't want to share my village.

No, it was a toothless mother dragging a young beauty by the hair, a young boy clinging to the girl's sash. The shrieking woman had travelled from a faraway village to collect her runaway daughter who'd eloped with her fifteen-year-old sweetheart.

The love in their eyes eclipsed the dreadful determination on the mother's face as she argued with the boy's family. The crowd, who formed a circle, made it impossible for her to drag the girl off, but she never let go of the long black skein of hair as the sun went down and the row entered its second hour. The crowd remained, and in carnival mood.

As one relative lost his temper, he was dragged back and another pushed in to reason, ripples of laughter running through the listening crowd. Boys hung in trees, men squatted in rows on a bank, smoking and talking with babies strapped to their backs. Women gathered in gossiping groups with children playing in the dust around their feet. A father laughed when I asked if women gave birth lying on their backs.

When the headman arrived he stood and surveyed the sorry scene, commenting that it was the first feud in the entire 150-year history of the village. It would escalate into bloody enmity between two villages for the angry woman would not even accept his arbitration because he was not her village's headman.

As darkness fell, the mother was allowed to push her daughter into the back of the pick-up truck with the young boy still clinging to her sash. Several minutes later three young girls who had left the crowd returned in all their hilltribe finery – new embroidery so bright it flashed in the dusky light, heavy silver round their necks, their hair tied in buns draped with best beads. They had been offered as brides to the other village so that our young Romeo could stay with his Juliet – and yet their faces were a picture of delight as they climbed into the truck.

And then came the flash. Sudden silence as the crowd looked up for lightning before someone shouted and they all turned to stare – at me. Men dashed forward, grabbing my camera and gibbering into my horrified face.

"It's all right," said my guide. "They ask you to send them pictures – they've never seen photos of themselves."

MICHAEL GEOGHEGAN

ECHOES IN NUREMBURG

I climb the huge white steps of the grandstand at the head of the Zeppelinfeld, the arena where the Nuremburg rallies were held, and sit down with a beer and a bread roll filled with salmon and onions.

It's the last day of September, a late summer's day, and the air is warm and still. It's impossible to imagine the banners, the double-headed eagles, the swastikas, the shadowy floodlit masses, the smell of sweat in the air, the red and the black, the blood and evil.

Now the empty, graceless terraces, stripped of their fascist decorations, are crumbling and overgrown, and the field itself, the size of four football pitches, is used for showjumping. The only sounds are the distant swish of cars and motorcycles, and the patter of tennis balls on the back wall of the main stand.

The buildings have been partially renovated as a permanent reminder of Nazi rule, though no mention of this monument is made in the tourist brochures. The platform from which Hitler addressed the Party faithful has been newly concreted. I am sitting ten metres above it but feel reluctant to mount it – as are, it seems, the few other visitors, a mixture of elderly Germans, American servicemen, and the children of Italian immigrants, for whom this is a quiet place to sit necking.

A large German family arrives in two cars. A teenage son rushes up to the platform and smirkingly flashes two very convincing Nazi salutes to the rest of his family below. Two of his brothers follow him up to the platform. They strike heroic poses – one hand on the hip, one forearm clenching the handrail, bums jutting out arrogantly.

At the top of the steps is the original iron door, through which the Nazi dignitaries entered the arena. It is now pitted with rust and graffiti. A lot of the graffiti is old – Barrett 1946, Davis 1947. The more recent graffiti, which is presumably cleaned regularly, is a mixture of peace symbols and neo-Nazi slogans: SKINPOWER REGENS-BURG WEHRSPORTGRUPPE 4.9.85, written in black felt-tip with SS-style lettering: KAMPF DEN DRECKSHIPPIES; HORS-FORTH BOYS WERE HERE AUGUST 85.

As I leave, a black Mercedes containing three boisterous young men in black T-shirts and dark glasses drives slowly along the driveway in front of the grandstand. As it passes Hitler's platform, now occupied by three Filipino wives of US servicemen, it swerves as the driver takes his right hand off the wheel to jerk a salute, and roars off like a drag-racer.

I wander back through the beautiful Volkspark: lakes shimmering in the late afternoon sun; soft, springy lawns; cool avenues of oak and birch trees; the crunch of women's shoes on the gravel. Elderly, silver-haired Germans with mottled faces and canes are sitting in the sun; Turkish families are picnicking on the grass. There are young Americans listening to pop music, and Yugoslavs washing their cars on the avenue leading to the Volksfestplatz, which serves as a racetrack for young Germans in gaudy, customised Opel Asconas. And in the middle of all this is a huge redundant building shaped like three-quarters of the Coliseum, in the neo-Classical style favoured by the architects of the Third Reich. It, too, is absent from the tourist guides.

I continue through the smaller, more intimate Luitpoldhain park, with landscape lawns and fountains, bright flowerbeds still in bloom, and Italian families playing football on the grass; past the ugly new Meistersingerhalle where an orchestra is unloading its instruments from a double-decker coach; over the Platz der Opfer des Faschismus; and through quiet, tree-lined streets towards the centre. Most of the apartment blocks are four- or five-storeyed, in pastel shades, and built in the late 1940s or early 1950s over the ruins of the war-destruction. A few old houses survive – some cleaned, showing off Nuremburg's pink sandstone; others still blackened and scarred. There are small businesses and shops, a tiny door announcing a FRISEUR, old people sitting in windows, a wedding reception, street nameplates in Gothic script, and a small, fenced-off enclave with young trees and a hand-written sign saying WER SEINEN ABFALL WIRFT HIER UBER DEN ZAUN HEREIN – DER IST EIN SCHWEIN, except that the pig who throws his rubbish over the fence is drawn rather than written. This is a characteristically German way of conveying a message – both poetic and crude.

The anonymous belt between the suburbs and the city-centre could be anywhere: railway bridges, parking lots, insurance offices, computer companies, lunchtime bars, a Greek restaurant – all deserted on a late Saturday afternoon. Eventually I reach the Königstor, one of the medieval gateways of the walled city. The circular tower is still intact. With its flattish, conical roof it resembles one of those Bavarian beer mugs with lids attached.

In the shadow of the Königstor is a reconstructed medieval artisans' courtyard with cobbled alleys. Coach parties of middle-aged Germans with pot-bellies and suede shoes emerge and collapse into the outdoor cafés along the Königstrasse. Cream Mercedes taxis line up. The main street is crowded: groups of black American soldiers in shorts and baseball caps carrying ghetto-blasters; white American soldiers in cutaway T-shirts and baggy Levis, with Yugoslavs girls; young Germans wearing US Army surplus clothes; swarthy German-speaking boys with embryonic moustaches, the sons of guest-workers. A group of "marginals", wearing cheap fashion-clothes and straggly 1970s hairstyles, probably alcoholics, possibly junkies, are sitting smoking, getting through the day.

Two hours later dusk is falling in the old city. It is Saturday night. Remember, people had told me, Nuremburg is the centre of Franconia, the heartland of Germany, the most German of German cities, the home of Hans Sachs and Albrecht Dürer. Wagner chose to live in nearby Bayreuth; Hitler chose Nuremburg for his mass demonstrations of German nationalism. I visualised an old city-centre replete with baroque churches and cobbled streets overhung with craftsmen's guild signs, perhaps a dreamy river.

I set off for the evening, taking the first left off the Königstrasse, and plunge into a neon maelstrom of sleaze and machismo. Luitpoldstrasse: sex shops, sex cinemas, peep shows, cabarets, gambling halls, video games, discotheques, *Currywurst mit pommes frites,* Americans, Germans, Yugoslavs, solitary men weighing up the porno movies, soldiers arguing with bouncers, girls in disco-jeans smoking and looking cool, curly-haired Italian kids rolling their shoulders as they strut along, taxis drawing up from the barracks out of town, stylish black soldiers with girls, and hordes of kids around the discos, trying to get in, trying to get out, pushing, shouting, drinking, hundreds of them spilling into the street, letting themselves go, dreaming that tonight will be the special night, the night they get laid instead of getting hungover. And in the shadows, the older, lonely men, who have given up on the dreams, drift relentlessly towards the movies, hoping that they won't meet a neighbour or that they haven't seen the same film before.

I retreat into the Königstrasse and walk through a shopping precinct with neo-cobbled streets and phallic concrete fountains. Young people sit around talking; older people are window-shopping in Hertie or Kaufhof or Karstadt. In the Lorenzerplatz a huge dark church towers over the square. It feels somehow absent rather than present – a big black space ignored by the passers-by. Opposite, a medieval corner-house survives – now a pharmacy with Gothic lettering and gilt pestle and mortar. I pass the Fountain of Virtues, warlike angels with water spouting out of their armour-plated breasts; then another sex shop, a "disco-theater" and, round the next corner, a breathtaking medieval almshouse built over the river, floodlit from below, the reflection of its golden-pink sandstone shining in the dark water.

The atmosphere seems to change once you cross the river. The Americans and their rock music are left behind and the only sound is the whine of a gypsy violin. An elegant middle-aged couple dressed in green serge trimmed with leather make their way to something cultural at the Hall of the Holy Spirit in the Hans-Sachs-Platz. The streets begin to climb and wind; there are monuments and churches, fountains and statues – of Hans Sachs, of a local margrave – tottering, half-timbered houses, tiny alleys, coats of arms, a wooden carving of Saint George and the Dragon above an inn, and finally, up in the stars with its towers and turrets, walls and tunnels floodlit, is the Imperial Castle.

It's quiet up here, leaning over the ramparts looking down on Nuremburg. Below is the house where Dürer made engravings of the Four Horsemen of the Apocalypse; out on the edge of the city Hitler barked out his vision of the master race. Nobody cares very much for either of them now. A door opens just below me and the sound of disco music and beer glasses echoes into the night.

ITALY'S DEEP SOUTH

It is wholly appropriate that to get to Basilicata, the innermost of the Southern Italian provinces, one has to pass through Eboli, an uninspiring town which has achieved some dubious immortality in the title of what is still the best book about the South, Carlo Levi's *Christ Stopped At Eboli,* recently movingly filmed by Francesco Rosi. For Levi, this town whose patron saint is none other than Saint Vitus, marks the point where the Europe of the kind we know ceases, where history turns in on itself. The lines that divide North from South in Italy are mostly intangible – lines of time, ethnography, exploitation, prejudice, psychology. Levi was sent, during the Italian Abyssinian war – one of Mussolini's symbolic nationalist fevers – to Gagliano, Grassano and Stigliano, three small towns in this inner recess of Italy. Confined as a political prisoner, he wrote his book as a record of extraordinary contact with the mentality of the South. He wrote, like many who write about the area, with an air of enforced desperation:

> "No-one has come to this land except as an enemy, a conqueror, or a visitor devoid of understanding. The seasons pass today over the toil of the peasants, just as they did three thousand years before Christ: no message, human or divine, has reached this stubborn poverty."

Even to get there by rail you have to take a drop in quality from the *rapido* (supplement payable) to the *direttissimo,* a "most direct" train that does not dawdle. For dawdling you take the *diretto* or, even worse, the *accellerato,* an all but accelerated walk, as its name implies, which stops not only at, but in between, stations – indeed, wherever anyone wants to get off. However, this is Easter and they have laid on a special *rapido* from Naples to Potenza, and we clatter off over the former malarial plain of the Sele, near where the Greek sanctuaries of Paestum stand, and turn inward towards the mountains, leaving the tourists at their furthermost point south. Outside the entrance to the Paestum temples the coaches and hired cars turn round and head back for Salerno, the Sorrento peninsula and Naples. Augustus Hare declared

that "civilisation may be said to cease altogether at Salerno", a senti-
ment that is echoed by most travel agents.

Basilicata was named after the title of the Byzantine administrator of
the region, the *basilikos,* but the alternative, and more nationalist,
name for the region is Lucania, after the original tribe of the area. It is
the most mountainous of the southern provinces, with only two small
strips of coast – one at the Gulf of Policastro on the Tyrrenian sea, the
other at the southern Ionian, near the Greek colony of Metapontum.
The brochures make as much as they can of this potential tourist trap.
But the reality is that most of the province is plain, twenty-two per
cent barely cultivatable hill country, seventy per cent mountains.
Seventy per cent of the population is engaged in poor agriculture, as
the statistics have it, barely concealing a large, illiterate peasant community. The province consumes a third as much meat as the rest of
South Italy; it has half as many hotels, and spends twice as much on social assistance. It has suffered from many disastrous earthquakes and is
constantly prey to erosion, landslides, and flooding by torrential rains
that wash whole mountainsides away in a hard winter. It is on the way
to nowhere. The Via Appia Antica just crossed its northern borders,
while the Autostrada del Sole manages a small trajectory near the sea.
But the region is grandiose and absorbing, and its people are proud
and warm-hearted. The Lucanians spoke a strange pre-Latin language
called Oscan, which resembles nothing more than an invention of
Tolkien: *"mr atiniis mr kvaisstur eitiuvad multasikid kumbennieis
aamanaffed"*. They seem to have lived in defended upland com-
munities, much like the present population, and there are remains of a
Lucanian town at Vaglio Basilicata near Potenza. Like everyone else in
these parts the Lucanians were eventually absorbed by Rome, which
produced the *basilikos* to administrate the region. Mussolini characteristically wanted no verbal relics of past empires cluttering up his
map, and so Basilicata became Lucania again in 1932. Now it answers
to both names.

My personalised Basilicata began somewhere after Eboli in the
compartment of the special Easter *rapido,* when the black old peasant
woman leaned across to the student and asked if he would write
"Hotel Principe" on a slip of paper, for her to find her way in Potenza.
He did it almost automatically, leaning over to me explaining
"anafabeta" (illiterate). The young national serviceman in the opposite
seat thought, at this point, that I should hear the troubles of Basilicata,
and the eternal southern chant began. This recitation of the miseries
of the South is now a reflex action on the part of the inhabitants en-
countering a northerner. Part of southern psychology is to excuse the
fact that life does not really come up to European standards. And so –
the poverty of life, the lack of work, the intellectual deprivation, the
poverty of the land, the ignorance of the government in the North, the

frustration of being young, and a southerner. The leader of the chant
in this case soon became a student of economics at the University of
Naples on his way home for Easter. Now economics, combined with
agricultural science might, you imagine, go somewhere to solving the
problems of this inland region. But, and here the chant rises higher,
there are few jobs and far too many graduates. In fact, as elsewhere in
Europe, university graduates swell the numbers of unemployed. The
more educated you are, it would seem, the less work is available.
Paradoxically education, instead of producing the type of mind to
plug the gaps, to create the necessary organisations, can only produce
a complaining citizen who bewails the lack of a job for his particular ta-
lent. This inability to think in terms of innovation where innovation is
so desperately necessary is a very present characteristic of people who
have always had to accept rule from above. And so the solution is often
emigration north, marriage perhaps with a foreigner.

The student explained all this in the loud and confident voice that
education brings. The old lady and the soldier remained impassive.
Let him talk, nothing would change. But at the mention of marriage
the dowager sat up.

"Why don't you settle down with a girl from your village? A girl
you have known all your life. Keep the family together, honour it.
Keep the village whole, the mother and father happy, a little" – and she
used a typically southern word – "sistemazione". We don't have its real
equivalent in our rational north, but it indicates a desire for order, for
certainty, particularly in family matters. A person who is "un-
systematised" is untrustworthy. This closed, secure state of affairs will
come about only by keeping the Others out. I recognised in the old
woman's words the age-old cry of an invaded and threatened people.
The student merely laughed, but it seemed to me that this constant
running away from the South, to which many of its intellectual class
resort, deprives the region of any really innovatory force. Yet education in the south of Italy can in a sense only be an education in envy –
for all that progress, industry, and freedom beyond the Alps.

The train had now passed through many a defile of the Lucanian
Apennines, and comradeship and philosophy had to end. We arrived
at Potenza. Invitations to drink with the soldier at the Polo Nord Bar
in an inland village, to sample homemade pasta with the old lady, to
visit the student to talk more about the South with a friend who was an
historian. I looked down at the name of his home town. Ironically it
was Grassano, where Carlo Levi had begun his exile.

"Levi? No I don't recall the book at all. But of course it's all changed
now."

Of course. I looked up the hill to where Potenza, the provincial capital, clung to the mountainside, and I began to trudge up to the centre,
to the unloved city. Edward Lear, travelling through it in 1828,

thought it "as ugly a town for form, detail, and situation, as one might wish to avoid". Indeed, since a series of earthquakes it is a thoroughly modern city, as the guidebooks put it somewhat disparagingly, as they also have to describe Warsaw.

The former medieval centre of the town is 2,700 feet up on a hill above the valley of the Basento, surrounded by the mountains. All around the hill are modern blocks of flats put up since the war, so that from afar there is an unmistakable air of old-fashioned modernity – terrace upon terrace of blocks rising to the top of the hill, the whole reminiscent of a nineteen-fifties re-interpretation of the Dalai Lama's palace. For miles around this vision of the amphitheatrical city is visible, stamping itself on the area as a capital city ought. Here, it shrieks, is progress, Potenza! But it's also in the earthquake zone, and there is an air of impermanence to everything. The buildings are cracking and crumbling, paint is peeling, repairs are blatantly necessary. There seems to be an immense garbage problem at every corner. Finally, at the top, there is no point of orientation. Where is one? The narrow medieval streets lead to the central square, the Piazza Matteotti. But how to get out of it, and where to? Having climbed to the city centre, it appears that you are in increasing spirals going down the hill again. Nothing is signposted, or if it is, then the signs soon give out. The tourist office is closed, and Potenza seems to circle in on itself in quiet desperation. Here we look to the Middle East. Everybody knows, therefore why advertise.

In the Via Pretoria the evening *passegiata* had begun. Old men in heavy overcoats and grey feathered hats met each other, stopped, moved to the end of the street and, as if propelled by some magnetic force, reversed and walked back. For the Italian, and the South Italian in particular, the evening *passegiata* is the stage for the daily public performance of self. Respect, honour, obedience are given their arena. The promenade of the citizens, dressed in their best, their daughters, grand-daughters, wives, sisters, cousins, sons from the university, all respectfully acknowledging the status and rank of each other. The public face of *sistemazione*. What is not shown is the grinding poverty at home, the quarrels over money, emigration, marriage. Sometimes the sadness of a spinster shows in the street, sometimes the bereaved husband, but usually the Italian genius for the good show triumphs over all. There was a feeling in Potenza that, despite the cracking modernity of the buildings there was a way of life that was very old going on. In defiance of earthquakes, Potenza's way has not changed. After all any city that can survive sacking by Alaric the Goth must have some guts. Down in the monastery church of Santa Maria del Sepolcro I came across a monk playing Mendelssohn's *Italian Symphony* on the organ – a strange event in a city that is on the same altitude as Istanbul, Ankara and Yerevan.

Down in the Piazza Crispi, the Middle East took over again. Crowds of people, mostly peasants, black-clad, waited for buses to the outlying areas, to Mount Vulture to the north, Melfi, Lagopesole, Barile, all once belonging to the great Frederick the Second of Hohenstaufen, "Stupor Mundi"; to Metaponto, colonised by the Greeks; to Venosa, the home of Horace and the unhinged Prince Carlo Gesualdo, he of the strange madrigals; to the Albanian colonies. As the bus jerked out of the square, laden with peasants, chickens, and me, I fancied that here in Lucania was a strange melting-pot of civilisations that defied intrusions from the North. Far away under a railway bridge a couple pressed together passionately, hoping to be unseen by their elders on the road above. In a field an old woman was hoeing, the tool rasping as it hit rock not far from the surface. The sun began to shine bright and hard, and I remembered Carlo Levi's story of exiles in Chicago who would meet on a Sunday in the countryside, and beneath a tree would let down their trousers. "What joy! We could feel the fresh air around us . . . we felt like boys again, as if we were back in Lucania." In these parts change is associated with so much misery, and so many disasters, that it is necessary to cling to what few certainties there are, even if these only turn out to be simplicity, poverty, suffering.

ANTHONY SKITT

DOWN AND OUT IN PARIS

Lisbon stinks of coffee. The smell of it made me violently ill. This is all I wish to say about Lisbon. It is a very ugly city and a very poor city. There is really no point in detailing its poverty and its ugliness. I mention the place only because it happens to mark the beginning of my journey, which ends in Amsterdam, an equally unattractive place. Fortunately Paris lies between them.

Another thing that happened in Lisbon was that I had my rucksack stolen. I put it down in the station, turned to consult a timetable and it was gone. All my plans had to be changed. I decided to go to Amsterdam, as I had met someone the day before who lived there. I would have to borrow some money from him in order to get back to England. The problem was that he wouldn't be back in Amsterdam for another four days, so I had somehow to spend four days in Europe with about ten pounds English currency and one set of clothes. It meant washing in station toilets and sleeping in trains (I had a rail pass), and even for one night in a squat.

I boarded a northbound train at lunchtime, and spent the next thirty hours on various Portuguese, Spanish and French trains.

It was early evening when I arrived in Paris. The Gare du Nord was a hive of insect activity; swarms of anxious travellers buzzed and bumped their sweaty way towards exits and toilets (which were inevitably locked). With head bowed I crawled through the crowd towards the arches that opened out on Paris.

Once outside, and comfortably seated with a glass of cool white wine and a cigarette to smoke, I began to enjoy the atmosphere. The air was warm and dry, the sky a delicate wash of pale blue and fairy pink. A light breeze blew, carrying with it exotic fragments of European language, eastern spices from the smoky kitchens behind me, and the jangling melody of wineglass and laughter.

I was shaken out of my trance by the shrill voice of the waiter demanding payment. As I made my weary way down wide boulevardes and shady side streets to the river, I realised that I was, officially, a vagabond. Or would be by the time I had paid for my next meal. I stared hungrily at the tourists gorging themselves in streetside restaurants, and even more ravenously at the gorgeous prostitutes, pouting for customers in the doorways and alleyways on every side. Some of them were fantastically clad in black leather and leopardskin, some in nothing but underwear. Occasionally a distraught shopkeeper would rush out and plead with furious hands for the girls to move on. Sometimes they were forced to. Often they just laughed, with wide mouths and heads tilted back like hyenas; they laughed at all of the men who dared to look but obviously were not going to pay. Men like me, I suppose. Voyeurs/tourists, what's the difference? There is an official bus tour of Paris that includes a visit to the red light district.

I arrived in St Denis, just across the river from Notre Dame, at about nine-thirty. It was growing dark; overhead, the sky was like a purple pincushion, with only the brightest stars shining through the multi-coloured glare of the Parisian night. Having no money, I simply stood and watched. Fortunately, St Denis offers plenty of entertainment, even to its vagabonds. In every courtyard and square of this tiny area there were buskers, tap-dancers, budding ballerinas, small street theatres performing plays in English as well as French. I saw two fire-eaters, numerous clowns and a particularly striking juggler, dressed in a vivid primary-colour harlequin suit. There was also a very shrewd mime artist who followed sightseeing tourists around, mimicking their every move until they paid him to "entertain" someone else.

Café bars and restaurants swallow up half the tourists. The other half wander lazily around, studying every menu in sight with the intensity of visitors at an art gallery. I sat down on the corner of two narrow alleyways and lit my last cigarette. Somewhere to my left, less than a hundred yards away, was the Seine. I decided to sleep on its bank – the left, of course – for that night at least. The air was warm and thick with the smells of roasting meat and spicy sauces. In front of me an old tramp was reeling about clutching a bottle of wine. He was thin, ragged and had a long, grey beard and an equally long and equally grey pointed hat. He looked like a fairytale character, Rumpelstiltskin perhaps. Then he did something fairytale characters never do; he unbuttoned his trousers and urinated in the middle of the street. The crowds parted in perfect order, and flowed smoothly past seemingly unperturbed.

Passing tourists obviously mistook me for a poor, helpless Parisian beggar boy, with my baggy sweater and thin brown arms. I was handed delicious kebabs, full of meat and spice and salad. The old drunk joined me, and between us we managed to make every well-fed passer-by feel either sick or terribly guilty. After a very successful half-hour, my new-found friend offered me a slug of his precious wine. With a grunt he took it back off me and slipped it under the folds of his overcoat.

The gay parade of St Denis eventually dwindled into a sorry trickle of drunken, bellicose tourists, bumping and burping their way back to the plush hotels on the other side of the Seine.

I suddenly became aware of a new character squatting beside me. He was small and tight, built like a boxer. Long curls and ringlets of shiny black hair covered his head. His wide animal-brown eyes were watching me. He spoke very loudly, alternating between English and French. He spoke contemptuously of the tourists; there was nothing he loathed more than compromise, he said. His own life, he assured me, was lived to the hilt. It was with apprehension and excitement that I agreed to go with him to a certain bar, patronised by local Parisians who, like himself, lived life "all the way up". I was intrigued.

He took me across the Seine, which was shimmering with snakes of golden and silver light. The streets on the other side were now empty. The night air was cool; lights shone in rooftop apartments and from one of them a piano played, bluesy and mournful.

We arrived at a bar, somewhere in the middle of Paris well after midnight. The street was black and empty, the bar glowing like a fire at the far end. We sat outside at a table strewn with empty wine bottles and overturned glasses. It reminded me of the painting by Van Gogh. It had the same magic, the bright yellowy light, the curve of the table legs, the flickering shadows all suggesting something strange and dreamlike.

He paid for all of our drinks; I in turn listened passively to his ideas and dreams. I learnt that his name was Jean-Luc and that he lived at the moment in a squat. His ideals were vague: to live from moment to moment with no plans, no security. He clowned around with intellectual ideas and laughed uncontrollably at the mention of Sartre.

An effeminate young man stole the limelight for a moment. He appeared suddenly in the middle of the street, wearing a floppy hat and carrying a stuffed pheasant. He began talking to it then rubbing it suggestively up and down his leg. Jean-Luc roared with laughter and clapped his hands together. I smiled and finished off the last of the wine.

We left, hours later, confused and elated. I learnt as we made our drunken way back to the squat that tonight's entertainment had been funded by a number of careless tourists who had been foolish enough to leave their wallets in their back pockets.

The room was at the top of four flights of stairs in an old, unused building. Inside were at least five other people, all just settling down for the night. Amongst them was the old drunk; he smiled in recognition and then curled up to sleep. Jean-Luc gave me his mattress to sleep on. I was no longer afraid or apprehensive, and slept soundly till late the following morning. When I awoke Jean-Luc was gone and so was the old man. I made my way outside and found myself in bright dazzling sunlight in a crowded square dominated by the absurd Pompidou Centre. Somewhere out there Jean-Luc was busy, working silently and anonymously, lifting everything he could lay his hands on. I don't think he was free at all. He had to work for a living, for his late-night excesses – his "freedom" – as did everyone else.

I arrived in Amsterdam the following morning. It was cold, and a grey industrial rain was falling. Nothing much happened. It rained on and off all day. I was hassled by dope dealers wherever I walked.

I soon found my friend, who was very kind and understanding, and left shortly afterwards. On the ferry the other passengers were chattering incessantly. A canal trip here, cathedral there. They all sounded as though they'd been on a school outing. I took comfort in this. Despite my lack of money, my discomfort and isolation, I knew I had travelled, seen and experienced other lives. These people around me hadn't; they'd just been on a "holiday".

STEPHEN HINCHLIFFE

WORD PERFECT IN THE SUDAN

Different people speaking different languages often express ideas which cannot be translated. Sometimes it's easier to borrow words than to try translating. That was how English friends in the Sudan coped with explaining to me the sights, flavours and values of Sennar, a hot, dusty settlement on the Blue Nile where they were teaching English for a year. Some extracts from my personal dictionary follow.

Khawadja. Self-knowledge dictates that *khawadja* is a word to be learnt early. It means "foreigner" or "Westerner" now, but comes from a synonym for "rich man". For most Sudanese, the two concepts are rather similar; what amazed me was that the natural dignity of even the poorest Sudanese prevented my wealth from creating any social difficulties between us.

A *khawadja,* whether in Sennar or in the relative sophistication of Khartoum, is self-evidently a stranger to whom a welcome must, unobtrusively, be extended. I had, on the basis of a gruelling week alone in Morocco, decided that a *khawadja* and his money were likely soon to be parted, and had girded myself up psychologically for a difficult transit from Khartoum airport to Sennar.

I began to feel slightly baffled when the airport taxi driver, having indulged in bargaining which, although effective and precise, was ridiculously good-natured, refused a tip. With petrol at thirty-five English pounds, a gallon, the man seemed imprudent by my standards.

I rather came to rely on the way in which, whenever I hesitated over which bus to board or which way to turn at a thronging street corner, someone would appear from the crowd. At five in the morning, trying to find the right bus to the truckstop for Sennar, it was heaven to be sat down beside a glowing charcoal stove with a glass of hot, sweet red tea then hauled aboard the correct bus as soon as it drew up. My stock of small change scarcely diminished, as all attempts to pay for tea or buses were met with a standard reply: "You are a guest in our country."

Perhaps that's the best free translation of *khawadja*. Even if he's carrying the average national annual income in his money-belt, it's still the right thing to do to feed, water, advise and transport him, just because he's a long way from home.

Fool. I can't deny that the people who asked me how I was going to carry all the food I'd need in my rucksack did set me wondering. Little did I know that, away from the famine areas, food is abundant and that to dine on *fool,* the Sudanese staple, is to enjoy a simple but profoundly satisfying experience.

It doesn't sound instantly lovable – mashed, stewed Egyptian black beans with vegetable oil – but the atmosphere of the *fool*-shop is perhaps the key to being converted. To leave my friends' little Arab courtyard at twilight and make our way down the dusty road brought a keen sense of anticipation. Which acquaintances would be at the shop, chatting unhurriedly as the *fool* bubbled away slowly? And would there be eggs or fried chickpea balls to mash into it? The social niceties over, the metre-long ladle would reach down the long neck into the bulbous base of the *fool*-pot, and up would come our dinner. To be mopped up with fresh-baked bread seasoned with chilli and salt, a feast with no E-numbers and no need of them.

The same went for every other item of food in Sennar; the meat, bought on the hoof each morning and eaten by nightfall, the salad fresh from the fields, the fish straight from the Nile. The chlorinated water on tap to wash it all down with seemed just enough of the twentieth-century for Sennar's cuisine.

Fuddle. I had been fuddled many times before I even heard the word in its Sudanenglish form. Fuddled to tea, fuddled to bus fares, fuddled till I was befuddled. The word comes from an Arabic word meaning (loosely) "You're welcome", or "You're invited", and became a common verb among the English in Sennar, meaning to treat, invite, look after or welcome. Whole days could be spent, just as the Sudanese spend them, fuddling and being fuddled. Thus are social bonds forged.

It is a two-way process – it isn't wise to refuse a fuddle, even if in a rush and not relishing half-an-hour with a Sudanese family drinking tea and eating a second dinner. My best fuddle was when I had to register with the police in Sennar, a prospect I viewed with some apprehension. Despite my friends' reassurances I did not relish the idea of signing on with the authorities, having had some argument with the Ministry of the Interior in Khartoum about my travel permit.

Sheltering from the noonday sun in Singah's 'high street'. (*Word Perfect in the Sudan*)

My fears were scarcely dispelled when I entered Sennar's police station. A wild West-style set of prison bars revealed the morose and shabby haul from the previous night's patrols, whilst the company on "my" side of the bars seemed no more appealing. They had guns, too.

My earnest explanation of my credentials, accompanied by a display of passport and travel permit, did not, apparently, compete as an attraction with the communal breakfast. I could see the point, and so could the prisoner. Ample *fool* with a generous supply of stewed meat on the side; the police had no option but to fuddle the *khawadja*.

The tastiest morsels having being pointed out for my attention, I tucked into my second breakfast. Then, every scrap gone, I was taken to see the commandant. Despite the advantages of literacy and a little English, he seemed no more *au fait* than his men with the procedure to be followed. To be on the safe side, I was instructed to report back again upon leaving town.

Which I duly did. No written details were taken this time either; I had been summoned only to be fuddled again to breakfast.

Tukkul. *Tukkuls* were among the things which reminded me that Sennar was very much on the fringe of the Arab world, with a heavy African influence. They were the grass huts I never thought I'd see outside a geography textbook, which the non-Arab, non-Muslim Southerners had built on the edge of town, hoping to find prosperity by moving north towards the capital.

Debari, the Southerns' suburb, was, I suppose, no more than a squalid shanty town. But at night it had a certain romance. With no electricity, and surrounded by tall woven grass stockades, its darkness was pierced only by flickering oil lamps in the *tukkuls* and the glint of the guard dogs' eyes as we passed through, trying to look nonchalant.

Even though the writ of Islamic law was supposed to run here, the police weren't inclined to get involved and I was treated to an evening of *aieesh,* or grain spirit, at a Debari speakeasy. The stuff isn't strictly consistent in quality, but it's not hard to tell whether your bottle has been watered down. Just splash a little on the table and light it – if it burns with a gentle blue flame, you're in for some heavy drinking. Just don't get any on the walls of the *tukkul* if you're a careless smoker.

Alhamdulillah. This word relates to the particular contentment of lying out in the courtyard, drinking tea and wondering which of Sennar's inhabitants would be next to knock and be fuddled. It might be the local beggar, or a Western-educated Arab like Aga, the head of English at the boys' school, calling in to talk about his happy days in England.

ABOVE: Bound feet (*left*) and hitching a ride in Xian.
BELOW: Harvest-time in southern China. (*Changing the Itinerary*)

Or Paul, from deep in the south, recognisable as a pure Dinka tribesman by the fact that, in his mid-teens, he was already two metres tall. He didn't like living with his parents in the Arab city of Khartoum and found Sennar smaller and friendlier, if still not his home. His tribe's culture revolves around cattle, after whom the men are named and for whom they compose and sing songs. Telling us about his cattle was a good way for Paul to feel nearer his true home.

Muslim and non-Muslim alike, we could all honestly make the ritual response *"Alhamdulillah"* when our well-being was asked after. More than just "fine" or "OK", I didn't have to feel literally "Allah is watching over me" to express a positive feeling that all was right with the world. There was tea in the pot and lemons to drink it with, and the *fool*-shop stove would be glowing along the road as today's dinner slowly stewed. Perhaps *khawadjas* romanticise Sudanese life as much as some Sudanese idolise the West, but during my short stay in Sennar I could truthfully say *"Alhamdulillah"*.

MIGGY CHENG

CHANGING THE ITINERARY

Being rerouted to Karachi due to bad weather sets the proverbial ball rolling. "Here we go again," I think. "We'll miss our connection to Beijing and they will not be happy." Some of them are already bitching that they have been promised a fluent German-speaking tour escort. That the tour has been marketed as English-speaking means nothing, of course, and if I – not the company I represent, but I – used a decent airline, we wouldn't be stuck in this godforsaken hole. Now their entire holiday is ruined. They have been *so* looking forward to it. They have saved for *years*. And . . . "don't tell me I'm tired. I want to go home."

We miss our connection. A very nervous air traffic supervisor at Islamabad nods his head from side to side and mutters "Oh blimey" repeatedly as I demand hotel accommodation during the twelve hours' layover. We get it . . . eventually.

At seven in the morning, arrival at Beijing doesn't exactly fill me with joy. What they don't know is that the other members of our group, who will join us at the hotel, are holding the group visa. I have a stack of duplicate application forms which are to be discreetly handed over to the immigration officers for processing here and now. A time-consuming matter which I am quite sure won't go down well with either officers or tourists.

Just as they are beginning to look around them and wonder why they are the only ones left hanging around the arrival lounge, I appear with a pile of passports stamped with individual visas and announce that breakfast is being served in the airport dining-room. That little arrangement is necessary due to the fact that there are no coaches waiting, and there are no coaches waiting because there are no hotel rooms ready. No prearranged itinerary is on the cards either, Mr Zhou – our man in Peking – tells me. We have arrived *late,* not early, but there is no time for argument and anyway, one of the first rules I learned about the Chinese is that one does not argue, one grovels.

After dinner at the hotel, I grovel for the use of a room in which to hold a briefing. We have been assigned to the "military" hotel, at least an hour's drive from Tian-an-Men Square. Expecting a bilingual onslaught I take a few slugs from what must be an essential part of any tour escort's luggage – the Scotch bottle. It helps.

I apologise for the late arrival, the absence of a national guide and for China International Travel Service's choice of hotel – hastily adding that all tour arrangements in China are at the final discretion of the state tourist organisation who "make every effort to ensure that your stay in China is enjoyable and memorable".

"Enjoyable. *Ha!*" they cry. "Memorable? Oh yes, we won't forget this *hostel* in a hurry. Hairs clogging the bath plug-hole. What could be worse?"

"No bathroom at all," I am tempted to retort. But then I remember there is a chance Kashgar may be deleted from the itinerary altogether due to the recent earthquake. They *have* to be made aware of this. Why hadn't I hit the Scotch bottle a little harder? I take a deep breath and plunge into my usual routine. I beam at them. I am sure they realise that this is not so much a holiday, more an experience. I am certain they undertstand that as they are among the very first foreigners to journey along the Silk Road since Marco Polo, facilities will be a little primitive at times. I know they will meet any necessary changes of itinerary with the intrepid traveller's sense of adventure . . . and have they heard about the earthquake at Kashgar?

Despite the rumour that thirty per cent of the local population are homeless, we do have a hotel. And bathrooms. Not a single groan when the bus breaks down en route to the Three Immortal Buddhist Caves. News that dinner will be at an authentic Uijur home actually meets with a cheer. Only once do I hear Big Mac mentioned.

"More or less a successful evening," I think as we ride back to the hotel for a performance of traditional song and dance. Wrong! The "artistes", for whom I have paid sixty yuen, cannot sing (much) and cannot dance (at all). Peering beyond the make-up I realise I have seen those faces before. Making an abortive attempt at entertainment, no doubt for a small percentage, are the hotel domestic staff.

Urumqi – capital of Xinjiang Province. We wave farewell to our "Japanese-speaking" local guide, bundle into the buses and rumble across the Taklamakam to Turfan. The local guide greets us with an expression I can do without. "Little problem," he whispers, and they all lean forward to catch his words.

"How little?"

"New hotel not officially open yet."

"Let's unofficially open it then."

"Cannot. Sorry."

"Can. Sorry. Will." Did. There are no curtains at the windows, no lights, no loo rolls. But there are beds and by evening there are sheets on them. I used to think this sort of thing happened only in Spain.

The overnight train to Liuyuan has no water – for drinking or for the toilets. "You charter carriage, you bring own water." Oh sure. I can just see them shuffling along the platform, slopping water from buckets hooked on bamboo poles over their shoulders.

Dunhuang. I am on my way to the hotel desk to protest about the lack of hot water when one of the more ambitious of my flock (having wandered out of the hotel to explore alone) comes charging through the revolving doors spurting blood all over the foyer and yelling that he's been bitten by a mad dog. A couple of surgeons on the tour – their honeymoon for heaven's sake – stitch him up and drag him off to the hospital whilst I go off to determine whether the salivating beast is rabid or not. I miss out on a hot bath *and* dinner.

Oh my Buddha. At Jiuyuan I have to announce a change of itinerary. We will not be staying overnight but flying directly to Lanzhou. That might just have been accepted graciously if we had not been given the wrong flight time. We dash to see the westernmost part of the Great Wall with barely enough time to snap pictures. We wolf down a meal hurriedly enough to give the tin man indigestion. And for what? A four-hour wait at an airport where they have to take turns to sit down.

Pass the valium – it gets worse. Lanzhou and another change of itinerary. Train, not plane, to Xian. No time to visit the Thousand Buddha caves. Isn't that what they all took this entire trip for? They are not happy. Not one bit. They are seething. I promise a special Tang Dynasty-style banquet on the eve of National Day in Xian as an attempt at compensation. A mistake. Restaurant, food, service and atmosphere are all wrong. We are not in a party mood. And the following day all the city sites are closed. On his recent visit, Japan's premier had publicly prayed for lost Japanese souls in China during the Invasion. There were fears that the students would run riot and foreign tourists would be at risk. "All tour buses must leave the city immediately after breakfast and not return until evening. The acrobatic show is cancelled."

At Shanghai the hotel is so far out of the city proper that they refuse to get off the coaches.. The flight from Guilin to Guanzhou is delayed. Forget about a much-needed shower and gin and tonic at the White Swan to put us in the mood for our farewell banquet. We speed directly to the North Garden restaurant. But the banquet is good. The banquet is *very* good. "They're mellowing nicely," I muse as I stand to speak.

"Friends. Allow me to propose a toast. As this is our last meal together I'd like to take the opportunity to thank you all for hanging in there with me when the going got rough. I know there were times when you wondered whether it was all worth it. Those times are behind us now and it *was* worth it . . . wasn't it? I'm sure you agree our journey has been an interesting and *valuable* experience. One on which you can look back with many a pleasant memory. I see you are enjoying the suckling pig and the Mao-Tai, so on this happy note I drink your health. To you all . . . and to no more changes of itinerary. Cheers!"

I didn't know then that our tickets for the morning's train to Hong Kong had not been reserved and that the train was already well overbooked.

TASHA WILLIAMS

MINCEMEAT AND MASHED POTATOES

Our bus was bulbous, brightly decorated and flashed green, red and yellow lights in unexpected places. A child's tiny sandal dangled from the front bumper as a good luck token. We had driven through the night, and most of my companions lay in tortured attitudes of sleep.

In the bleak light of dawn we emerged from the gorge into desolation. The glacial-fed waters of the Indus wove a channel through wide mud flats, and on either side the river in spate had deposited high banks and cliffs of shingle and solidified debris. Beyond, boulder-strewn desert stretched to the extremities of the valley. Barren mountains sloped steeply towards distant peaks which, snow-striped, could be glimpsed through slits in the mountain wall. There was not a tree to be seen, not a blade of grass.

As the others stirred and shivered, the first signs of cultivation came as a relief after that world of primeval chaos: a field of maize, a small orchard, puny settlements, a patch of willows by the river's edge.

By the time we bowled into Gilgit in Pakistan's northern provinces our eyes had grown accustomed to a variety of greens punctuated by the gold discs of sunflowers. The mountain backcloth, receding in layers like the flies of a stage set, was the desiccated colour of elephant-hide or wrinkled rhinoceros-skin. The lack of cold purple shadows – no gloom, no melancholy – made them seem unrealistically accessible.

Gilgit is a long, busy, straggling bazaar, a crossroads between Baltistan and Hunza, and also between the secret valleys of the Karakoram and the Chilas route to the Punjab. There was a time when this route linked the sub-continent with the Silk Road through Sinkiang. It was a heady thought that we might continue through Hunza on the Karakoram Highway and, if we ignored the frontier which was there to stop us, end up in Kashgar, Yarkand or Khotan. I was possessed by a longing to do so.

The bazaar was filled with vibrantly coloured sweaters and windcheaters, mounds of dried Hunza apricots, bags of fresh almonds and piles of Chitrali hats in white or natural wool. We discovered an excellent bookshop run by an Urdu poet. There is a polo ground, and down by the river a neat public garden – the Chenar Bagh – and the longest suspension bridge, so they claim, in South-East Asia.

It was hot and dusty. I chose the quiet courtyard of the Stay and Dine Inn to pass the time over a pot of *kawa* brewed from green tea (which is bartered with the Chinese for dried fruit) flavoured with cardamom and almonds. The enclosure presents a patch of sparse grass edged by hibiscus, sunflowers and roses, and a spindly but refreshing fountain. Through an archway I could see the glare and bustle of the Cinema Bazaar. One morning as I scribbled postcards a small plump hand slipped into mine and I found myself looking into the solemn walnut-brown eyes of a four-year-old, who trustingly held onto my hand. His mother smiled and nodded from her veranda.

The Suzuki trucks in which we travelled to Karimabad, the capital of Hunza, were comfortable enough. The Chinese-built Karakoram Highway penetrates the long snake-like gorge of the Hunza river. Lion-dogs strut along the parapets of the principal bridges as a reminder of the builders and of the proximity of the border. The side roads into Hunza were buried in dust to a depth of a foot or more, and in places we had to rearrange boulders into the semblance of an even surface to avoid breaking a back axle or slithering into the bed of an errant stream.

The road wound round the northern side of the broad Hunza valley through an abundance of apricot, peach, mulberry, pomegranate, apple, almond and walnut trees. Like feathery headdresses, thin rows of poplars edged the fields and milky-green glacial water cascaded over precipices and spilled into complex irrigation channels. But the water, when it emerged from the tap, was black and thick with sediment. Our hands and faces, and when we were foolish enough to wash them, our clothes, gradually turned grey.

Up against Ultar mountain old Baltit fort, now abandoned by the Mir for a new palace, looked blankly down the valley like the eye of a blind man who might one day miraculously regain his sight.

"What is the name of that dish we ate last night, Faqeir, that looked like cold spaghetti and meat sauce but wasn't?"

"That dish is a traditional Hunza dish."

"Yes, but.what do you call it?"

"It is called," Faqeir said, "mincemeat and mashed potatoes."

We had gorged ourselves on a sumptuous meal of subtly spiced dishes, followed by small green peaches and accompanied by tall mugs of thick apricot juice. Later we lounged on low platforms ranged along the walls of an inner room. A local band squatted cross-legged on a higher dais.

The group comprised two large drums, a pair of *tabla* and a wind instrument, somewhat like a shawm, which was occasionally exchanged for a flute. The shawm-flute player set the pace, enticing dancers onto the floor with flashing eyes and curling movements of his wrist.

Faqeir danced with outstretched arms and shuffling feet. As word of the party spread, neighbours gathered at the door and, dissembling reluctance, took to the floor one by one. Each had his own style, proud, head flung back. Five and ten rupee notes were thrust into the dancers's hands and worn like a fan jutting through his fingers. The pace quickening, the money was flung to the band and the dance ended abruptly with the performer melting away through the door.

The inhibitions of the English (or do I mean British? – no, English and Scots) showed itself in the reactions of our group, lolling, lounging, sprawling with response: one young man read a paperback throughout the performance.

The women of the household peeped and giggled through a square aperture in the centre of the ceiling. The evening ended with Faqeir doing a slow stamping Pashtu war dance. Incongruous – gentle, soft-eyed Faqeir, who earlier that day had cupped a moribund butterfly in his hands and by breathing gently on it had given it the kiss of life.

Long after we had retired to bed we could hear the trilling flute and the rhythm of the drums.

I took to rising at 5.20 to watch the first rays of the sun capture one by one the pinnacles of Rakaposhi, Durrand, Ultar. Then quite suddenly the light slid into the valley. Even at this hour people were stirring; women in twos and threes wending their way to the fields. Both men and women work all hours of daylight at this time of year, gathering in the harvest and laying out fruit and vegetables on the flat roofs to dry for winter storage. Six months of hard work, six of play, I was told. For having secured the harvest and made fast against the long winter, what is there to do but eat, drink, make music and dance?

The longevity of the people is legendary and is variously ascribed to ingesting large quantities of apricots, or to eating the apricot kernels, or even to gold in the water (not that black sediment?).

"What age do people live to here, Faqeir?"

"Over sixty."

"Well, there are plenty of people in England over sixty."

"I know of a woman," said Faqeir, "who is ninety-two."

"I know of someone in London who is ninety-three."

"It's claimed," desperately, "that a man in the Nagar Valley is 104."

When the time came to leave we retraced our route along the Hunza and Gilgit rivers, then plunged further into the Indus Gorge eastwards to Skardu. The road, a miracle of engineering, clung like an eyebrow to the mountainside high above the boiling river, here tightly compressed into a narrow chasm. This must be the longest, most brutal gorge in the world. Great boulders the size of a two-storeyed house perched at ninety degrees, restrained only by a few small rocks which it would seemingly take little to dislodge. Involuntarily I held my breath as we drove past.

As darkness fell we closed our eyes to avoid the sensation of perpetually careering at great speed towards the precipice, only to be hurled at the last minute round a hairpin bend towards jutting rocks magnified in the headlights, and so to start the next dash for the precipice. We slowed down only to pick our way round boulders or over a landslide or, where half the road had subsided into the river, to bounce and sway up against the mountainside.

The brightness of the stars in a jet black sky, the roaring river below, the sense of our busload being alone in space and time, all added to a dreamlike quality, as though the journey was destined to go on for ever.

LOW COUNTRY LIFE

"*A Foggy Day in London Town,* in B-flat," says Coops. "One . . . two . . . one, two, three, four," miming grotesquely. And off the four of us go, skittering through the chord changes. Two Brits and two Dutchmen, we have never even met before yet alone rehearsed. We don't speak each others' languages. We are performing in the Trafalgar Pub, Eindhoven, southern Holland, on an August Saturday night, by now halfway through a good, romping version – even though I say so myself – of *Just One of Those Things.* The Dutch are clapping, the proprietor is smiling. I titter at the piano as Coops, bass clarinet under his arm, makes his standard intermission announcement: "And now the gentlemen of the ensemble will take a short break and repair to the bar to mingle with members of the audience who will, no doubt, express their appreciation in the time-honoured tradition." And they do. Our first gig is a success. The Alan Cooper Trio (there are, in fact, four of us) is a hit on the eve of our two-week Dutch tour. The proprietor is an admirer of Thelonious Monk. He feeds me *genever jong* as I play *Round Midnight* for chorus after chorus until my hands won't move through fatigue and gin.

The train to Maastricht is crowded with kids. They hammer out tattoos on the ashtrays, reassemble Coke cans and shout at each other. Coops and I try to doze in our corner seats but it is impossible. "Where are we going, dear boy?" says Coops. He's in his absent-minded academic persona today.

"Three days in Maastricht," I reply. "It's a medieval town stuck on a pimple of Holland, between Belgium and Germany."

"Hmmmm," he says, then straightens his military tie, dusts the jacket of his ancient and threadbare grey suit and puts his fisherman's hat on the rack above his collection of instruments – B-flat clarinet, E-flat clarinet and bass clarinet, to be precise. All this is routine for him. He flits about to the Gulf, Hong Kong and the States all the time. But this is my first tour for twenty-two years, since 1963 when I was a young piano player with the Scottish jazz group, the Clyde Valley Stompers.

"And now," says Coops, grinning skeletally, "a tune which our pianist Jamie Evans and I used to play in an east London public house called the Rumboe. That is, on the odd occasion we remember being there. Ladies and gentlemen, "Somewhere over the Rumboe." Blank looks from the Dutch, Belgian and German audience. But they warmly applaud our version of *Somewhere over the Rainbow*. A French girl buttonholes me and calls me "a genius of the piano".

We have a new, young Dutch drummer tonight. He's smoking a giant joint and drinking far too much. "Can't we play some avant-garde music?" he says. Coops acquiesces, lizard eyes narrowed and beard twitching. "No piano please," says the drummer pointing me barwards. "Alan will please play the big bass clarinet and make elephant noises." Coops and I collapse helplessly. A tour joke is born, to be repeated and enjoyed, night after night.

In Venlo, a south-east border town, the rain pelts down on the asparagus fields. Western Europe is suffering its worst summer for decades. Dutch and German TV stations show scenes of caravan and camping sites sinking into mud. It's an eye-opener for us, who have been taught to think that British weather is always nastier than anyone else's. The Sunday afternoon gig is in a pub-cum-brewery. And at three o' clock, a time when English pubs are closed and dead, we launch into *Can't We be Friends?* But the audience is very talkative, which irritates Coops. He makes his stock anti-noise announcement. "Ladies and gentlemen, the next tune, *Groovin' High,* will feature the bass clarinet. Not many people are familiar with this instrument. This is because there aren't many of them, few people play them and most people are talking too much most of the time to be able to listen any-way."

It's a long way, by Low Country standards, from Liège in northern Belgium to Amsterdam, slap in the middle of the Netherlands. As the train rattles along the landscape, housing and lifestyles change gradu-ally but markedly, "I like the Belgians," says Coops, drinking Pils beer and stuffing down ham and cheese, doggy-bagged from the hotel that morning. "They're just like us. A nation of stroppy piss-artists who'd rather go down the pub than mow their rotten lawns." The strait-laced Dutchness, un-netted windows to show off their ubiquitous house-plants and dour furniture, takes over the view from the carriage window. I feel excited by the prospect of seeing Amsterdam again. My last visit was in 1978, and during several trips in the Seventies I had always felt at home there. We roll through the suburbs and as soon as we set foot outside the station, Coops decides he doesn't like it. "Junk food, noise, traffic and children. Appalling place, dear boy."

"But," I cajole, "there are lots of lovely paintings here – Rem-brandts, Van Goghs, all the old and new Dutch masters." He's slightly mollified but grumpy. Our hotel is just off the Leidsestraat, only a few minutes' stroll from the Bamboo Bar where we are booked for two nights. We have both developed a craving for the delicious Dutch street snack, raw herring with chopped onions. But here in tourist-stricken Amsterdam we can't find any. It's all hamburgers, chips, mayonnaise, ketchup and imitation *saté*. . .

The first person we bump into on German soil is Johnny Parker, veteran jazz pianist and long-time crony of Coops. They egg each other on with tales of the old days. "So Coltrane comes down to my place trying to buy my straight soprano," brags Coops. "So I told Louis to try this Swiss laxative," trumps Parker. By mid-afternoon, in a famous Dusseldorf beer hall, we are well into a jazzers' convention, drinking small glasses of dark *alt* beer served by genial blue-clad waiters who replace every empty glass with a full one unless prevented. A few yards away the dignified boats and barges sail down the broad sweep of the Rhine with grace. The afternoon passes hilariously. Back in England they close the pub in the afternoon just as you start enjoying yourself.

The weather changes in Amsterdam. The sun beats down and the canals shimmer. We have two days off and Coops, grumbling about "children and hamburgers", heads back south to base. I decide to stay on and enjoy the city. It's good to be on my own for a while, just wandering where I please . . . I realise how responsible I have been feeling for Coops, always having to find things to keep him amused. I look at the Rembrandts in the Rijksmuseum and dote over the wonderfully restored *Nightwatch,* now de-gloomed into its former grandeur. Outside the museum, a mock-up of the painting has been set up on the pavement with holes cut in place of the main characters' heads for end-of-the-pier type photographs. Is that funny or sad?

Dead cats and other nasties now float in what I remember as clean canals. The girls of the red light district, posing in their shop windows, haven't changed. Nor have the sex shops, apart from their wares becoming more explicit. As I settle my hotel bill, the resident cat purrs at my feet. I stroke it and see that my hand is adorned by four tiny black fleas.

Saturday afternoon in Rotterdam. It could easily be Croydon or Hemel Hempstead, all shopping precincts, parking lots and modernity. Hardly surprising, as the Germans flattened the place early in the Second World War. We eat in one of the thousands of Chinese-Indonesian restaurants, magnificently dragon-decorated but my chicken and the sauce covering it have been introduced only in the previous two minutes. The Hook of Holland, our boat and Blighty beckon. I'm still in shock after being a pretend-professional musician for a fortnight but Coops is already making phone calls, doing deals and setting up gigs and trips. My desk awaits me on Monday morning.

ROY MANLEY

FROM RUSSIA WITHOUT LOVE

The train stops just short of the Finnish border. Soviet officials now fill our corridor. In the next compartment a woman starts crying. I look through the window at a watchtower overlooking scrubby coniferous forest.

They have finished with me. I stand up and begin to repack my belongings which are strewn over the seats opposite. Dirty clothes, magazines, papers, letters. The man had spent twenty minutes with me.

"Clubman's Club?" he had asked, looking at a directory. "Women?"

He had gone slowly through a copy of *Australia Society*. "Water is more dangerous than Alcohol," he had read the headline aloud. "They are speaking of dirty water? Yes?" Yes, they were.

An individual tourist, I reflect, gets individual attention. A few compartments away a group of Americans had received the most cursory of examinations.

When I had arrived at Leningrad Station I had been pursued along the platform by a short, sweating Russian in spectacles. "Mister Manley! Mister Manley!" He had caught me up and told me to wait while he collected two other individual tourists, Americans. He had returned without them. "I hate Americans," he had said. "You know what Oscar Wilde thought of Americans?" He quotes *A Woman of No Importance*: "When good Americans die they go to Paris."

"Indeed? And when bad Americans die, where do they go to?"

"Oh, they go to America." He spoke with an American accent.

The Hotel Leningrad was full of Americans. It was outwardly an American hotel, bland and competent, concrete and glass. My bedroom gave me a distant view of the Winter Palace. It was midsummer and the scene varied little through twenty-four hours. I stayed up to see the white night and saw only a grey river mist broken by the dark shapes of river boats.

I found Leningrad an empty shell, a painted, vacant woman, a city without a spirit. It was a Vienna or Paris, built for magnificence but shorn of all those things which make grandeur live. Bereft of markets, cafés, incident, intimacy, vitality, humour, that jumble of material and personal qualities which give a place heart. It was a mausoleum. For a few hours I was able to lose myself in the Hermitage. There, in the wit of Picasso, the zest of the Impressionists, the human dignity of Guardi I found a life I could not see in the streets outside. Would they have been able to paint in modern Leningrad?

As an individual tourist, unprotected by a guide, I came closer to the treatment Russians give to Russians. Sitting in the Hermitage buffet, a small room hidden from the hordes and shown me by a friendly Rosa Klebb, I watched waiters screaming at latecomers and slamming the door in their faces. The waiters in my hotel restaurant just shrugged their shoulders and directed me from one serviceless table to another. I had been to the Soviet Union before and had expected bureaucracy or, rather, the worst signs of it. I had expected the three separate stages to be endured before buying a coffee or a sandwich – identifying and pricing the object, paying for it and then obtaining it. I had expected the complex regulations which found me wandering lost between hard currency (sic) and rouble stalls, shops and bars in the hotel. What I had not foreseen was the drab mental brutality of it all. ˙

It was four Iraqi airforce officers, each with an immaculate moustache, who rescued me from the indifference of the hotel waiters. They were on holiday from the front and had spread their money around. Their generosity did me a service. They saw what was happening to me and summoned their waiter. He attended to me immediately, sat me down at a table next to them and handed me a menu. And he smiled! The Iraqis toasted me in Russian champagne.

Next night there was a cabaret. I had to pay to watch high-kicking girls who might have graced a Hollywood musical of the Forties. A young and generously proportioned woman came over to my table and asked me for a light. Would I like to join her and her friend? I ordered a bottle of wine. They spoke enough English to make their intentions clear.

"You know," said one of my Iraqi friends a little later, with a gesture taking in the huge restaurant, "every single woman here is a prostitute. But it's not the same as it is in your country or mine. It's very dirty."

"Dirty?" I asked.

"Yes. Dirty," he replied, raising a hand to their obedient waiter and tapping a bottle.

"You see. You can't take them to the hotel bedrooms." I saw. Old, scowling men in ill-fitting uniforms patrolled the public rooms. Women who dispensed our keys sat on each floor and overlooked the lifts and stairheads.

"So we have to go home with them and they have to get their husbands out of bed so we can use them."

That afternoon, ignored by taxis, I had stood outside a small hotel and been surreptitiously ushered into a large black saloon and whisked towards the Leningrad. Before we reached it the driver asked for money.

"We all have to make our private business," he said, pocketing three roubles. He dropped me hurriedly and well away from the hotel entrance.

The train starts. The officials have gone. We have crossed the border. Soon we shall stop at the shining little Finnish frontier station and buy sandwiches and sit, eating them, in the sun. I have finished stuffing my things into my bag and briefcase.

I look into the next compartment. A young woman sits in a ransacked waste and talks to a pony-tailed child. Her face is still streaked with tears.

"Remember, you're an American now, not a Russian. The Russians are shit, shit!"

The little girl's face is expressionless. "And we're never going to come back here again. Never!"

Nor, I think, as I turn away to watch Finland slipping by, am I.

Room for a few more in Leningrad's Palace Square. (*From Russia Without Love*)

The ruined city of Pagan, with its temples and pagodas the size of European cathedrals. (*On the Road from Mandalay*)

ANGUS GAUNT

On The Road From Mandalay

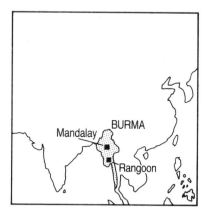

After three months in Asia I could have picked several better days for my first attack of the runs. We'd arrived at Mandalay the day before and were now to make the seven-hour journey by road to the ruined city of Pagan, eighty miles away. There was no question of delaying the trip. The Burmese government allows you only a seven-day visa, and this was our fifth day.

We'd bought our tickets that afternoon from a man in a wooden kiosk near the market. It had a newly painted sign that read "EXPRESS BUS. MANDALAY PAGAN" in red and blue capitals.

"Bus go tomorrow morning, five o'clock," he said, taking our kyats, freshly changed on the black market, and allocating to each of us a seat which he ticked off on a chart. "He's well organised," I remember one of us commenting.

Four of us had taken up together for the week: an Australian, two Danes and myself. We had all spent some time in South-East Asia and, after what we would come to recognise as the comparative luxury of travelling in those countries, were feeling a little apprehensive about the rigours we'd been assured awaited us on the subcontinent. Burma is where the transition becomes clear.

At five in the morning Mandalay seemed quiet and snug. The streets were littered with sleeping dogs and in the coffee houses faces clustered around solitary lights and sipped their first cups of the day. There was no sign of a sunrise when we arrived at the kiosk. There was no sign of a bus either, just a couple of red pick-ups with a small crowd milling about under the yellow glow of a street lamp around which hundreds of insects were making orbits. From time to time a cart would trundle by in the shadows. We put down our bags. The scratching of crickets still dominated the night and the air smelled warmly of cow dung, coffee and cheroot smoke.

"Good morning, sirs!" Our man was waving from beside one of the pick-ups with a fan of bank notes. "Bus is ready, sirs!"

San Anton's day in Andalusia. (*All the Fun of the Fiesta*)

He seemed to be relishing his duties.

One of the things about travelling on the cheap is that you learn to adapt. And if not to adapt, at least to expect the unexpected. Which was why our objections were short-lived, almost disappointingly so.

"No. We're on the Express Bus."

Half a dozen words to be exact.

"Express Bus – here!" He grinned hugely.

There really wasn't any more to be said. These pick-ups, the size of a family estate car with a wooden bench down either side, are found throughout the region. They are convenient, though scarcely comfortable, for journeys of half-an-hour and less. They are variously known as bemos, jeepneys, tuk-tuks or whatever. Never had I heard them referred to as Express Buses.

"How many passengers will there be?" one of the Danes asked without expression.

"Fourteen passenger. Get in please. We go now." From the interior several faces were looking at us placidly. At a squeeze I estimated that one of the benches would accommodate about four European-size bums.

"Get in now. Bus go in five minutes." Two on one side, two on the other; we occupied all the space that remained. Unless you were under five feet six the roof was too low. Our host whisked several tiny stools into the space between the benches. He counted in English.

"Fourteen!" he said in triumph and went to supervise the loading of the other Express Bus.

People climbed in and sat on the stools. The Burmese, fortunately, are not a large race. Like cinema usherettes, young men with trays of sweets and absurd plastic toys hovered hopefully outside. When we set off, half an hour later, there were exactly fourteen of us in the back, not counting the conductors who preferred to perform acrobatics on the tailgate. Dawn was now breaking, the dogs were uncurling and the city was coming to life. My buttocks were already aching and, after toying with the notion that I would either die or go insane before finishing the journey, I had resolved to take a perverse pleasure in enduring it.

What do I remember about it? I remember everything. There was the climate; at six o'clock I was wishing I could get up onto the roof to fish out my pullover; at seven the sun was up and I was wanting to take off my shirt and at eight the heat inside the van was intense and all our clothes were soggy with perspiration. After that it grew hotter. Then there was the realisation that numbness in the rear quarters by no means precludes pain, and the moment when we found out why the two conductors were necessary. They were indulging in a little private enterprise – we were to take on more passengers. They stopped for everybody. There was always space for one more. I wouldn't have minded but hardly anyone seemed to get off. At one point there were thirty-one passengers on board. I know because Kym, the Australian, counted them.

But there were also rest stops. While the others leaped out to quench their thirst and stretch their limbs, I spent the time inventing embarrassing sign language to discover the whereabouts of the nearest hole full of writhing maggots where I could snatch my ninety glorious seconds. And there were the people. I remember their serenity, their seeming indifference to discomfort and their cheerfulness which made me feel both ashamed and murderous. Without a word they crouched into spaces I hadn't even noticed, and settled down as though this were an everyday occurrence. But then again, they weren't suffering from my problem. The only consolation I drew from the entire seven hours was that it was physically impossible for my buttocks to be parted.

Even when we broke down at noon in the middle of a desert they simply filed out and positioned themselves in the shade of a parched-looking bush as though it had all been rehearsed. It was a bad breakdown. Under the weight it was carrying the vehicle appeared simply to have collapsed. At home it would have been terminal, but they set to work with hammers and wrenches and within an hour we were able to continue. It's like that in Burma. Things fall apart but somehow they are kept serviceable and life carries on.

A couple of hours later I was lying on my bed in a guest-house in Pagan, already congratulating myself at the experience, isolating the salient points and honing the phraseology for my next letter to my girlfriend. A huge green gekko jumped from the rafters onto Kym as we lay there. Unsure whether it was a genuine danger or just a practical joker we spent fifteen minutes with a broom-handle encouraging it to leave by the window. In the end it consented and crawled at leisure onto the outside of the hut. Then we put up our mosquito nets.

Pagan is Burma's Pyramids or Taj Mahal, but it seems to possess an extra dimension of its own – twenty-five square miles of brown plain spangled with temples and pagodas the size of the great cathedrals of Europe. Green scrub now grows in the gaps where eight centuries ago Burma's capital thrived. We spent the morning viewing some of the structures in a horse-drawn *tonga,* fortifying ourselves at roadside stalls where old men chewed betel and sold us booklets on Buddhism that are available for nothing from the Department of Religious Affairs in Rangoon (it said so on the inside cover) and bottles of Vimto that tasted flat and unpleasant because they were made up from the dregs of other unfinished bottles. I thought it clever of them to sell the same bottle so many times, but I made sure to pour away what I couldn't drink.

In the afternoon we hired a jeep, a group of us, for the four-hour journey to catch the night train back to Rangoon. We didn't pick up any passengers, although several tried to flag us down. It seemed like the most shameful luxury.

ALL THE FUN OF THE FIESTA

It was hotter than we had ever known it. The village, as we climbed the hill, smelt like an African kraal, of dust and animal droppings, and the white buildings reflected more light than the eye could bear. Beside the fountain stood an elaborately caparisoned mule, being watered by a boy. As the water splashed from the bucket it formed long rivulets down the dusty alley, each one lined with thirsty wasps. What was the mule's name, we asked in a gush of English sentimentality. His name was Mule, the boy replied.

Up on our flat roof the temperature was cooler, with a breeze blowing up from the coast and the vine arbour providing an indigo shade. Across the valley the ruins of the Arab castle stood out so clearly that it seemed one could pick out every sprig of cistus between the tumbled stones; and sounds, too, reached us with a heightened intensity in the mountain air. Half a mile away a man was loosening the earth around an olive tree, and the fall of every pebble sounded like an avalanche.

Close below us, outside the next house, Elisa was hard at work despite the heat, touching up invisible defects in the whitewash with a small brush. She then carefully dusted down the exterior of the house like a Victorian tweenie polishing a tallboy, and finished by sweeping the alley on hands and knees. Why was she working so hard, we asked. Because of San Anton, she said. The Fiesta, tomorrow evening. The village's chief event of the year. The procession would go right past her house – and ours.

We looked apprehensively at our street wall, which now took on a new importance. It could certainly do with a coat of whitewash in honour of San Anton. We asked Elisa how to set about it.

Easy, she said; all we needed was *cal*. From a shed down the alleyway she produced a sack of it: innocent-looking lumps of white chalky stuff. She also loaned us a bucket, a couple of brushes and a large oildrum. The latter we half-filled with water, as instructed, and dropped in the *cal*. Only then did we realise what it was. Quicklime.

The effect was cataclysmic. The quicklime's fearful pent-up energy was instantly released in a maelstrom of chemical activity. The water seethed like a geyser, and the oil-drum leapt up and down on the paving like a Brobdingnagian jumping-bean. Bemused by the infernal forces we had unleashed, my wife and I cowered at a safe distance until the seething white broth had subsided and cooled. Then we went to work.

The trick, Elisa explained, was to dip the brush into a bucket of the whitewash and then to flick it onto the wall in a fine spray. We flicked, reloaded our brushes, and flicked again. after a few minutes of this, every inch of our clothing was encrusted as stiff and white as the cerements of a corpse, while the wall apparently remained its grey knobbly self. But we were doing better than we knew. Fresh whitewash is grey-blue until it dries, and after a few minutes in the sun our wall was dazzling white. We admired it through screwed-up eyes. We were ready for the Fiesta.

It began at about seven in the evening with a series of explosions that rattled our teeth. From the platform in front of the church Manolo the mayor was discharging rockets, lethal silver-nosed monsters that looked as though they could down a B-52 at 10,000 feet. He fired them casually over his shoulder while hob-nobbing with a circle of friends. We decided to wait behind the corner of the church until he had finished.

Somebody tapped me on the shoulder. It was Juan. Would we like a glass of wine, he asked, to prime ourselves for the festivities to come. We followed him to his *bodega,* a tall lean-to at the back of his house, windowless apart from a small aperture high on one side. Walls and roof timbers were uniformly coated with a layer of whitewash so thick with age that every outline was as blurred as a half-melted ice cream. Along the floor, and almost filling it, was a row of enormous barrels.

Juan mounted one of them like a bare-back horseman, removed a brick which was capping a hole, and reached down with a scoop cut from a length of bamboo. This he emptied into a couple of glasses, which he passed to us after fishing out some mosquitoes with his finger. We sipped the familiar straw-coloured, druggy liquid, halfway between nectar and cough mixture. We were starting on the second round when Juan's wife put her head through the door. It was time to go. The procession was about to begin.

All day the village had been humming with suppressed excitement, like a hive about to swarm, and now all the eighty-odd inhabitants were gathered in front of the church. The double doors parted and San Anton emerged, a dour figure with a black pig at his feet, on a wooden platform borne by four men. They inched him through the narrow passage behind the church and past the freshly limpid wall of our house, now gleaming in the evening sun. In front of the figure walked the women in dignified devotion, many of them barefoot. Behind came the men, smoking and chatting and comfortably shod. In and out ran the children, brandishing fireworks.

The little cortege straggled down the hill and round the end of the cemetery, then along past the main wine-store on the road at the bottom, and back up the dusty track on the far side of the village. At the top, near the end of the circuit, there was a brief interruption. One of the men stepped suddenly onto a bank above the procession and burst into song. His voice was high, a threnody of rising and falling and vibrating notes, driven from his lungs in gusts of passion. The walkers stopped suddenly, like a freeze-frame in a film, until the last words died away. Then the shuffling feet continued down the headlong alleyways and back to the church, where the saint was safely parked for another year. And immediately – like a click of a switch – the village reverted from religious to temporal celebrations.

Down on the road below the houses it looked as if a mule Derby was about to begin. The contestants were lined up with two young bloods astride each mule. Ahead of them, across the road, was a high wire to which were attached reels of brightly coloured silk, each with a ring at the end. In turn, with a clatter of hooves and a tornado of dust, each mule cantered under the wire while the pillion rider reached up with a knife and tried to thrust it through one of the rings. If he succeeded, the silk unfurled with a flash of colour and he rode off in triumph, flourishing it from the end of his dagger like a jouster flaunting his lady's favour. If he failed, he tried again. All this took a while. By the time the last ribbon had gone, the velvet dusk had descended.

Suddenly, with a screech of amplified guitars, the twentieth century arrived. The small dusty arena beside the pump had been converted to a dance floor, and a pop group from the village over the hill now exploded into action. At first only the children danced, while the adults fuelled themselves in the makeshift bar. Some of the little girls wore flounced gipsy costumes, with combs in their backswept hair, earrings, and beauty spots on their five-year-old cheeks. They swayed solemnly to and fro, doll-like in the lamplight, moving their arms in slow, ritualistic gestures. Gradually the adults joined the dance; the women grouped together, and then the men, still without any communion between the sexes. Not until midnight had come and gone did men and women pair off, and not until dawn did they touch. Then at last the brown hands clutched, and dark heads drooped against slowly gyrating shoulders.

By then we were tired. As we walked slowly back up the hill, the church tower and the roof lines were beginning to emerge from the dark lavender sky, and the angular dimensions of the houses were hardening. High overhead, in the greater radiance of the upward air, the swifts were already whirling and flickering like sparks rising from a fire. Another Andalusian day had begun.

GEORGINA CARRINGTON

IN THE FOOTHILLS OF ANNAPURNA

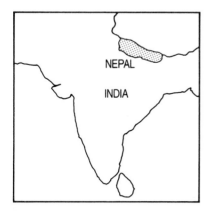

It was birdwatching that brought us to Nepal. A while before, we had met for the first time at Heathrow – a random assortment of Dutch, American and British, brought together by wanderlust and an interest in natural history. We planned to trek to 10,500 feet in the foothills of Annapurna.

We went by taxi to the place where our guides were waiting. Pokhara sprawled along its dusty road; open shop fronts revealed bright heaps of vegetables alongside specialist trekking equipment, bales of fabric and stacks of *doko* (the woven, conical baskets used with a headband to carry everything here).

We walked for seven hours a day. Mileage became insignificant; the statistic that proclaimed itself in our aching legs was the height climbed or descended. At first the going was easy. Tall clumps of delicate bamboo occasionally blocked wide views over gentle landscape. Brainfever birds' throbbing calls hung in space; shadows were sharp on the white dust. We stopped to watch a man ploughing with two water-buffalo. The trail began to ascend steeply as we followed the main trade route to Jomosom, in the north. Small terraced fields wrinkled up the hills, and lean oak and kapok trees, coated in lichen, towered beside the path. A mule train climbed towards us from the next valley: twenty beasts, slow under enormous loads, with coloured plumes between their ears and small pieces of mirror on their bridles catching the light. The bells round their necks made a continuous mellow sound. We stood on the wall to let them pass.

"*Namaste,*" called the mulateer, astride the last mule, and we returned his traditional greeting. Minutes later we were on the wall again as a group of people came twisting down the track to overtake us. In one *doko* basket huddled a frail old woman. She looked very sick. An ancient treddle sewing machine passed by on somebody's back. "*Namaste.*"

My constant companion was a young Sherpa called Nima, who was the same age as my oldest son. His English was good, and he was a great communicator, always prepared to try and bridge the gaps arising from language limitations and different cultures. Sherpas are a mountain race from north-east Nepal, quite different in appearance and speech to lowland Nepalese. Their reputation as mountain guides is such that now all the trekking guides are known as "Sherpas" regardless of origin.

Sometimes the trail was so steep that my head was level with the heels of the person in front. We had grown accustomed to the effects of altitude – pounding heart and panting breath – but our guides insisted that we rest regularly. Our porters rested too, leaning against the specially constructed places along the way which enabled them to take the weight off their shoulders without removing their burdens. We had two Sherpa girls with us, carrying loaded *dokos*.

"Never offer food or drink of which you have already partaken, as it is considered polluted, and could cause offence," our holiday literature warned sternly. But Dalli, sitting on the wall beside me, was very pleased to share my water, polluted or not. She drank deeply, and wiped her hot face as she eased her basket.

"Let me try," I asked, and after her initial surprise she put the folded cloth across my forehead and placed the headstrap in position round the *doko*. I stood, feeling the weight in my neck and shoulders. I managed a short way before handing it back to the grinning Dalli.

The narrow gorges were negotiated by swaying suspension bridges. If you dared to look down through the gaps you could see the white ice-water from the mountains surging far below. Sometimes clear little cascades fell beneath a tangle of rich vegetation. These steep-sided streams were another promising place for birds. Our Sherpas waited about resignedly whilst we slid over wet stones, struggling with cameras and binoculars.

We breakfasted each day as the sun rose over the mountains. Disembodied peaks of flame and indigo would suddenly glow in the mist above, changing rapidly to pale, glistening gold, as the light crept slowly towards us. The evenings had their special magic, too. Dusk came, grey-blue and sudden; activities in the nearby village ceased. As the smell of supper and wood-smoke pervaded the rapidly cooling air little groups of glimmering orange lights appeared, bright holes in the opaque hills opposite. Where there had been no sign of habitation by daylight, unseen villagers were lighting torches and cooking fires as they settled down for the night; the darkness deepened under brilliant stars.

We had to limit campfires as the area was suffering badly from deforestation; everywhere, thin white runnels on the hillsides told a familiar tale of soil erosion. Occasionally we did indulge in such luxury. Flickering light reflected on Asian and Caucasian faces; somebody would produce a little drum called a *tabla,* and quick brown fingers drummed a rhythm; then the singing would begin. They sing,

I was told, to keep away the demons. Demons and gods were a part of life here; the Sherpas believed the Yeti to be a demon, to be respected and left in peace in his remote fastness.

One evening a woman appeared at the edge of our camp. She carried a child of about six, on whose arm was a great running sore, surrounded by swollen purple flesh. It must have been causing her great pain. The girl leant against her mother's shoulder, silent and still. The woman's face was expressionless. Only her eyes moved, searching the group for the slightest sign that someone may help. What could we do? We had no suitable antibiotic, and if we tried to help with what medication we had, would we open a floodgate of people seeking help from the benevolent strangers? I remembered reading that it is not uncommon for a family to lose as many as three children through sickness. The antidote to their hard life was a strong, practical network of feeling that bound the people together. They needed each other's caring to survive. The feeling extended to us, too, as we blundered through their traditions in our heavy boots: they welcomed us with serene dignity, ignoring our clumsiness.

One day we heard the sound of drums and loud, wailing cries.

"It's a funeral," exclaimed Nima, with the air of one announcing a carnival. He borrowed the binoculars and we hurried to the nearest viewpoint. A small procession, dressed in mourning white, wound down the hillside. In front went the drum, a large one this time, and behind followed a man with the deceased, seated on a large chair, tied on to his back. The corpse was shrouded in white, and covered from head to foot in crimson rhododendron blooms. From the valley below a wisp of smoke ascended, and the sound of hammering, as the funeral pyre was prepared.

"They will burn all his possessions," Nima told me. "Not the chair," he added. "Special chair for funerals." A few days later we heard the distant sounds of what Nima assured me was a wedding; to me it sounded identical to the funeral.

As we entered the rhododendron forests the fog closed in. The air was so moist that our clothes were soon wringing wet. Through the mist we could see the huge trunks and spreading umbrellas covered with crimson and pink blooms among which innumerable birds moved; even if we managed to focus our binoculars the lenses immediately clouded over with droplets of moisture. We discovered an early orchid in the layers of dripping moss on the trees. Light meters protested with querulous bleeps when we tried to take photographs. Fragrance surrounded us, emanating from a small bush with leathery leaves and tiny white flowers. We had to be careful not to lose our footing. Beside the track the ground fell away between ghostly trees to unseen depths.

The last day came. It was a long day's walking, and for the first time

I felt completely drained of energy. A man in a sarong stood outside his house watching my slow progress. As I drew level he said in hesitant English: "You look tired, my sister. Rest here a little. I will bring tea." I followed him. In the dimness I could see his wife sitting on her haunches by the hearth where the inevitable blackened kettle steamed. She poured the Nepalese tea – buffalo milk, water, tea and sugar, stewed up together – into an ancient mug, and smiled as she offered it to me. It was surprisingly refreshing. I sat outside with my host. Flies buzzed everywhere; I tried not to think of dysentery as two thin children, clad only in grubby T-shirts, peeped round the door, shy dark eyes beneath unkempt hair. I was not sure whether this was an official tea-house, and I offered the man the usual three rupees. But he shook his head.

"No, you are welcome, my sister. Go safely. *Namaste.*"

A very special place is Nepal, untouched yet by the twentieth century; you can sing to demons under the stars, and a total stranger is your brother.

PAUL HARVEY

SPRINGTIME FOR CZECHOSLOVAKIA

Irena lived in a late-Seventies block of flats on the edge of town, half a mile from the Russian barracks, part of an ugly outer-urban sprawl. After buying me lunch in a new concrete hotel called, romantically, The Interflora, she drove me back at high Skoda speed through the centre of town – choke full out, engine howling in second gear as we skidded across wet cobblestones, clipping kerbs and narrowly avoiding the numerous potholes and dug-up sections where slow attempts were being made to repair the water mains, shattered by the minus-twenty-five February temperatures. The only vehicles Irena took any notice of were the thin double trams, locked inscrutably into their own system, clanging their way up and down the narrow streets making unmistakable tram noises. Saturday afternoon shoppers shared the pavements with soldiers in iron-grey overcoats wandering about in twos and threes.

"You can tell the difference by their boots," Irena told me before I'd had a chance to ask the question. Some of the Russian soldiers (pull-on boots, no laces) looked Mongolian and very young.

"We hate them," she remarked casually.

Olomouc, former capital of Moravia and reputed to be Czechoslovakia's second most interesting city, doesn't look its best in mid-March. The botanical gardens are bare and there are few signs of the famous flower festival exhibitions in the cold grey wet transition between winter and spring: on the four days I was there it rained every day, finally removing the last traces of soot-encrusted snow from the pavements but leaving everything streaked with a post-winter dampness. Even the drainpipes, clinging half-heartedly to cracked walls and rusty gutters, looked as if they'd had enough.

The Gothic and Baroque buildings in the centre of town seemed somehow to reflect the gloom with their peeling plaster and crumbling façades: a once-proud city of towers and spires, balconies, alleys and doorways, with the university – a jumbled collection of yellow buildings and small courtyards – standing on a rock above the River Morava gazing severely down on a gold-domed Russian Orthodox church, now boarded up, its green roof tiles slipped and broken. Everyone I met kept apologising for the shabby state of the buildings and I had the feeling that if I went back in ten years' time it would look like the set for some grand-scale horror film, all broken banging shutters and cobwebbed windows. I tried to explain to Irena that I didn't mind, that this was how I felt it *should* be – the real Central Europe – and anyway I preferred that kind of place to ordered museums and shining monuments. She gazed at me with ice-blue eyes and murmured, "I see."

Olomouc is full of churches, huge and chillingly ornate, freezing inside and – as far as I could see – deserted during the week. Our Lady of the Snows was full of gilded pouting angels, but despite the heavy rain I was the only visitor, devout or otherwise. St Michael's Church – "a gem of Baroque Moravian architecture" – was firmly shut and St Wenceslas Cathedral, founded in 1109 and rebuilt at the end of the last century on a vast neo-Gothic scale, was dark, impressive and so cold inside it made your head ache. In front of the church of St Maurice I met Lenka, a music student who had promised to show me what she described as "the biggest organ in Central Europe", all 2,311 pipes of it, the largest more than thirty feet tall, the smallest eight millimetres of solid silver. Built in the 1740s and housed in the only remaining Gothic interior in the city, it's now electronically operated and can imitate anything from bagpipes to a brass band. Lenka adjusted her fur coat, blew on her hands, opened it up and let rip: the noise nearly blew me off the balcony, a stupendous megalomaniac combination of centuries of Bach fugues and the Incredible Dr Phibes. She said it had taken her seven years to learn to play it, and the only problem was when there was a power cut. That and the temperature during the winter.

Irena took an unofficial day off work and we wandered through the damp streets while she told me about being a student at Palacky University in 1968 (and what happened afterwards: "It is strange how the history books of a country can change, isn't it?"). Two soldiers (lace-up boots) were taking photos of their girlfriends in Peace Square, also known – at various times in its turbulent career – as Lenin Square and Hitler Square. Hiding from the rain in a smoky bar we missed the twelve o'clock chiming of the Town Hall clock. The original sixteenth-century clock was badly damaged in 1945 and has been restored, somewhat incongruously, with mosaic figures of model socialist workers.

"I am glad we are late," Irena growled. "Look at them, they are ridiculous."

Opposite the clock, angels and bishops stare moodily down from the Holy Trinity Column in what is now the middle of Red Army Square.

As a change from wet feet and sightseeing I was smuggled into an

English-language class where we drank home-made slivovitz and one of the students, a lugubrious-looking individual called Miroslav who played the bassoon in the Moravia Philharmonic Orchestra, invited me to a concert the following evening. Irena produced a suit from somewhere – I had nothing appropriate to wear and the Czechs dress up to go out – and on a cold wet evening Miroslav, who once behind his bassoon couldn't stop smiling, dragged me in off Red Army Square where I'd been waiting under an umbrella watching a group of Czech soldiers trying to stand up, and escorted me up to the balcony of the Fucik Hall to watch the performance. He was wearing immaculate white tie and tails and the cloakroom lady kept shaking my hand and shouting "Welcome!". Irena arrived looking stunning, and the entire audience spent the interval walking about studying each others' clothes.

Olomouc has a population of about a hundred thousand but it's a small town: I kept bumping into people I'd already met, and Irena appeared to know everybody.

"It is necessary to have connections, you do not understand," she told me when I remarked on the fact, though even the normally impassive Czechs leapt to their feet and gallantly opened doors for her at every available opportunity. In the Post Office while I was trying to phone Prague, Irena was getting free phone calls in exchange for correcting a German text for the manager, and when we went to a bookshop she had a friend who sold her books at half price.

The morning I was due to leave – the day Chernenko died – I woke up to the sound of Russian troops singing marching songs from the nearby barracks. On the radio the Voice of Moscow was retelling their fifty per cent of the story of the Vietnam war, and every half-hour or so large green helicopters flew overhead as they did every day. Nobody I saw in the streets ever looked up.

Irena drove me to the station, past the monastery that is now a military hospital, along the main road north where tanks rumble across at night. We flew round corners and bounced over cobbled junctions, ignoring traffic lights and scattering innocent pedestrians, speeding through puddles and swerving to avoid the steaming manhole covers. As we parked outside the station Irena reversed into a 1964 Mark One Cortina, crushing a wing.

"Never mind," she purred, "it is not important. I know the director of the insurance company. They are all bastards."

She kissed me and wouldn't let me pay for the ticket. It was still raining.

The train going west to Prague was empty and unheated, and arrived two hours late at a different station; but the weather in Bohemia was a few days ahead of Olomouc and the capital was clear and bright. Springtime for Czechoslovakia . . .

DAVID BRIERLEY

WHERE REALITY SLIPS AWAY

"Perdone, señor, que hora es?"

I showed her my watch and said: *"Habla usted ingles?"*

She sat on the bench and asked what I was called. "My name is Cintia," she told me. "And that is Ñeri." A five-year-old was kicking a stone round a statue in the middle of the square. "I thought I was going to have a boy. That is why I gave her a boy's name. It doesn't matter."

This was in Santa Cruz, in Bolivia, where reality slips away.

On one side of the square is the cathedral, built of sandy brick. On another side is a building in Banana Republic Extravaganza style with a sign in English: Palace Theatre. A third side has a gleaming bank, but you don't change money there. You go to the fourth side where the money-changer offers black market rates. He is gross, a parody of a bloated capitalist. He has a couple of minders, toughs with eyes like Dobermanns', following every move you make. When I arrived the rate was 108,000 pesos to the dollar. This morning it was 124,000. This afternoon it will be more. Inflation is running at twenty-two per cent a day.

"I thought you were German," Cintia said. "You look German. I speak German too. My great-great-great-great came from Germany. Was the end of the eighteenth century. He do very well, become *marquesa*. But he fight the Spanish for independence and he lose. Maybe the Spanish kill him. Maybe he kill himself."

She shrugged.

The square had the usual pedlars of Latin America. I declined offers to have my shoes shone, to have my photo taken, to become a zillionaire in the lottery, to drink lime juice, to acquire a lavatory brush, to buy a razorblade to shave off my beard.

"Would Ñeri like an ice cream?"

"Yes," Cintia said.

An ice cream seller was summoned. He honked an old car bulb horn. A small parrot with blue and yellow wings stood on his head.

"I have many famous ancestors," Cintia said. She tells me of another great-great-ever-so-great who was commander-in-chief of the armed forces in the 1880s. The Chilean army was advancing up the coast, but her ancestor refused to sign the mobilisation order until Carnival was over. Too many parties and dances. So her not-so-great lost Bolivia its access to the sea.

"You like Santa Cruz?" she asked.

"I like this square," I replied truthfully. I liked the palm trees and cannas, the acrobats and Mennonite farmers in identical blue overalls and straw stetsons. I liked the university girls with their T-shirts: Lover come back, Why don't you ask me, Love me now before the rush. I liked the arcaded sidewalks, waiting for Butch and Sundance to make their final dash into a hail of bullets.

"Have you eaten?" I asked.

"It doesn't matter."

"Perhaps we could have dinner tonight?"

"Okay," she said.

In the afternoon I walked out to what the map promised was the *Jardin Botanico*. It was a patch of unimproved jungle, a dirt road puddled from lunchtime rain, a row of thatched cafés, a broad brown river. The jungle looked surprisingly like jungle: forest giants, struggling saplings, undergrowth, vines, parasite plants that dripped aerial roots, a singing of insects, birds that chattered and chucked and screeched but never sang.

On the way back, on a deserted stretch of road, a pick-up truck stopped. It held half-a-dozen unsavoury thugs, grinning and beckoning. I lengthened my stride whereupon two jumped down, raced over and thrust identity cards into my face. *Policia Boliviana,* I read, and in bold letters: Interpol. My papers were inspected, my pockets searched, my clothes sniffed. Drugs? Why pick on me? Let them raid the market or the building on the way to the airport signposted: *Comita Regional de la Coca.*

The restaurant was on a bluff overlooking the river. A sword of grilled meats was brought, enough to feed a football team. She ate the lot.

"Did I tell you about the great-great-great who was president?" Cintia asked. "The president of Brazil sent him a gift of a white stallion. It was so magnificent that my great-great-great called for a map and put his thumb on it and sent it to the president of Brazil with a message: In return for the magnificent stallion, I give you whatever part of Bolivia is covered by my thumbprint."

We drank *singani,* the local firewater. It rained hard, a tropical deluge, and after it stopped the air was hotter and more humid than before. When we left the restaurant she took her shoes off and began to walk. The city was a dozen kilometres away.

"There are no taxis," I said.

"It doesn't matter," she said.

She bustled down the centre of the road, a dumpy figure, no taller than my chest. The first car stopped and gave us a lift.

We sat on the same bench in the square. There were people about. Girls walked in threesomes, their arms linked. I refused another shoeshine and the chance to become a zillionaire.

"When do you leave?" she asked.

"Tomorrow afternoon. I fly to Rio and then to London."

"You should stay for the election. My great-great-uncle is standing."

I think it was her great-great-uncle. It could have been her great-great-cousin.

"He was president thirty years ago and he wants to be president again."

"He must be old now."

"He is older than Reagan. He is seventy-seven. But I have another cousin who is younger who is also standing for president."

"You have *two* relations who are standing for president?"

"Yes," said this dumpling of a woman. When she laughed she showed a lot of teeth and her whole body shook. "But it doesn't matter."

An old woman stopped in front of the bench and began to moan and then to mumble and finally to shout at us. I understood nothing. Perhaps it was gibberish.

"If you give her some money," Cintia said, "maybe she goes away."

I gave the woman ten thousand. She screamed so I gave her another ten thousand. She stared at the notes, muttering. Then she crumpled them up and spat on them. Then she dropped them on the paving and trampled on them and ground them under her heel. Then she picked the notes up, smoothed each one with care and tucked them inside her dress, between her breasts, and walked off.

Cintia gave a sigh, too big for her body. She spoke to herself more than me: *"El mundo es loco."* Then she grinned at me. "It doesn't matter."

This was my last day in Santa Cruz, in Bolivia, where reality slips away.

SALLEHUDDIN BIN ABDULLAH SANI

SADDLE-SORE IN INDONESIA

"Whoosh . . . Balibi. Whoosh . . . Pinla." The two Torajan horses picked their way over the broken rocks towards the town of Bittuang. We were high in the mountains of Sulawesi, a large amoeba-shaped island amongst the fourteen thousand that make up Indonesia. The horses were small, tough and wiry – like Daniel who had hired me the horses and was my guide on this trip. In theory, he should have been sitting on the other horse but, owing to my lack of equestrian skill, he spent most of the time running behind, driving on my mount with cries of "Whoosh" and smacks on the rump.

It was raining with the relentless fury that characterises tropical rain. Leeches had begun to insinuate themselves under our clothes and gather like lace around our wrists and ankles. Not for the first time I wondered what I was doing spending my holiday in such an unlikely way. I had determined to get away from the normal tourist run and go somewhere completely different. This was certainly different. My unreliable guidebook had vaunted the attractions of a gentle expedition into the friendly mountains. It was advisable to go on foot but the very rich or infirm might hire horses, as I had done. As I surveyed the fierce torrents, precipitous scree slopes and thigh-deep wallows of mud that gathered on the plateaux, it was hard to imagine any Westerner surviving, let alone travelling, on foot.

We rode for sixteen hours that day, perched on Torajan saddles that were like bundles of firewood covered with rags. There were no stirrups, no reins. You just hung on with your knees and grabbed the mane at moments of crisis. Fortunately, the horses knew their names and the Indonesian for "right" and "left". You steered by voice and let Daniel act as accelerator and brake.

The jungle around us stretched away into the mist, unbroken save for rivers and the odd clearing where a woodcutter lived and worked. Occasionally we would come upon them – visions of despair – crouched in shelters, puffing cigarettes over smoky fires or listening to transistor radios. Some had planted gardens of manioc and installed complicated systems of rattles and tin cans that clanged and rustled when a string was pulled. "Against savage beasts," explained Daniel.

Owing to some misunderstanding about supplies, we had brought no food and so had to ride all day without eating. I was glad I had my water bottle, but Daniel waved it away. It seemed he did not need to drink either.

The jungle was an odd mixture of the known and the unknown. Many of the plants were familiar as house-plants in England – only here they were larger and more rampant. It was like being a dwarf in someone's sitting-room planter. At the tops of hills, giant ferns gathered to overhang the path and drip wetly on us and the steaming horses. One smacked me in the face and cut my lip. I was now covered with blood from plants and leeches. Daniel, as ever, seemed impervious. "Whoosh . . . Balibi. Whoosh . . . Pinla."

We met some travellers coming from behind – two women and their children – leaping and slithering over the rocks and mud. They speedily overtook us, much to Daniel's disgust, though weighed down with basket backpacks and sheltering from the rain under natural umbrellas of banana leaves. We exchanged cigarettes and smiles. They helped us over a tree-trunk bridge covered with moss, the horses shying and sliding in a way not encouraging to one who had never ridden before.

We came to a huge stone staircase of tumbled rocks, each step some two feet high so that the horses had to clamber and skid, banging against the trees on either side. The path had sunk into a deep rut so that our feet scraped against the mud walls and our boots filled up with red clay. Then came a roofed bridge of logs over a waterfall of great beauty. We stopped to tighten the saddles and I found my legs had gone numb and I could no longer stand up. At such moments there is only one thing to do. You light a cigarette and take a photograph. Daniel immediately stopped scowling at the saddle I had dislodged with my untutored buttocks, and grinned cheesily into the lens. Click! He resumed his scowl and muttered darkly against the horses, the weather and me.

We set off again uphill into the glowering stormclouds. Here was a new attraction. Trees had tumbled from further up the slope so that they leaned drunkenly over the track, forming narrow natural arches. The horses only took account of their own height in choosing which way to go and made no allowance for their riders. I received numerous dank blows to the head. Can horses grin? I was sure mine did.

Night was falling when we emerged into a clearing. A large house of planks sat on stilts in a meticulously sculpted landscape of paddy-fields. Water flowed from level to level through bamboo pipes. Children shouted excitedly. At last. A promise of rest and food. Daniel rode grimly by. We had taken too long, been too slow. We must press on before it got too dark for the horses. We plunged into forest again.

I do not know how I would react to the unexpected arrival of two complete strangers at my house late at night – especially if they looked as I must have: wild-haired, mad-eyed, caked with mud and blood. Fortunately, the house at which we finally stopped had firm notions of Indonesian hospitality.

I clambered from the horse and fell over. The owner of the house watched laughing from the veranda and called for his wife. My horse looked round at me in reproach, then *it* fell over. Everyone laughed and we were invited in. I took off my shoes and huddled miserably in the place indicated on the bare floorboards. We went through elaborate greetings, my host – a young woodcutter – pausing to casually swat leeches that had begun to detach themselves from me and arch nose-to-tail into the dark corners. The rain beat against the tin roof and the wind howled through the windows – plugged with old newspapers and the flag of the Republic in an act that combined patriotism and utility. There was no fire. I had no dry clothes. Children crept silently into the corners of the room and eyed me in respectful silence, draping themselves, bat-like, in thick sarongs that were wound about legs, bodies and heads to leave only dark eyes gazing in deep wonder. As usual, I felt I was disappointing them with my trite phrases delivered in poor Indonesian. One by one they stole away.

Daniel came in from tending the horses and settled to a huge dish of rice that he devoured with awe-inspiring appetite, as if he were one of those creatures obliged to consume twice their own weight of food a day or perish. We ate in virtual silence. I felt broken and exhausted, shivering and feverish. I knew it would take another two or three days before we got back to the world of electricity and bottled beer, petrol engines and television that I had so joyfully abandoned to package holiday-makers.

Someone brought in a storm lantern and the men settled in corners on woven sleeping-mats, eyes shining like little boys as they told each other stories. As I was about to succumb to unconsciousness, two of the children crept back in. One pointed to me. *"Tuuriis!"* he explained to his friend. It all seemed very unjust.

DAVID GODOLPHIN

In Pursuit of the American Dream

"Kiss mah grits," said the waitress, conversing with a regular customer as she served me up a 99-cent breakfast in the diner at Orlando Airport.

I was frequently to hear Americans exhorted to kiss each other's fried porridge, in a parody that seems to be the last legacy of the Southerner who occupied the White House in the dark days before Ronald Reagan. Kissing grits has supplanted the fashion for kissing ass, which is surprising in an upwardly mobile society.

An hour later I was drinking (what else?) Florida orange-juice beside a motel swimming pool while the early-morning sun gently warmed away jet-lag. The lady on a nearby lounger ordered the waiter to put a slug in her juice.

"I always have screwdrivers for breakfast," she confided to me by way of introduction. A strawberry blonde, she wore a two-tone lilac bikini over tanned cellulite. She was close to seventy years old. "Join me," she invited, or possibly commanded. I joined her.

She was from San Bernardino, I learned, visiting her son in Orlando. She stayed at the motel because "my daughter-in-law is a twenny-fower-carat bitch who makes Joan Collins look like Miss Ellie".

We talked travel. She loved Paris. The Pompidou Centre has more class than the "Louver". The metro is so quaint, and the shops around the Shamps Ulysses are almost as good as those in Palm Beach or Beverly Hills.

She had done "Iddaly" but did not share my passion. Rome is badly in need of renovating. They should widen the streets of Florence and landfill some of Venice's canals to put in a subway system.

Conversation turned to politics. Jimmy Carter had been pathetic but she couldn't support Reagan because of his policies on social security. She described herself as a "liberal conservative" and plainly warmed to my reminiscences of the Edward Heath administration.

Lunch in the motel's coffee shop – fresh melon, lobster salad, ice cream – cost a little over five dollars. My single room, with a bed designed for Bob and Carol and Ted and Alice, was twenty-eight dollars a night. Notwithstanding a pernicious exchange rate, Florida is cheap.

Superficially, Orlando resembles Crawley or Milton Keynes, except that there are palm trees and no hills. The climate has plainly been modelled on the Garden of Eden. Florida is beautiful.

The people are bronzed, fit, not young but still active, and candid. My neighbour at the luncheon counter boasted equally of his golf handicap, a part-time job as superintendent of a condominium to supplement his pension, and three full-time girlfriends. He was sixty-four; the youngest of his girlfriends was fifty-seven.

Florida is bracing.

The epitome of the American Dream, in pursuit of which I had, after all, braved the airways over the Atlantic, can be experienced at Walt Disney World, an exercise in total fantasy expertly stage-managed with scarcely an ugly glimpse of how anything works.

As well as all the souped-up funfair attractions designed to impose new limits of endurance on your stomach, there are mechanised pageants which glorify the past, present and future achievements of the land God gave to Mammon.

A cinema with a 360-degree screen affords an enveloping thirty-minute tour of the US, climaxed by a swoop across the Hudson River at twilight. Before you rise the towers of Manhattan; behind you Liberty bears her torch in the gathering darkness. A choir, in the style of the Ray Conniff chorus, sings *God Bless America,* and in the breathtaking splendour of the moment you are sure that He does.

On my last evening in Florida, after six gruelling days pursuing the American Dream from Disney World to Sea World, Epcot, Cape Canaveral, two waxwork museums and an alligator farm, I chanced to dine in my first Stateside McDonald's. A couple from Texas shared my table. Inevitably, we ended up talking politics.

The husband, a grizzled caricature of LBJ, was a staunch supporter of the latest elderly cowboy on Pennsylvania Avenue. He had a favourite word with which I hesitate to soil the pages of *The Sunday Times,* but in his opinion Jimmy Carter had it between the ears and Ronnie Reagan is gonna drop it in large amounts on the Eye-ranians and the Commie Dagoes and anybody else who tries to put one over the US of A.

"Am I right?" he asked his wife in conclusion, "or am I right?" His wife nodded unenthusiastically.

I ventured to express nostalgia for the Kennedy era, the "New

Camelot", when I, like many Britons, believed we were at the dawn of a second Renaissance.

The Texan heard me out. Then:

"Crap on the Kennedys," he said vehemently. "And crap on the Pope," he added, for good measure.

In my taxi next morning, en route to the airport, the driver's girlfriend, a big, black, breezy hooker from Carter country, suggested from the front seat:

"Honey, whah don't Ah clahmb over an' sit theyuh in back with you-all?"

"My dear," I told her, "you can kiss my grits."

TIMOTHY LEADBEATER

SANTORINI

It was like catching the island with its trousers down. What possessed us on the last morning to walk to the airstrip is a long story, but after half-an-hour's desperate trekking across fields and beaches, we found ourselves at the back end of the runway. And there, hidden amongst the strange pumice dunes were derelict factories and a power station, all brick chimneys and broken windows.

But, characteristically unabashed, a taverna and rooms-to-let were taking root amongst them. The islanders of Santorini make a living out of life amongst the fragments. The island was devastated around 1,500BC by a volcanic eruption five times more powerful than Krakatoa. The centre of the island disappeared like the top off a boiled egg. The destruction brought Minoan civilisation (some say Atlantis) to an abrupt halt, but it has been the making of modern Santorini. The geographical shards that remain form an exotic spectacle more breathtaking than the statistics. Hearts, and words, falter at the edge of the red-and-black thousand-foot cliffs, topped off with creamy-grey pumice, which plunge deep into the *caldera* on the "inner" coast of the island. Restaurants spill over the cliff edge, like a sprinkling of salt crystals, in their eagerness to offer the best view of the biggest ruin in the world. Behind them, terraced vineyards of rich grey soil ripple away down to the "outer" coast like beaches of stranded green starfish.

Once, the only way up and down the cliffs was by mule, but this route is taken only by tourists now. The mules have an attention span slightly shorter than the distance to the next bend. It belies their thorough knowledge of the route: they know when the journey is over all right. Mine rounded the last bend and firmly resisted my attempts to park it expertly in line with the others. Growing tired of my exhortations, it stepped off the path, over the balustrade and on towards some succulent cacti just below the cliff edge. A mule master appeared from nowhere shouting somewhat superfluously "Mister! Mister!" He was less concerned than exasperated by another incompetent penny-pinching foreigner.

Greek is a language well designed to express stress. If there are languages of love and seriousness, then Greek is the language of minor crisis. The patriarch of our favourite taverna wore a T-shirt with the popular Greek slogan "No Problem". Yet if one of his family of waiters and cooks indicated a table to be cleared or a couple to be served he would break into a monologue of misfortune, seemingly that minute befallen him and in the face of which he was helpless.

Nevertheless the jobs get done, and the bigger the better. When a commercial port was needed, a two-lane hairpin highway was concreted onto the cliffs. The *frisson* of fear has been retained for the benefit of tourists, however – most journeys to Athinios port seem to be necessary at night. We rode up in a bus packed to panic point – one woman shot out between the conductor's legs and refused to reboard. We rode down in a taxi whose driver was obviously less concerned about the fears of his passengers than the fares waiting in town.

Town is Thera, or haphazardly Fira (and on one memorable occasion we boarded a bus for Vera). Passengers decant into the main square and lodging touts scurry slowly from bus to bus. We were approached by a little girl.

"Room? You want room? Very nice. Very close," she urged. She watched attentively as we debated how close was nice. We agreed to take a look.

"All full! All full!" she announced merrily, and skipped off.

It is not just business which stirs the islanders, however. There is something suspiciously competitive about Santorini's 400-odd chapels – more than any other Aegean island, naturally – and something positively hubristic about their siting. White as wedding cakes, they cling defiantly to the most precarious promontories of the island.

Most bizarre is the monastery of the Prophet Elijah. It shares the island's highest peak with a military establishment. Visitors clad in sombre brown robes over their offensive holiday clothes are confronted in the monastery's courtyard by the over-reaching feet of next door's radar mast. At night from far below, the arc lights of this Siamese twin make it appear like a mad scientist's laboratory.

Cheekiest is the chapel of Agios Nicolaos on the sulphurous upstart of Nea Kameni in the centre of the *caldera*. It's not unlikely the plans were drawn up before the rocks were cool. All around are jagged skylines of black lava. The rocks are thrown together but fused solid – this is young scenery – but here and there thin patches of grass have taken hold like adolescent fluff. At the top of a cinder track of rasping ash is the most recent crater, with rocks of yellow, green and rust-red. The courier coaxes people to insert their hands into a smoking crevice. The fumes are hot and moist. The smell has the whiff of apocalypse.

Beyond Nea Kameni lies Therasia, the other island forming the broken rim of the great wheel. From Thera, when the horizon disappears in the mid-afternoon, the whole archipelago seems to float on the heat haze. Beams of sunlight probe mysteriously through the clouds, moving slowly across the floor of the *caldera* like vast spotlights.

All Santorini's houses are vaulted for protection in tremors, but Therasian ones are the prettiest: subtle pastel stucco, peach or pink, with striking sky-blue lintels and window-frames. Attractively, they are not for the tourists – barely a dozen make it up the cliffs from the boat each day.

We ate at a small egg restaurant. Therasia had the only chickens of the island that we saw. A fresh cheese omelette arrived with lemon juice and a small box of oregano. Normal service was interrupted when all the family turned out to wish the priest good day as he rode past in grey robes and black hat. He sat side-saddle on a mule with a small passenger. On our way down we found him discussing business with the mule man.

The best restaurants are at Perissa beach. As the peasant green-grocers (resident) and the jewellery-makers (seasonal) moved their stalls under the lamps, we would promenade along the row. As we drank the evening's first small glasses of scouringly dry Santorinian wine, the buses would begin to come in empty and go out so full the waiters would laugh and shout the attention of rivals in neighbouring restaurants. Finally, as the moon rose, fishing boats would put out from the lee of the huge rock which looms over Perissa by day.

The very last restaurant of the island is reached through a small grove. Chairs and tables sink into the black sand. There we had char-grilled red mullet, fresh from the night before, followed by alternate mouthfuls of honeysweet melon and volcanic rosé, walked off with a moonlit climb to the small chapel of Panaghia Katefiani, most roman-tic of the island . . .

But Santorini's wheel inevitably comes full circle. As we were sit-ting one night in the roadside overspill of tables at another restaurant, a tanker lorry pulled up and a filthily-clad workman jumped down. He heaved and hauled corrugated pipes through the consternated eaters to the kitchen – and toilet – area. Waiters and owners looked on benignly. It takes two to be embarrassed. The man returned and switched on the pumps. Only then was there a reaction: from the waiters next door. Exhaust fumes were blowing their way. Our waiters remained impas-sive – what's the problem? The resigned workman (No Problem! No Problem!) remounted his cab and without stopping his pumps edged the tanker forward, gently overturning several tables, and brought it to rest against the back of the first occupied chair.

At this point it was observed that there was a leak in the system. A pool was growing beneath the feet of a solitary woman diner. She was English. She ignored it. By the time she decided to move it was too late to do so without stepping in the pool. Eventually, transfer being complete, the dripping pipes were hauled back and the lorry reversed out.

Much later the same night we leaped off a track behind the village as it hurtled on past into the darkness, unloved and defiant. Being caught with your trousers down is one thing; making a living from it must be desperate.

LEON TAYLOR

THE HOLLANDER AND THE BALD IBISES

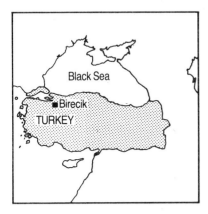

The bus drops me off on the bridge. I can just make out the Euphrates rippling below. It is ten o'clock at night in Birecik, eastern Turkey, twenty-five miles from the Syrian border and host to one of the world's last colonies of Bald Ibises. Or so my guidebook says. Every so often a brightly-lit truck rumbles past, blinding me with its headlights and then showering me with dust. A torch flashes in my face. I can see the outline of a peaked cap behind it. I smile nervously, *"Otel?"* and hold up my baggage. The peaked cap confers with two confederates and then points to some dim lights in the distance.

The man behind the desk speaks no English, wears mirrored sunglasses and proudly shows me a squalid room with four beds in it. One is occupied by an amiable old Turk who jumps out fully dressed, offers me a cigarette and tries to talk to me in what I guess he thinks is pidgin Turkish. Shamefully I can speak only a dozen words or so of Turkish, I'm tired after a day spent on buses and don't feel up to this. I settle on a double room where I have to pay for the other bed to stop the hotel owner putting another guest in. He is optimistically anticipating a full house and I'm not very good at bargaining.

It is the thirteenth day of Ramadan and I've existed all day on dry, but tasty, bread. I search for food but everybody else has already eaten, the shops and restaurants are closed. Involuntary starvation until tomorrow sundown, again.

I sit dejectedly sipping a glass of black tea in the hotel café. A local schoolteacher at the next table questions me, relaying my replies to his friends. "Why have you come to Birecik? To see the river?" I've come to see the Bald Ibises. He doesn't understand Bald Ibis. I try to mime one and flap my arms. "Chicken?" "Eagle?" I fetch my field guide and show him the picture. The company burst out laughing. Silly tourist. "Where have you come from?" Kayseri. "How long was the journey?" Fifteen hours. "Fifteen hours on a bus to see a bird?" More roars of laughter. The teacher leans over conspiratorially.

"There is a Hollander in the hotel. He has only come here to swim in the river!" He turns to his friends, taps the side of his head with his forefinger and nods towards the hotel. "Hollander!" His friends chuckle appreciatively.

The men return to their wives, I to my poky hotel room with stained sheets and solid pillows. There is a night porter sitting at a desk outside my door. He adds up figures in a ledger and listens to his radio, humming to Western pop tunes. My room has two large windows that face the night porter's desk. The tattered pieces of cloth that pass for curtains barely cover half these windows, so light from outside floods in. Why does this hotel need a night porter? Who is going to turn up, looking for a room in the middle of the night, in this town? If I'm to sleep, I will have to do something about this. I smile at the night porter and point to the light above his desk. I rest the side of my head on my hands to try to demonstrate sleep. He smiles back and, thinking I don't know how to switch my room light on, does it for me. A little later I hear him leaving his desk. I creep out and turn his radio softer. He won't notice the difference. He returns and turns it louder. I wish I'd learnt more Turkish.

I wake at six after a pitiful three hours of sleep. At times like this I long to be back in England, but then I think of the awful weather . . . I breakfast on bread and tea in my room. I don't want to offend the fasters. I guess the Hollander is eating the same fare in preparation for his swim. The Bald Ibises nest alongside the river about two miles out of town. It is still early but starting to get very hot. After I've walked a mile or so I'm offered a lift by a kind fellow driving a horse and cart. We painfully lurch between potholes in the road for the remaining distance and stop outside a wire enclosure. My quest nears its end.

Two dozen scraggy birds, each with a few feathered tufts sticking out of the back of its otherwise bald, lobster red head, hide in the shade, or steal out to strut awkwardly, pecking at the dusty ground with their long, curved bills. Those in the shade now and then call vociferously to one another, *"kay – kay"*, or leap in the air frantically flapping their wings. They don't seem to mind me, so I settle down to enjoy their company and doze.

I wonder why these birds live here in this battered wire enclosure in the middle of nowhere. The enclosure has no roof so the birds could go elsewhere if they wanted to. They do have a scenic nesting spot beside a grand old river, but why the Euphrates? What is the attraction of Birecik? I suppose it's not bad as small towns go. Its hotel leaves a little to be desired but the people are friendly. The men I was talking to last offered to accompany me here. I imagine a crowd of local people marching on these innocent birds to find out for themselves why it is that foreigners travel such long distances just to look at them.

My reveries are disturbed by an angry individual in tattered clothing running towards me and gesticulating furiously. Why have I undergone a lengthy bus journey, a sleepless night and semi-starvation to be pounced on by this despot? My attitude must be wrong. Maybe I should be looking at these birds from a more respectful distance, from outside the enclosure. I don't know what I've done wrong but I know my presence isn't desired so I hold my head high and strut nonchalantly out of the enclosure and down the road. The despot stands, hands on hips, watching me until I am out of sight.

The hotel door is locked. This is a hotel that manages to have a member of staff on duty all night but nobody around during the day. A smartly-dressed man in his mid-twenties lounges against the locked door. He looks rather like a spiv. I wonder what he wants to sell. He speaks some English and runs through the European leaders giving his opinion of each. Mrs Thatcher, bad. Mr Kohl, bad. Mr Papandreou, good. Mr Mitterrand, he is not sure. A few people have now gathered around; he plays up to them, showing off his knowledge of English. Am I married? What is my profession? Do I live in London? Would I like to buy a cheap carpet?

I ask after the Hollander; I'd like to meet him before I leave. I learn that he is answering questions at the police station. He'd climbed on to one of the bridge pontoons to measure the current and had been picked up. Perhaps the hotel owner is helping him? No, he has gone shopping.

Three hours later I'm back on the bridge. I'm waiting for a bus to Urfa and from there I'm catching another to Nusaybin. I can just see the head and shoulders of a body swimming in the river some distance upstream. It can only be the Hollander. If he goes on to swim across the Tigris we may still meet because that's the direction I'm heading in too. I'm off in search of the Pale Rock Sparrow.

JILL RANFORD

FRIENDS IN HIGH PLACES

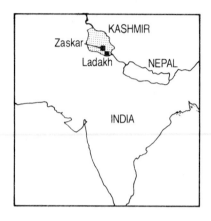

Even our Tibetan horsemen Chonjor and Tamdin erected a tent today, a smoky white, torn canvas strung between two poles with sacks stuffed around the perimeter and a hole for a chimney.

The mountains from where we'd come put on a kaleidoscope of colours as clouds and then pools of evening sun moved across them. Very soon the sky's luminosity had darkened, and through the chimney aperture in Chonjor's tent we saw the first *karma* (stars) appear.

Our four Western figures were huddled around the bubbling pots of salt tea and vegetables, unaccustomed to the chill night air of high mountains, but grateful for the warmth of our down jackets. Meanwhile, our Tibetan friends, dressed in thin woollen pullovers and smoke-engrimed shirts and trousers, had donned just a windcheater each and with bare hands tended the fire, lifting sizzlingly hot pans from the smouldering dung pats.

However silent a gorge, or lonely the slopes beneath a pass, our friends would create a home from the scant resources around them. A trickle of water sufficed for cooking, an armful of brushwood or yak dung for fuel, and some tufts of edible grass for their horses who carried our month's supply of food.

On reaching the Himalayan kingdom of Zaskar, Chonjor hoped to sell some handmade rugs and buy a strong Zaskari horse. Nick, Alan, Bruce and myself simply wished to cross Ladakh (in Kashmir) walking from Leh through Zaskar to Darcha in the south. We wanted to rediscover our roots with nature and meet these mountain people on their own terms. Our influence was inevitable, but we were far from being the first visitors. At one isolated village our hosts had never seen an onion, and sniffed and fingered one with incredulity, but even here a handful of Westerners had set foot before.

Although trekkers frequently visit Zangla, Zaskar's second capital, we soon attracted the attention of villagers carrying home barley sheaves at the end of a day's harvest. A circle of grubby faces watched us, some very young with runny noses and tousled hair, entreating us light-heartedly for *kaka* (sugar or sweets), and others with ancient skin as brown and wrinkled as parchment.

These hospitable people, though still wide-eyed with curiosity, accepted our presence next day at a religious gathering held in honour of a visiting head lama from South India. We were invited to meet this enlightened being in a small room of red and yellow awnings. From his wooden "throne", adorned with painted lotus blooms, he surveyed us without expression. Our souls felt suddenly naked in the face of such proven spiritual wisdom, and all we could think to do was smile self-consciously up at him from our floor-level rugs.

When a stream of villagers entered to pay their homage, he blessed each one in turn. The final man, wearing European clothes, appeared servile in the lama's presence. As he bowed in triplicate, his head touching the ground each time, the Holy Man's chubby cheeks and slit eyes creased up in a stifled yawn! On his final bow the man swung instantly round to us and introduced himself. "I am the son of the king of Zangla," he said in perfect English, then launched into the history of Zangla's fortress which commands the Zaskar valley from its rock outcrop.

The room in which we were seated was actually on the roof of the king's residence. Like all Zaskari houses it was built of mud bricks with wattle ceilings, but was larger and on higher ground than other dwellings, and its flat roof was not dishevelled with drying pea plants and pats of dung.

The two-hour sermon was delivered in a courtyard outside. Attending it were the king and his son, all the local Gelugpa-sect monks in yellow peaked hats and *gonchas* (maroon robes) and dozens of villagers dressed in homespun gowns, Pashmini shawls and felt boots. Women were bedecked in their best jewellery, ear-rings of silver and cornelian, necklaces of amber and coral. The wives amongst them wore *peraks,* fantastic head-dresses of leather reaching from forehead to waist, studded with crude lumps of turquoise and coral and flecked by large ear-flaps of curly black yak hair – heirlooms of unrealised wealth.

After the sermon a monk poured sacred water from a silver jug into each cupped palm, then distributed red ribbons and tsampa *chilups* – balls of roasted ground barley. His Holiness blessed the people, their livestock and crops and touched all heads and hands as he left the courtyard. Following him was the frail, ageing king supported by his son. He looked up at us through watery eyes and greeted *"Julay"* – hello, welcome.

After days of wading rivers in towering gorges of tortured rocks where no prayer stones line the path and no goatherd passes by, such welcome filled our hearts with warmth. Even in the humblest abode we were greeted with a plate of tsampa powder, barley flower chapattis and butter tea.

Our presence was never resented, not even in the shrine rooms of *gompas* (monasteries), where the wise and smiling faces of Buddhas and Bodhisattvas flickered surreally in the gloom, their gold cheeks glowing from the fluttering light of butter lamps.

In the sunlit courtyard at Bardan Gompa red-hatted (Drugpa-sect) monks bustled around us with copper kettles of rancid butter tea, as green and thick as pea soup. From a dark room at the corner of the courtyard a guttural growling chant welled and waned as if emanating from the earth itself. Peering in at the doorway, we saw eight senior monks consumed by the rhythm of their daily *puja* (prayers) infusing the room with their souls and the mysterious forces and spirits they invoked. Above them an arc of miniature skulls glowed in the darkness, reminding each mortal of his own physical transience, for while his soul will thread through the generations, his body will crumble. Only the denial of ego and the attainment of Nirvana (enlightenment) will finally free the soul.

Through meditation one attemps to understand evil inner forces and harness them to produce good. Embodying these fearful powers were black masks of demon gods, hung around the room, their grimacing faces so horrific that they must be covered from human sight.

These spellbinding visions burnt still deeper on our minds as we listened to the sonorous undercurrent of voices. No melody took shape, but the animistic chanting, from long pages of prayer books, was as vital as a heartbeat, as inevitable and embracing as the constantly churning river in the valley below.

Suddenly the chant would cease, the drums would swell and the chattering cymbals resonate with louder, fuller sound till they clashed to a climax from which a new rhythm was born.

We confronted the sunlight, deeply moved by our brief experience in that dark room, and even more respectful of the quietly flowing spirituality of our Tibetan friends, the inner strength that is the life-blood of their thoughts and helps them thrive in an environment that would defeat a weaker mind.

Chonjor, the younger of the two men, has particularly adapted to his new country where, as a refugee, he must live in a Tibetan camp on the poorest land – which in this high scorched domain of desert mountains is completely infertile. Like a lammergeyer eyeing up food, he seizes any opportunity that comes his way. Perhaps in the West he would be a successful salesman but here in the East he treads mountain paths, his hands clasped behind his back, fingering each of his 108

ABOVE: Tibetan horsemen, Tamdin and Chonjor, brewing salt tea to drink with *tsampa* (roasted ground barley).
BELOW: A Zaskari woman loaded with barley at the end of a day's harvesting. (*Friends in High Places*)

Camp at the foot of Lapporten. (*Kebnekaise Mountain Station*)

Alexis, Boo and Ben growing up fast in the jungle. (*Boys' Own Expedition*)

prayer beads. Occasionally he interrupts his gentle murmur of Buddhist mantras to chide a horse out of line.

In contrast to Chonjor's kind eyes and sensitive mouth, Tamdin has the nut brown, angular face of a Mongolian. Normally he wears his greying hair in plaits gathered up with red string, but once we saw him washing by a stream, his hair a wild grey mane reaching to his waist. It accentuated those sculptured cheekbones and wild but mischievous eyes so much that his impish grin of protruding spaced-out teeth seemed not nearly so prominent. Incongruously this bandy-legged horseman was fascinated by gadgetry, so we supplemented the trekking fee with a pressure cooker and some containers.

Our gratitude is much deeper than a few such items could ever show. We had seen vast shale slopes, painted rock colonnades, cascading white monasteries and moonlit rivers, but without hearing the mesmerising rhythm of *puja* in the ridge-top *gompas,* without the hospitality of the villagers, and above all without our Tibetan friends, these would have been just visual memories. We began to glimpse through their eyes, to understand and respect. But awakened in all of us is a seed of awareness . . . perhaps the seed of a lotus bloom.

DAVID HAY JONES

KEBNEKAISE MOUNTAIN STATION

Three of us got off the train at Abisko in the mountains of Swedish Lapland: two men and a dog. I sat on my rucksack while the dog and his friend strolled over to the station building. When they were out of sight I stood up, glanced at my map and took a compass reading. It's difficult to look confident in the mountains, so I always check map readings when there's no-one to question my judgment.

I was going to walk south through Lapporten to Kebnekaise – Sweden's highest mountain, 7,000 feet above sea level – and on to Nikkaluotka, a Lapp settlement by a beautiful ribbon lake. If the weather was good, it would take about a week. If not, I told myself that ten days would do.

Abisko is 200 miles north of the Arctic Circle on the line to Narvik in Norway. It sees plenty of trains, carrying iron from Kiruna and Gallivare, but not many people – just a handful of Lapps and mountaineers, and a dog or two.

In early summer Abisko's lake, Abiskojaure, is still frozen and the high ground is covered in snow. The sky is a crisp, clear blue. The mountains are darker. This far north the snowline is low at 3,500 feet.

I was travelling in the second week of June to take advantage of the midnight sun. If you walk at night, the snow is harder, enabling you to cover five extra miles each day. In June it's best to avoid the valleys because the thaw is well under way. Rivers burst their banks, carrying snow and ice until it melts. Walking in the valleys means days spent wading through water and melting snow. I choose to climb up to the mountain sides and beat a path with my ice axe, only coming down to the valleys to sleep. At this time of year you can walk for a week without meeting anyone. I like that, and rarely use the marked tracks that scar some valleys in Lapland.

When you walk south from Abisko, the obvious landmark to aim for is Lapporten, gateway to the Lapps. It's haunted by trolls and must be treated with respect. Lapporten's bleak mountain walls and lifeless valley floor don't encourage you to stay. A nod of respect, head down and keep walking, that's how Lapporten should be treated.

The climb up is simple but hard work. First there's a slog through a jungle of birch and willow trees. Look out for a walking stick here – a sturdy birch branch that will help you on loose rocks or in deep snow.

It's important to talk to yourself, coax yourself. Talk aloud about the sort of walking stick you want to cut, or what you're going to eat later in the day. Pick on an easy song and chant it over and over again in time with your walking. It numbs the pain of aching legs. When you lose sight of the railway line and the station, the loneliness hits you. Keep your mind busy. Never sit around for too long doing nothing. When you stop walking, pitch the tent immediately, take some photographs, collect firewood – if there is any.

Ritual in the mountains can save your life. The tent is put up in the same way each day. This has a practical value, too. If it's dark, or you are cold and wet, you can get inside the tent quickly and forget about the mountains. The thin sheet of canvas makes loneliness easier to bear. It breaks the silence. I love the hiss of the gas fire and the orange glow inside the tent. For a while you can forget the nagging feeling of uncertainty that follows you on each solo trip.

Mountaineers make poor philosophers. They romanticise danger and like to be afraid because it makes them cautious. Only a stupid few are prepared to forget commitments to their team members and friends and family at home. When you are in control you can sleep well. I dream about fresh food. I can taste the meat. I can feel its texture. The fruit juice is sliding down my throat.

From Lapporten to Kebnekaise the snow was deeper than I expected. One night, fighting hard to get out of the valley, I waded for three hours up to my waist in snow. One leg forward – rest – push – second leg forward – rest – push. I could feel the cold water inside my boots, which was fine as long as I kept moving. Anger follows tiredness – lashing out with my ice axe at snow that's too soft; cursing rocks that trip me up in mid-stream. All sorts of daft ideas seem sensible: throwing away my rucksack to lighten the load; eating all the food or feeding half of it to the lemmings; making snow shoes out of my walking stick and climbing rope.

I fell down a hole up to my ears in snow and just wanted to sleep. Only five minutes, I thought, then I'd be strong enough to carry on. Talk to yourself: "Yes, you can sleep, but only when you get out of this mess. Today it's soup . . . no, mashed potatoes and a tin of sardines . . . drinking chocolate and porridge . . . something special, but first get out of the snow."

The map said there was a Lapp hut about four miles away. If I walked without rest I could be there in two hours. I'd only stop for water and a chunk of chocolate every half-hour. Then I could sleep, make a fire, dry my clothes. If the hut was closed, I'd break in with my ice axe.

I could see the hut after I had walked for three hours. I fixed my sight on it, packed away the map and compass and pushed harder. There was smoke coming from the chimney. If it was another climber he'd let me sleep. A Lapp would probably tell me to sleep outside – and charge me the next morning. Perhaps I should offer him some food. What did I have to give him? Soya meat, packet soup, Oxo cubes, porridge – nothing worth having. I could pretend to be ill. I could try limping, say that I needed to rest for a while. Whatever he said, I was going to sit by his fire.

A man came running out of the hut to meet me. He was Danish and wasn't making a lot of sense. He looked tired and out of place. "Have you got any food?" he asked.

"Yes, why?"

"I've got nothing at all. I've eaten everything. Two days stuck here. The weather's been real shit."

"Is that a fire?" I asked, wanting to get inside.

"Sure. Come on in. I need someone to talk to."

It was soon clear that the man had no idea what he was doing. He shouldn't have been in the mountains. I asked him where his gear was. "Over there," he said, pointing to the corner of the room. There was a tiny rucksack, a summer sleeping bag and a pair of Wellington boots. "Is that all?" I asked.

"Shit man, I didn't expect this. I came straight down the path from Abisko. It was beautiful the first two days. Which way did you come?"

"Over the mountains through Lapporten."

"What was it like up there?"

"Cold and too much snow."

"Where are you going?"

"Kebnekaise."

"Can I join you?"

"I'm climbing. You haven't got the right stuff. You wouldn't like it."

"But I haven't got any food. You can't leave me here. I won't give you shit, man. Let me come."

I wasn't keen. I didn't trust him, so I offered some advice instead.

"Look, there's another hut thirty kilometres down the valley. If you keep high you should be able to make it in a day. Keep away from the rivers. Two days' walk from the hut there's Kebnekaise mountain station. You can buy some food there. I'll give you enough to eat for three days. I'll catch you at the hut. If you leave before I get there, write a note."

It was five in the morning. If he left at six, he'd probably reach the hut after twelve hours – six in the evening. That would give him time to cook, sleep and leave by six the following morning. I'd take about nine hours to reach the hut and planned to start walking at five in the evening. We should meet up.

He left as I was dozing off. I kept an eye open to check that he didn't steal my boots or food. Silly bugger, he should have stayed at home. I fell asleep.

The heat from the fire woke me at four. The air was so dry it tickled my throat. I got up and opened the window. It seemed fine outside: no sun, but no sign of a storm. The Dane wouldn't have far to walk now, and I doubted whether there would be much snow between him and the mountain station at the foot of Kebnekaise. I hoped the man had learnt his lesson.

An old reindeer trotted towards the hut. I watched as he nosed around near the rubbish bins and firewood, but I couldn't stay still enough and he was soon gone.

My clothes were dry and stank of burnt wood and sweat. I'd put them on later. It was warm enough to wander around in my under-pants while I packed my rucksack and prepared a bowl of porridge. I'd be away by five. It promised to be a good evening's walk. I was strong and my shoulders had stopped aching from the fifty-pound rucksack.

Before leaving the hut I left a few packets of food behind. Someone might need them. For the first three hours I couldn't get into my stride. I was trying too hard to avoid getting my socks wet, and I hadn't put enough clothes on. Not wanting to stop and pull on an extra sweater I decided to walk faster. I couldn't think of a song to sing, though.

I can't remember the shape of the mountains, nor how the river flowed on the way to the second hut. There was a lot of snow and I thought of my advice to the Dane about keeping away from the river. All I cared about was to reach Kebnekaise quickly so that I could buy at least ten bars of chocolate. Only one brand would do: Marabou milk chocolate made in Sweden. I thought about the many kinds of choco-late bar I would be able to buy: fruit and nut; hazelnut; almond; nut chip; white chocolate. I ranked them so that I would know what to buy in case the shop had no milk chocolate. I wondered whether they sold fresh fruit. I fancied an orange. It was too much to expect them to have pineapples or mangoes, but they might have pineapple juice. By the time I saw the hut I had decided to buy a packet of blueberry soup, a carton of pineapple juice and a bar of almond chocolate. This hut was much bigger than the first one and could easily house five or six people. Perhaps the Dane had met some other climbers. That would have cheered him up.

The door was locked so I used my ice axe to prise open the window on the roof. There was no sign that anyone had been there recently: no ashes in the fire; no smell of cooking or sweaty clothes. There was plenty of chopped firewood in the corner of the room. The hut might have been empty for weeks or even months. I made some soup and went to bed.

As I predicted, the walk had taken me nine hours. I can't remember it as hard work but it must have been. The Dane had probably camped halfway, thinking me stupid to recommend a twelve-hour walk in one day. Many climbers say that five or six hours is enough. But the Dane was desperate to get out. He would arrive, I thought, while I was sleeping.

Because I didn't think there would be much snow between the hut and Kebnekaise (for the next day or two I wouldn't climb above 2,000 feet) I thought it would be no problem to walk during the day and enjoy some warm weather. I was prepared to wait until noon to see whether the Dane turned up. If he didn't, I'd tell the rescue services at Kebnekaise. He'd no longer be my responsibility then. I didn't fancy sending the rescuers out for nothing, and the Dane was quite likely to be wrapped snugly in his sleeping bag dreaming of roast beef, bottles of beer, or whatever he liked. Anyway, it was his own fault.

I must have been exhausted because I woke at three in the afternoon and just didn't feel like moving. I had a good excuse to stay in bed, and read the labels of my food packets. Up at five and away by six, I thought. The Dane didn't turn up.

I hate unreliable people. If the Dane showed his face I'd tell him to stop pissing people about. If you have an arrangement you stick to it, snow or no snow.

I was ready to leave at seven. Everything was packed and stacked against the wall of the hut. I was scribbling the man a note: "It looks like I got here first. I will tell the rescue people that I arranged to meet you but you didn't turn up. When you get to Kebnekaise tell them you're the missing man." I dated and timed the note and pinned it to the door.

I'd have to try to reach Kebnekaise in a day. It was thirty-eight kilometres away: fifteen hours' walk if I pushed hard. If I only stopped twice I might be able to do it in thirteen hours. The Dane could be dead by then. What was the alternative? I wasn't going to leave my rucksack behind and run to the mountain station. What if it started to rain or snow on me? No, the Dane would have to put up with it.

The walk was easy and I would have liked to have taken my time. I was right, there was very little snow on the ground and it made a huge difference to my mood to see some greenery and a river without ice. It made me want to finish the walk in twelve hours. I wanted to know how fast and for how long I could keep walking without rest. There's enormous pleasure to be had in stretching yourself despite fatigue and lack of food. I imagined that I was a reindeer covering the ground in graceful, bounding strides. Kebnekaise, no sweat. I'd show that bloody Dane. He'd had a head start and still he couldn't keep up. I was master of the mountains and couldn't be beaten. All I needed was Lapland water, a few cubes of chocolate and a tin of sardines. Kebnekaise mountain station, easy, easy.

Ten hours later I was leaning against the wall of one of the huts at Kebnekaise. My right leg had seized up and I couldn't bend it, nor could I sit down or walk about. The toes of my left foot felt like they were bleeding. The toenails had dug into the flesh. When I threw my rucksack off I was lifted a few feet into the air. I felt so light. I didn't want to eat, just rest and maybe sleep.

I didn't make myself very clear to the woman at the desk inside the hut. She thought I'd had an argument with my Danish friend and left him in the mountains. I tried again. This time she understood. Missing person near Kebnekaise. "It happens too often," she said. "Never travel alone. This isn't Switzerland, you know. You might have an accident and not see someone for two or three weeks." People were difficult to find in the snow, she said. I'd done my job and went away to pitch my tent.

Next day I'd walk the final leg to Nikkaluotka and catch the bus to Kiruna. I'd be back in Copenhagen in a couple of days. I wanted to get out.

The loneliness eats you. Only yesterday I'd sat reading the labels on my food. Why? Because it was the only contact I had with the world outside the mountains. Another week and I might well have gone loopy.

While I was having a wash outside the bus station in Nikkaluotka I heard a helicopter overhead. It landed a hundred yards away from me near the road. There was a body attached to the side – covered completely in a green blanket. I didn't want to look, but I needed to make sure it wasn't the Dane. The pilot was smoking a cigarette and tapping the road with the toe of his boot.

"Is someone ill?" I asked.

"Dead."

"Who is he?"

"Some Danish guy we found up near Kebnekaise. Poor bloke was stuck at the top of one of the mountains. I don't know what he was doing so high, but you can't tell these people."

I nodded. I was back in Copenhagen in two days. I have no plans to return to Lapland.

BOYS' OWN EXPEDITION

The night is pitch black, the jungle floor sparkles with fireflies. Monkeys screech and monsoon rain thunders on tightly stretched groundsheets. I lie uncomfortable, anxious, within a mosquito net on a hammock. Slung in similar positions between other trees are Alexis (fourteen), Boo (ten) and Ben (ten). Though it's 2am, I know they will be awake and won't hear reassuring words, even if shouted. Eventually, to our relief, daylight emerges hazily through the jungle canopy. Date: August 15, 1985. Location: deep in primary jungle, Kota Tinggi, Malaya. Event: the climax of a 1,400-mile expedition in the Far East.

Having been in Singapore twenty years ago with the army, I had thought what a marvellous adventure playground Malaya would make for my two sons, Alexis and Nicholas (Boo). This Peter Pan and the Lost Boys fantasy became reality in 1985. Ben, a school chum, came to keep Boo company. The plan: fly to Singapore, buy food, hire a car, travel up the eastern Malayan coast to Thailand camping on beaches and in jungle, and return via the west coast arriving in Singapore eighteen days later. Kit to be supplemented by friend at 22 SAS and to include machetes, web belts, water bottles, hammocks, maps, paludrin, purification tablets, medical kit etc.

August 1
Departure photograph and champagne send-off, Plymouth. Surrounded by piles of baggage which made nonsense of the 22-kilo allowance. Dressed in assortment of civilian/military clothing. Suddenly I feel nervous. Margaret (my wife) and Jane (Ben's mother) look at their children more lovingly than usual. A brave hoot and we're away!

A thirteen-hour flight, dumping of kit at our hotel and into the heart of bustling Singapore: Bugis Street. The only part that remains smelly, alive, exciting and Chinese.

Where are the transvestites? The children ogle at the street traders.

"Look at their black teeth," says Boo. No transvestites, but pirate tapes at 50p each tempt us all. From this point we become the subject of constant, often amazed curiosity.

Difficulty hiring a car with a Malaya permit at such short notice. Purchased four bolted bars to make roof rack and some perished bungees. Canned food and cereals, burner fuel, bought locally, fit into boot leaving the four-man tent, two water jerry-cans and four back packs to put on the roof rack. Decided to keep a diary, writing a day in turn.

August 4, Nick
Johor Baharo customs, Singapore/Malaya.
   "Which hotel will you be staying at, sir?"
   "We're camping." Look of disbelief.
   "Sir, people don't camp in Malaya. It's dangerous." A suspicious glance into the boot and at the enormous hump on the car roof and we are through. Mersing: palm-fringed bay. Erected tent for first time: went up a dream! Boys went swimming at dusk. Lost a beach ball and a flipper. Boo badly cut foot, Mustn't get irritated. Hot, humid; all being bitten by mosquitoes and giant red ants. Tent unbearably hot. Horrendous night for us all. Ben cries for his mother. They'll have to get used to dressing before going for a pee, closing the mozzy net, and undressing on return. I think the boys, especially Ben, will mature tremendously this trip.

August 5, Alexis
Woken by the wailings of a mosque through a mega-wattage microphone. Sat on a log and read *Pet Sematary* by Stephen King. Ben appeared naked, to be confronted by a car of inquisitive Malays. Embarrassed, he tried acting naturally, covering his bottom with one hand and his personals with another whilst beating a hasty retreat. Snorkelled, then breakfast when the new primus expired. Travelled on to find new camp site further north. Fabulous fishing cove. Supper beef stew. Started making raft with driftwood/bamboo. At dusk lit camp fire.

August 6, Boo
5am. Alexis and I re-kindled the fire. Large group of locals helped launch the raft which had a sail and was held together by paracord. Christened her Physicotic Hernia. After a swim we went exploring past lots of swamps searching for anaconda snakes and crocodiles. Discussed the army and jungle.

August 7, Ben
Went to buy eggs. On my return a Mongol boy was kicking coconut shells barefooted and throwing them at lizards. We gave him a mug and a tin of burnt spagehetti. Drove into Nensi. In 'Café' had ten Cokes,

six portions of chicken and four of bean sprouts. Wrote cards. Went on to Kuantan. Discovered we'd lost diaries and a camera. Had a better night's sleep on new airbeds. Talked about how far we were from England.

August 8, Nick
In 1966 Kuantan was a small village. It's now a modern city. Camped within sight of five-star Hyatt Hotel. It's too tempting. We booked in the following night. Entered the foyer like a bunch of Kampuchian refugees. Dirty, unkempt, with not a case between us, but with me holding aloft my gold Amex card. The kids are soon cleaning themselves in the swimming pool, sipping iced orange from semi-submerged stools set in the water. Reminded Alexis it was his birthday two days earlier.

August 9, Alexis
Woke in a cool, clean, comfortable bed. Nick complaining that I'd left a window open and a squadron of mozzies had attacked him. Loaded up, refilled jerry-cans and drove north towards Kuala Terenggau. Whilst pitching tent got caught in an incredible monsoon. Dark sky, violent winds, and the rain stung. Boo and I played with the locals in the sea. Long walk that evening into the town and drinks at the "Musik Bar". Dimly lit booths and full of Malayan ladies. We realised too late that this was a brothel. Boo and Ben very interested. Returned to the beach and collapsed.

August 10, Boo
After forty miles, stopped to cook breakfast in bus shelter. Beef and scrambled eggs. Roof rack broken and lilos burst. On asking a man where to put our rubbish he pointed to the ground! At Kota Barharu Nick got car stuck in sand and Ben and I put up tent. Cracked coconuts with machetes and drank milk. Watched Everton beat Manchester United on television at roadside bar!

August 11, Ben
Reached Thailand border where Nick had to put on long trousers before the officials would let us through. Travelled half around the world looking for Yala. Camped. Nick was watched by at least thirty grinning Thais as he burnt rice. A couple invited us into their house. What we call a shack they called a palace. The man played guitar and gave us tea and nasty cakes. Returning to the tent we fussed a bit, then went to sleep.

August 12, Nick
Tent surrounded by Thais. Boo and Ben showing off like mad.

Prepared muesli, shaved. Alexis packed while Boo and Ben dismantled the tent. What a help they've become! Back into Malaya via Betong. Annoyingly, border guards charge us sixty baht each because it's the Thai Queen's birthday. Then an epic journey through Pinang and Ipoh to Kuala Lumpur in the rain, with large logging lorries overtaking our overladen vehicle. Too late to camp so we find a hotel. Though exhausted, boys are in great spirits.

August 13, Alexis
Continued south for our Jungle Adventure. During journey played many games: speaking for a minute without repetition, hesitation, etc. Boo and Ben made list of numbers of wheels on lorries. Camped by roadside near Gemas. Nick, Boo and Ben were invited to someone's house. I went off with a boy on his motorbike! He told me about Malaya and how lucky we were not to have been attacked by drug-crazed robbers, which is now a commonplace occurrence. He gave me biscuits and a leaflet.

August 14, Boo
Left early for Jungle Warfare School, Kota Tinggi. A Malayan sergeant called Nick "Sir"! Made him sign for a map. We went into the jungle and had to cross rivers over logs. I practically died of heat. Nick rationed water. Ben wanted to go back. Found a place to "basha up" (make camp), only just in time, because it monsooned. A monsoon is rain four times English rain. After supper of tinned Chinese duck on mostly bone, lay in the hammocks. Ben nearly put his hand on a snake. God what an uncomfortable, cold night.

August 15, Ben
Terrible night's sleep. Headed back to the waterfalls. Took ages to get through heavy undergrowth and up Lombong Hill. Lots of obstacles like fallen trees and "wait-a minute" creepers, a sort of bramble with fish-hooks. Nick got splinters in his hand hacking a path. When we got back we jumped into the water fully clothed, then we laid everything out to dry. That night we made an enormous fire. What a brilliant day!

August 16, Nick
Over the next four days we travelled back to Singapore where we visited Tiger Balm Gardens and the magnificent national zoo. Had a day's water-skiing and finished with a final fling in Bugis Street tape buying.

Most certainly a holiday we'll never forget, a daring adventure that paid off. The boys *did* mature, and so did I.

TONY CROFTS

MATANZA

Six-thirty am. I'm already dressed and out of the couchette as the train slows to a halt in the darkness. Outside, nothing but gravel and a road on one side: on the other, the small halt with its sign *L'Hospitalet* and the bus waiting to bear us on the long winding climb, leaving behind an ever-lengthening panorama pierced with points of light. The snow stands in cliffs on the uphill side of the road, cut by snowploughs only hours before.

In Old Andorra, Peter is waiting with his Santana Land-Rover, and greets me heartily. Has there been a *matanza* yet? I ask. "There was one at Margarita's on Monday. I think there's another tomorrow at Mestre's," he answers.

Our goal is fourteen dizzying kilometres up into the Spanish Pyrenees. A community still living in an almost cashless economy, to a pattern already set in the fourteenth century. One of the last outposts of a peasant culture which is rapidly passing from the world, governed entirely by the seasons and depending little on manufactured inputs.

Their days, months and years move to the pace, and are sustained by, the products of their pigs, cattle, sheep, chickens and rabbits – which are, in a sense we have long forgotten, domestic animals.

It is those pigs which are the engine of the domestic economy. Bought as weaners in early spring, they are fed on kitchen scraps together with some bought-in meal; and in their pen below the kitchen are a living larder, evidence that the household will be able to feed itself in the following year. The climax of the year, and the time when next year's meat supply is laid down, comes in a hectic fortnight from Christmas Eve through into January, when the Festival of the Pig takes place. Or as the people themselves call it more plainly, *La Matanza*. The Killing.

Next morning, the appointed day, I find myself with the whole village, thirty-six people plus two generations of children and grandchildren who have come out from town for the occasion, gathered at the home of the mayor, whose *matanza* it is. Everyone has coffee, anisette, brandy, toasted bread and aioli for breakfast at 8 am. And then the work starts.

In the little square where three alleys meet, one man takes a spade and lifts away a few slabs of frozen snow, and makes sure the killing bench sits steady on its four short legs. It is a kind of long U split from the fork of two parallel branches, with legs drilled into their backs.

Up the steep alley beside the house, from the pens in the downhill basement, saunter the three pigs, with a neighbour, Cisco, shushing them from behind with a switch of scrumpled-up feed bags. They take their time, sniffing the stones and the muddy corners as if he wasn't there. Everyone stands round in a ring, closing the exits from the square between the houses. No-one hurries.

Andres, the slaughterman, has a long butcher's hook in his hand, about two feet long and sharpened at one end. The other end curves round the heel of his hand. He walks up to the first pig, hooks it through the jaw and drags it to the bench. The others all gather round to push it from behind, and then, once there, grab it by the legs and hump it up onto its side. The other two pigs continue their wayside investigations, taking no notice of the first one's screaming. Screaming like the brakes of a train. *Eeeee, eeeee.*

It doesn't stop as Andres put the broad-bladed knife into its neck and cuts the carotid artery. Margarita, the lady with the village telephone and the warm, kindly brown eyes, crouches with her bucket to catch the blood, whisking it to stop clots from forming. Andres opens the wound a little further so that it runs in a free jet. The pig carries on screaming, but its voice grows lower and softer. The men hold its jerking legs. The screaming is going to sleep.

In half a minute the bad dream is over, and it lies peaceful. Four sets of hands lift it across and lay it on a bed of arm-thick branches. Cisco brings half a bale of straw and covers the carcass reverently, as if tucking it up in bed, before putting his cigarette lighter to it. While it burns, filling the air with the smell of singeing hair, Margarita carries her bucket across to the steps by the front door of the house, where the owner's wife has placed a tin bath full of stale bread for black puddings. She pours in the blood and stirs with a big wooden spoon until all the bread is soaked. Andres hooks the second pig, and she follows back over with the bucket. The ash on the cigarette between the slaughterman's lips is barely a quarter-inch longer than before the first pig was taken.

Soon all three carcasses are lying on their stick pyres. Someone brings a long-spouted tin oil-jug full of alcohol, pouring a thin stream all over, drawing squiggly patterns of fire along the pig's side. The flames lick and join up, glimmering like brandy on a Christmas pudding. After that, water, and a scrape with an opened sardine can until all is smooth and clean.

Now Andres takes complete charge: he is the master butcher as well as the killer. The others merely wait on him like assistants in an operating theatre. As he works, others come to carry away each part as he frees it. A big bowl, large enough to bath a baby in, receives the entire coiled heap of intestines; the lungs and heart are bestowed like the Three Kings' gifts of gold, frankincense and myrrh, borne on open palms.

Men's and women's work is rigidly separated. The women take away and work the material, preparing the laborious transformation, while the men cut up and supply them. The ham is freed from the hip joint, lifted high and taken away; as much as a man can carry, ready for salting. Then the shoulder blade is freed and lifted out, cut away from the shoulder, the whole foreleg borne away likewise.

Twelve hams in a day, a year's meat supply. When cured, they will be hung in pillowcases in the airy upper rooms of the house; not cooked, but eaten raw. Fine Parma ham, the strong, resilient red meat beloved of peasants all over Europe.

Andres is working so fast that he is taking out slabs of meat more quickly than his workers can fetch them away. It is impossible to over-praise the skill and precision of his dissection. None of the crude chopping and sawing that our butchers do. Finally, all that is left is the pig's white waistcoat of backfat. Later in the week, this will be boiled up, together with any waste olive oil from the kitchen and some caustic soda from the pharmacy in town, to make soap.

Inside the house, the women have a long table set out. The town cousins are set there inexpertly to trim the meat off the bones, handling their knives clumsily, hacking and scraping, piling up the trimmings. Nothing will be wasted. To the left, at the sink, Pepita, one of the older women, is washing innards, dunking them in a big can of water. When she has finished she lays them aside and carries her can along past the toiling apprentices at the bone table, and empties it over the rail into the alley below. Beyond, the mountains can be seen, always brooding, always protecting. The winter sunlight dazzles in, and as the stream of scarlet liquid falls, it glows like molten rubies. On the table, a complete spine is almost clean. Guisepp, the son of the house, picks it up and puts it over his shoulder like a small pet dinosaur to bear it up to the bedroom for storage. All the bones are kept and dried for soup stock.

There must be thirty-five people in the house now, all working in a scene of incredible industry: purposeful, concentrated, happy – yes, happy above all. It is, after all, a harvest time; and by tonight the whole harvest of a year's meat will have been gathered and stored. Now all the men sit at the table; the women wait, or eat standing out on the balcony. We start with thin soup, meat balls and elbow noodles; then plates of white beans followed by boiled mixed meats, with thin slices of liver and chops after that.

Salad – sliced tomato, red pepper and olive in oil and vinegar – comes before plates piled with biscuits, puffy and sugar-sprinkled. Then the meal is cleared, the table scrubbed, and two big mincers set up at opposite ends. This is the women's empire, and they range themselves all along each side. The task of mincing three whole pigs – all but their legs – and blending in onion, salt, herbs and spices to fill the carefully-washed guts, will stretch out into the evening.

Some sausages are boiled; others simply hung in the upper rooms to dry in the winter air. Treated that way, they will keep fresh and tasty, redolent of mountain herbs, until July or August. Giusepp carries a trayful of them upstairs to lay on a sheet on the floorboards for a while. Probably to the room that was his sister's before she married and moved to town. Today they seem to have no bedrooms for sleeping in: only sausage-rooms and bone-rooms.

In between filling the gut casings with mince, little Miguel reaches up a hand and lets the moist trails of meat hanging out of the mincer rest in his palm, feeling it like a breast, squeezing it between his fingers, playing with it. No-one wants to stop him: he is experiencing food, the goodness of the land and its animals.

Drinks are brought round in a big pot, warm spiced wine ladled into glasses, so that all can quaff and refresh themselves. It is half past three, and everyone knows the work will not be finished until midnight. The numbers of people thin out, some come, some go, but several have gone off to feed or milk their animals. They will return later for the next phase, to relieve those toiling at the table. Everyone is tired, but all know the job must be finished before they can stop. Then we shall eat and drink together again.

And indeed, at midnight, we are all still sitting round the table, the mincers stripped for cleaning, the empty plates from a meal lying in front of us, the coffee cups being filled for the second time and the brandy bottle passed around. Little Miguel is prancing around in his grandfather's beret. He has picked up one of the mincer nozzles and holds it in his teeth like a trumpet. *"Pa para pa para,"* he goes. Time to celebrate.

PENELOPE FARMER

BALI AND THE BATTLE OF THE GODS

"If, unfortunately, your bowel is upsetting, probably you should only blame your psychosomatic boils."

BALI

AUSTRALIA

Arriving in Australia at seven in the morning with a dose of Bali belly, several shadow puppets wrapped in an Indonesian newspaper and a rucksack full of dirty clothes, I reflect wrily on the delicate Western stomach. The customs officer is fishing out my crumpled T-shirts and knickers. "They're wet," she says disgustedly. "Everything coming out of Bali today is wet." But they aren't just wet: there rises from them an unmistakable Bali reek – a rich, oleaginous compound of incense, spices, rotting vegetation and above all coconut oil, as ephemeral yet immutable as most things on that teeming island. I love it, I think. For days after I catch whiffs of it; am sitting again with Simon, lit by oil lamps, slapping at mosquitoes, on the hibiscus-fringed veranda of the Frogpond Losman, Ubud (four dollars a night for two, including breakfast).

"He used to be so dependent on his old guidebooks – somehow he thought they were his second bibles. . ."

Listening to the saronged English music student pick out her wistful tunes on a bamboo xylophone to a chorus of frogs from the surrounding rice paddies, Simon forgets that tourism has ruined Bali ("All the guidebooks say so"), forgets the hard beds, the intermittent rain, the dogs that bark non-stop, because the cheesecake our book sends us to gobble in the Lotus Café makes us smell like strangers.

"This isn't like India. You don't have adventures here. It's lotus-eating land," he says, taking my hand tenderly. "Sleep with me," one of the sons of the Frogpond owner is begging the music student. "Why not sleep with me? Why not?"

Last rites at a Balinese Hindu cremation tower. (*Bali and the Battle of the Gods*)

The backstreet charms of Corte, ancient fortress–capital of Corsica. (*The Face of Corsica*)

"To shock your lover after a fight, catch a snake, let it bite you. Green snake with red tail sends you to heaven. (No return ticket.)"

No need. We do not fight, though the stems of the lotus flowers are longer than we expect. Marriage, too, is a country to which we're not quite acclimatised. When Simon leaves for home, I am a lone woman traveller again, like those other lone women travellers who tell us the story of their lives over lunch in the Lotus Café. The music student also leaves; it is me the boy pleads with by the light of the oil lamps. Ostentatiously I turn the key in my bedroom lock, then lie awake, uncertain rather than lonely. At 3am my griping belly makes me flee to the bathroom. The tap is dry as usual. By the light of my fading torch the foliage invading the roof looks rampant and dangerous.

"BEWARE OF SARONG FEVER . . . wear your sarong neatly and properly, otherwise the Ubudians will consider you a 'not funny clown.'"

To hell with Bali belly: in the morning a festival rises up and engulfs me. I am, definitely, a "not funny clown" – whichever way I tie it my sarong refuses to look right. I give up and head for the temple at Mas, three miles down the road, past processions of women bearing on their heads elaborate pyramids of offerings. All wear neat blouses and sashes; their sarongs are smooth across their hips and stomachs, not bunched up like mine.

The crowded market at Mas sells sandals, plastic buckets and wooden ducks on wheels. Cheerful men in yellow sarongs and white temple hats are sitting at a table outside the temple, like ticketsellers at a garden fête. They sprinkle me with water. In return for a few ruppiahs I am admitted to the seething, hot-scented interior. The gamelan music is taped, to my faint disappointment; how practical they are on Bali, I think, remembering the huge Calor gas pokers we'd seen used to light a funeral pyre. Penetrating two inner courtyards, between gates carved with long-toothed demons, I find myself enmeshed in the hanging roots of the sacred banyan tree. Every image is flanked by pyramids of fruit and rice cakes; is wrapped in chequered cloth, honoured by incense sticks and ritual umbrellas. Thin priests in gold-edged sarongs sprinkle the praying people; processions of women bring offerings to be blessed; other processions take blessed offerings away. In such a multi-coloured throng the small boy wearing a cap with Mickey Mouse ears doesn't seem out of place. Not so some camera-snapping tourists – noting the pink and hairy legs of the saronged males of my race I view my Western pallor through Balinese eyes and do not altogether like it.

"One thing you should not lose is your balance. Know who is who, and what is which. A praying priest is not a photomodel."

A tall Italian with a face off a Roman coin does not agree; he is climbing an altar to get his photograph. As for me, in the heat of the midday sun I am losing my balance entirely. Queasily I catch a bemo back up the road to the Lotus Café and find myself reassured rather than irritated by the detailed directions I get from two middle-aged Californians, to a Milanese restaurant they know just off the Edgware Road.

"I know that it's not easy to chase away your headache. But I think it normal a living person is sick."

I am sick all right. Tonight, moreover, I fly to Australia; what I need is my bed. Instead, another lone woman traveller, a well-heeled one – her sarong fresh from the Bali Hyatt laundry makes mine look more crumpled than ever – persuades me to accompany her to the Battle of the Gods at Klungkung. Through the window of her hired car I gaze for the last time at this intricately green-patterned landscape: the villages hidden among banana fronds, the contours of hills defined by sinuous terraces, the elegance of coconut palms, the glint of water between the rice plants in half-grown paddies. I am desolate suddenly; dark is due shortly, by morning I'll be gone.

We climb into harder country, through a shuttered town past Muslim women veiled in black; clatter over a Bailey bridge across an agitated river. The Klungkung temple has no hibiscus bushes and frangipani trees; the trodden earth of its outer courtyard is bare except for puddles from recent storms. Perched on the edge of a bamboo-roofed platform, we watch the crowd arrive. It is Balinese mostly; there is also a group of orange people in pink, orange, red and purple, and some stocky Japanese, incongruously saronged. How white their skin is, whiter even than ours; they are no less outside this than us, I realise, feeling iller than ever as an American girl protests loudly at the smoke wafting from my cigarette-puffing companion.

"In case you are nauseated take a ginger root and chew it . . . First taste will be bad."

The gongs and drums of the gamelan band strike up a plangent racket. Women with images of gods on their heads sway down the steps from the inner temple, followed by youths, roughly dressed, bearing four or five stretchers made of long poles. On the stretchers are rectangular parcels, swathed in white cloth. The gamelans march them out of the courtyard. In five minutes the still more clamorous music marches the stretchers back – the images are now inside the parcels – behind a troop of pretty little girls in gold costumes and headdresses. Nothing else is pretty; no ornaments or carvings, no elaborate offerings or processions protect us from these gods. As soon as the girls halt and line up, the stretcher bearers take off, careering the parcels all over the courtyard. The crowd, trying to avoid them, hurtles backwards and forwards, screaming with excitement. Such elemental frenzy is altogether too much for me; fighting my way out, I have my own difficulties dodging the fury of the gods. I sprint desperately along the nearest dirt alley, then throw up against the wall of someone's house.

"Dear visitors . . . Fantastic dreams . . ."

Suppose an English woman found a foreigner vomiting at her gate: the Balinese woman, looking concerned, anoints me with some green liquid. In a moment my forehead, the back of my neck, are simultaneously cooled and burning. I stumble back to the battle, reeking of peppermint. Each crew of god-maddened youths is still charging its rivals; the packaged gods, juggernauts I think, lurch more crazily than ever on their stretchers. Stifled by the din, by the movement, by my own elemental reek, I remember the comic tourists in the painted festivals and processions on the walls of the gallery in Ubud. I remember the guidebooks' unequivocal dictum. "And they say we've ruined Bali," I whisper to my companion. "Then what has Bali done to us?" she hisses. "By the way, I like the peppermint." (I'm forced to flee again, and don't see the gods attain their temple. My friend, later, assures me they do.)

Quotations are from the official tourist map of Ubud, Bali.

THE FACE OF CORSICA

This summer the forest fires seemed barely under control, combusting only miles and hours from the last outbreak as if charged by underground fuses. Every night another swathe of luminous smoke rose across our valley; then the fire plane would wake us at daybreak, skimming down to land on the bay before rising engorged with its water.

Travelling anywhere on the island meant seeing these strange pauses in the maquis made by fire, the charred, bald ground where it seemed some atrocity might have just happened. Its tourist beaches and towns excepted, Corsica is a curiously unpeopled place. Passing the still-smoking pines impressed this loneliness on us as a sweet, black smell which stayed in our clothes and hair on the days we bumped and sweated in a succession of buses through its tense landscape.

On the road to Corte we stopped at a mountain spring. Beside it was a caravan selling cold drinks. Our bus driver and the caravan owner, a stately Italian-looking woman, explained how deep the snow became up here in winter. *"Ici,"* she said, slicing at one ample breast. It seemed hard to imagine.

Behind us, ten or twelve pigs nosed amiably in the shade, pink, black and shining. The driver and the lady, who appeared to be on intimate terms, paid no more attention either to us or to the pigs. We tried the spring. Icy splinters plummeted into our cupped hands. The shock!

Our driver, working perhaps with ulterior motive, filled his Coke-can from the spring and splashed it straight into his radiator, which exploded immediately and impressively.

Such immense stillness, to be out of the bus and face to face with the mountains, staring at their grey jaws prickly with pines like Desperate Dan's three-day growth. Mountains are what you see of Corsica first, from the plane, and their outflung fragments in the sea. I have never seen such mountains as those in the south: iron-grey, crazed with hairline cracks, torn into shapes manic in their arrested energy. The road plots its course through them with unnerving nonchalance. You imagine them twisting into even more fantastic gestures as soon as you've passed by, but somehow you don't want to look back. Then the mountains in the north are from another country, red as animal blood soaking into earth or the colour of cave drawings.

But here, beside the still sizzling bus, the mountains felt more familiar. They made me think of Scotland – a Scotland transformed by tactile heat, a humming presence in the air, but a landscape as brusque and secretive.

Walking the few miles back to the nearest village, we passed one of the police stations built strategically at the head of each important pass. Mammoth and self-contained, the windows shuttered, identical to all the others, it seemed malevolent to walk past, as if a concealed gun were sighted on our shoulder-blades. Further down, two hand-painted signs marked a barely-visible track between trees: *"Miel à Vendre"*, *"Hotel Calme et Douce"*.

We rested in the village square. Apart from three blonde cyclists who whizzed in melting colours across our vision, nothing stirred. This was not a tourist's stopping-place. A tin sign, crinkled and brown, advertised Poulain *chocolat*. We shared the square with a sleeping dog, an old man and a dripping fountain.

To escape the heat we discovered the yellow church. The Madonna and Child were black, except where the plaster had been chipped. Two jars of towering gladioli and a candle were all that disturbed the plainness of whitewashed walls and stone floor.

Walking round the back of the church we found an overgrown garden crammed with browning gladioli. A wooden door in the wall stood open, and next to it, propped up neatly, was a black bicycle. Clay pots of herbs and a white lily pressed through the spokes. I could almost make out a bed and a hard chair through the shadows inside the door, but then someone moved, I saw a pale flash, and ashamed I turned away. The priest did not come out, but I think he watched us as we wandered through the "city of the dead", between the marble "houses" on their immaculate pavements. Such peace and order; only ourselves and the grey cats moved. But outside the gate, a smelly dustbin overflowed with rotting flowers.

We finally made it to Corte on the next bus. Nationalist slogans slashed on two streets and boulders on mountain roads – hands brandishing guns – had made us curious about the old capital wedged on its rock fortress. Besides the cult of Napoleon (the firework displays and cocked-hat illuminations on his birthday, the busts ranging in size but not design, making it possible to buy a whole set rather like Russian dolls – the giant-size version being the Napoleon Monument in Ajaccio), there are also posters and cards for sale, though these are less easy to find, which show the "face of Corsica" emblem blindfolded, gagged and garrotted by the three strands of the French flag.

And Corte is still "the ancient bastion of Corsican independence", according to the tourist guide. But its grandest buildings are French imperial, declining in genteel palm-lined squares. So we climbed up to the Citadel, "focus of Corsican pride", paid five francs each at the stone gate and were solemnly handed our tickets.

Up the narrow, cobbled hill and around the corner we came to . . . what? We weren't sure. High barrack-like buildings surrounding a weed-straggled courtyard: high walls of dark schist. That stillness again. Only a movement when someone passed a window and light struck a fragment of broken glass.

The Citadel must be somewhere else. But as we thought this we were pushing open a heavy door, printing our footsteps in the dust inside. Guilty at first we began to explore, becoming braver and more childlike until we were jumping over missing floorboards, seeing dizzy storeys below, and pounding up rattly staircases. Some inner rooms had never had sunlight come into them: a shock, to put your hot, sweaty palm on a wall cold as a gravestone. Some rooms had fireplaces large as caverns. Everywhere smelled of lime. Doors, light-sockets, even some window-frames had been carelessly torn out. High up under the roof, exposed in places like a fishbone, you could look out over the mountains and the red roofs below. But where the roof held it was black as a cellar.

I found a row of coat-hooks behind a surviving door. Then a row of urinals, gleaming and streaked with tea-stains. But nothing else. It was a surreal experience to be able to look down the length of this entire derelict building, through doorframe after doorframe, as if into infinity.

At the top of the rise stood the medieval jail. Perhaps this was "it", but we found simply six coffin-shaped cells of blue stone the thickness of a man's body. Jacques had been there, September 4, 1951, though the paint looked too new. Far older words had been carved into the stone itself, but political slogans and crude intimacies jumbled themselves up among the cracks, bright and casual as the weeds, wild flowers and lizards outside. These, together with what looked like bullet-holes on a nearby wall, were all the signs there seemed to be.

Worn out by the heat and the climb, we sat under a tree, drinking warm Evian out of the bottle, not talking much. I watched a knot of smoke start to unfist on the skyline.

An English couple who knew us slightly stopped to complain: about the tourist guide, the loose boards, the hanging wires, the five francs. They talked about the standards of the National Trust. But I liked the barracks which, like Corsica, explained nothing of itself to strangers.

PATRICIA PERRY

DIGGING FOR SAPPHIRES

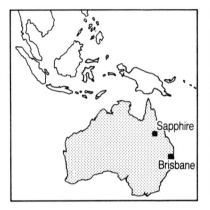

It is embarrassing to check into a youth hostel when your oldest son goes to work in a wig and gown. In Sapphire, however, there was nowhere else to stay except the Sunrise Cabins Youth Hostel. It did look enchantingly rustic . . . chalets built of smooth round rocks and rough hewn timber. Eucalyptus trees with coal black bark. Shiny galvanised water tanks like giants' coffee mugs.

We drove in hesitantly, sucking in our cheeks and stomachs, to the welcome news that the proprietors were engaged in giving birth somewhere less rustic and had left Mother-in-Law in charge.

We released our breaths and bellies. MIL was motherly and sweet and we had a fascinating conversation about how her twin sister had contracted skin cancer at the age of twelve.

"You'll have to wear a hat in the diggings," she warned, frowning at my M&S shorts and T-shirt. "We're right on the Tropic of Capricorn, you understand." MIL wore a pink straw hat, a long-sleeved dress and stockings. And that was just for watching telly in the reception lodge. When she ventured outside to show us to our cabin she carried a golf umbrella.

"We stopped off in Emerald and bought our Miner's Rights," said Bill proudly, waving two pieces of grey paper. "Of course, we've tried prospecting before. For gold in the Forty-Niner country in California."

I smiled fondly, remembering the little glass phial with its specks of gold dust. The kids used to take it to school to "show and tell". MIL looked less impressed.

"You know there's no emeralds in Emerald, don't you," she said. "It's called after the green grass."

"Of course," I lied. "But with Sapphire and Rubyvale it hardly matters . . ."

"Forget rubies, kiddo." She directed us to what looked like the hostel dump and returned to her telly.

Now when you go prospecting for gold in California in the Repro-

49-er country they give you little glass phials and lend you fancy aluminium pans.

When you go poncing about as a tourist in Sapphire, North Queensland, they lend you an ancient sieve, half a rusty oil drum, a pick and shovel of remarkable size, a twenty-litre plastic water container and vague directions about "Harry's Claim".

Harry's Claim was somewhere in the middle of a crazy lunar landscape of barren red clay. Hills and valleys, gullies and trenches and unfinished shafts marked the progress of generations of optimistic sapphire seekers. Abandoned machinery, rusty and gaunt. Rotting conveyor belts. Crumbling signs. All marked the abandonment of hopes and dreams.

As our dusty rented Toyota bumped over the diggings I peered worriedly at my eleven-dollar Miner's Right.

"This document is issued on the condition that the holder thereof shall, at the conclusion of any hand mining, fill in all excavations and do all things necessary to ensure that the land is not unsafe as a result of that mining (Sec 12 (4))."

We squinted through the dust clouds at the mini Himalayas.

"Jeez, they can't pin that lot on us," said Bill, braking swiftly before the Toyota toppled into a canyon. "I'll dig, you sieve and wash."

The soil had the consistency of stainless steel. The pick bounced right back when Bill struck a likely section of Harry's Claim. He cursed and counter-attacked. The sky was pale scabious blue. There were no sounds. No traffic, no people, no animals, no birds. Only the grunts and groans of the latest diggers. It was at least a hundred in the shade. Of which there was none. The sun was shooting burning bullets of cancer directly into our brain stems. We found no blue gems in our sieve, only grit and gravel. We retired to our Sunrise cabin and epic quantities of Riesling and Fosters.

Late that evening we sat in the communal kitchen with the hostel's other residents – two German lads who had been prospecting for a week. They were, they said, technocrats with the EEC in Brussels. They looked much like the motley crew that hangs round our house. We lent them four eggs and a hunk of margarine. We all hit the Riesling and Fosters again.

Automatically reverting to my mum role, I wiped down the battered table and emptied the ashtrays. Consternation! They had been displaying their finds. We all scrabbled on the floor in the dusky light and rescued the five minuscule chips. They were worth, they boasted, at least eight dollars and they intended to have them mounted. We nodded encouragingly, politely refraining from wisecracks about EEC fiscal policy. At least they had found something.

Dawn at the Sunrise Cabins was magical. From the pearly sky swooped flocks of lorikeets, chattering, twittering. Soaring jewels in ruby red, emerald green and sapphire blue. They perched in the trees, on the gutters of the cabins, waddled awkwardly on the stony paths. We held out peanuts and crisps and they perched on our arms and heads and shoulders to feed. The tiny filigree claws were sharp through the thin cotton of my nightgown. A brazen pair twittered in my ear as if confiding a secret. The perfection of the rainbow feathers, the curved beaks of jet, the glittering eyes, so close, so diamond bright. As suddenly as they had come, they flew away. The sun was coming up hot and strong.

Near the Blue Gem Store, which *is* downtown Sapphire, we ventured on to a dry river bed where a mechanised prospector had excavated with a front loader. We leaped down into the deep trench, picks and shovels rampant. It was soft gravel and sand and stones. Easy. Easy.

We found green ants, marginally smaller than lobsters. We found Coca-Cola cans. We found buttons. String. Dog turds. (Probably dingo, I suggested encouragingly to Bill, who was making noises about strolling down to the Blue Gem for a few tinnies.) A kookaburra chortled at us from an overhanging tree. He kept on and on. Giggling, chuckling. Laughing hysterically. Bill picked up a large non-precious rock, thoughtfully.

"Let's go visit that sapphire mine in Rubyvale," I said hastily.

The mine was excellent, a mini Disneyland. And cool. We wandered round seeing actual sapphires in the raw.

Then we realised our young guide had a familiar accent. The population of Sapphire and Rubyvale wouldn't fill a double decker bus. We'd come right round the world to the Australian outback in search of adventure. The lad was from North Yorkshire. We suspected we'd played bridge with his aunt.

We emerged from the mine into that baleful tropic sun, convinced it had already done brain damage, and headed for the nearby hamlet of Anakie. It seemed a suitable place for our state of mind.

The highlight of Anakie is a ten-foot-high fibreglass sapphire, but the pub is genuine. We had patronised pubs from Sydney to Daintree and thought them all smashing. In two months we never met an Australian we didn't like. After a few cold beers in the Anakie pub we positively adored everyone.

The stout man on the next bar stool was a sapphire miner. He only worked when he needed the money, he said. He sold all his gems to the Thais and to tourists.

"We noticed a little booth in Sapphire," I said, "something about Madame Lee buys gems."

"Too right," said the stout man. "Don't you believe a word about wonderful sapphires from Thailand. Crafty bastards buy them all here. You're English, aren't you – my wife's from Surrey."

"Fancy that," I said in my cocktail party voice. "How does she like life in Sapphire?"

"She went home on holiday," he said, gloomily swigging his lager. "Six years ago. Never came back."

It hardly seemed the time to ask for tips on prospecting. I turned to the barstool on my left. Its inhabitant, a wrinkly, twinkly man like an Australian leprechaun was wearing a seat belt, which was, in turn, fastened to one of the pub's supporting pillars.

His name was Sparrow, his barstool and seat belt were labelled "Sparrow's Perch" and the story was that he had dynamited the pub when they refused to serve him any more drinks. They'd only just re-paired the blown-up corner.

"I'm a boozy old fellow," he confided, "but I'm a great man with the explosives."

I turned to tell Bill the tale but he was already playing darts.

"Tell me, Sparrow," I began in my best North Yorkshire matron voice, "how much would you charge to blow up just a little tiny hole in the diggings? Cash. I've got my Miner's Right."

REVEREND ANDREW McLELLAN

SAVED BY THE BELLE

We were actually in the station when we discovered that we didn't have the family railcard. To reach our house from the station in ninety seconds you have to drive up a one-way street the wrong way, but we found the railcard and we caught the train. We caught the train with our big suitcase with the broken wheel, the other suitcases, the picnic bag, Irene's handbag, the overnight bag, the bag with the games in it and the two baskets the boys were carrying with the colouring books and the crayons and the teddy bears. We were still breathless when we flopped into our seats, but we were on the train.

I think it was three minutes after leaving Stirling when I checked the air tickets in Irene's handbag.

"Tickets?"

"Yes, the air tickets."

"Where are they?"

"In your bag."

"I don't have any tickets in my bag."

"Yes, they're in the big brown envelope."

"Big brown envelope?"

"Agh-agh-agh! Where does the train stop first?"

How could anybody take their family to the United States for two months and forget their air tickets? At least nobody was talking about the family railcard any more! Bit by bit, we formed our plan. It wasn't going to be easy, but at Edinburgh I would jump off the train and telephone the people who were living in our house to ask them to put the tickets on the next train. The reason it wasn't going to be easy was that we had to find Uncle Eoin on the platform as well, so there would not be much time. But it had to be done.

Uncle Eoin wasn't there. He is my elderly bachelor uncle who was coming to the USA with us. He wasn't on the platform when we reached Edinburgh and we had eight minutes. Three to get him on the train and five to telephone Stirling, we had calculated. But he wasn't on the platform and he wasn't in the superloo and the Glasgow train didn't know of anyone being ill and he wasn't at the Meeting Point and the eight minutes were up and it was back on the train with no tickets, no phone-call and no uncle. That was when Andrew said "Daddy, will you play Happy Families with me?"

Twenty miles out of Edinburgh I was considering hysteria and Irene was rummaging. Out of the picnic bag she emerged with a smile of triumph: "Look what I've found, dear!" There it was – an airline folder. She tore it open and gleefully pulled out . . . Uncle Eoin's air ticket. We didn't have him, but we had his ticket, and our own tickets were getting further away each minute.

We formed twenty plans before we reached London. We phoned his house, we phoned his friend, we phoned the club where he has his lunch. No-one knew anything and Andrew wanted to play Happy Families in King's Cross station. It was Irene who saw him first. You can always tell a Glasgow man on holiday by the way he wears his "Bunnet".

"Oh, you've made it at last," said he. "I reached Edinburgh too early for the train we were supposed to get, so I took the one an hour before."

The air tickets were sent down overnight, and we were on our way. On our way to Albuquerque, New Mexico, where I was "exchanging" with an American minister for two months: two months in each other's homes and each other's jobs. It was marvellous – Americans are so good at being kind – but we knew that nothing would be quite like the first six hours.

We hadn't heard about the other train. The scenic, narrow-gauge steam train which runs through the Colorado mountains, with magnificent pine forests lining the ravines which plunge down to the white spray of the waterfalls. In other places it chug-chugs through flat desert or open meadow, never touching more than eight miles an hour. With the cow-catcher in front and the lumps of soot in your hair, with the incessant noise of cicadas and the hot, hot sun turning the train into a steam room, you find yourself back a hundred years and you're not surprised to see a village bank displaying the Wells Fargo sign. For Ian and Andrew, Happy Families had made way for Billy the Kid.

Our journey was half over when the crunch came. Literally the crunch: *crunch! scrunch! crash!* and then stop. It's not a shock to come to a halt at eight miles an hour; but when you're just not anywhere it can be a surprise, especially when it is sudden enough to put your neighbour's sandwich in your mouth. One good thing about being stopped is that at last we could understand the loudspeaker messages. "The train has gone off the rails" is pretty easy to understand.

It was the ideal spot. On one side was a gorge which was quite impassable: and on the other, hills and bushes, bluffs and cottonwoods stretched to the horizon. Even Ian and Andrew, who watch more space cartoons than Westerns, knew what happens next when the train goes off the rails at the "ideal spot". Which hill held the Apaches? I began looking round the train for the wooden crates, for I knew that soon we would be breaking them open to share out the rifles. I knew, too, that one of them would contain a mysterious dead body; and I began to study my fellow passengers to see which one was the Colonel's lady and which one was called Doc.

The train really had gone off the rails and we were all shown the wheels in the mud to prove it. The next message through the loudspeakers was a humble one: "We don't know what to do". Then the two drivers and the conductor tried to lift this steam locomotive with its two hundred passengers back on the rails. Then came the message, "We're sending for help" – as we watched the driver jumping off the engine and running down the track as hard as he could. Help came eventually on one of the little rail-cars that are operated by pumping the handle up and down. Sad to say, Andrew and Ian had never heard of Buster Keaton.

It's Los Angeles we will remember, however. "Dana Point is the place to swim. Safe as can be, lots of sand, and gentle waves." It didn't look like that to us, but once we were in it was fun. Big high breakers, lovely warm water and hardly anyone else around. We had been in for ten minutes when Bob noticed that we were out of our depth, so we swam in. Five minutes' hard swimming – and we were still out of our depth. The came the big wave, hurling Bob toward the shore and sucking me back out as its prey. It's worse when you don't see well, swimming for your life and nothing to see but water and sky, waves and sun. Ten minutes, twenty minutes, and the conviction growing clearer that you're going to die. Bit by bit the strength goes, arms first, then legs, and there's no-one there. I remember saying to myself, "This is the sea – you can float", and then turning on my back. Then I remember very little.

Until there was a voice. "Can you hold on to this? I'm the lifeguard." I hadn't seen the helicopter, searching in vain; I hadn't seen the lifeboat, unable to pass the rocks. But I heard her. She pulled me three-quarters of a mile against the tide and I gave her no help at all. On the beach they said it was unforgettable: this golden California beach girl – dividing the ocean as she swam. Ariana was her name. There aren't many Arianas in Stirling.

The hospital bill was five hundred dollars. When they let me out I still tasted it and I still heard it and I still felt it. Mrs Black tried to help: "Andrew needs a good rest. Would he like to change rooms with me so that he could have the water bed?"

On the morning we flew home Irene left the passports in the supermarket. By that time we had forgotten about the family railcard.

RICHARD POOLEY

SHOOTING THE ZAMBESI

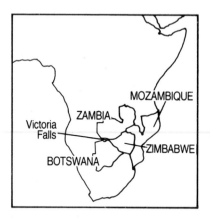

A white line still bisected the bridge, but its meaning had gone and the menace with it. Now the only sentry was a baboon sitting on a fence barking at a warthog on the other side of the road.

Early morning, sun up but cool, just two of us on the bridge at Victoria Falls, between Zimbabwe and Zambia. We looked down at the pale green Zambesi 300 feet below. Cecil Rhodes had wanted the bridge built close enough to the Falls to catch the spray. Usually it does. However, this was September and the "Falls" in front of us were just a curtain of rock. The rains had been good; not good enough, though, to make up for years of drought. Only on the Zimbabwean side did the river reach over and plunge in. Its noise was like distant motorway traffic.

We were about to go down the river on a rubber raft. We were to start at the bottom of the Falls and travel six miles down the Zambesi through zigzagging gorges . . . and over nine rapids. Why on earth had we agreed to it? Sarah didn't even like putting her head under water in the bath. As for me, the wake of a passing launch under a scull on the Thames was the nearest I'd ever got to white water.

"Triple A," the caricature Californian told our subdued party of eighteen outside the Zambian hotel. "A for scenery, A for excitement, and A for ease of access." Better than Omo. It took a little time before I realised he was talking about a river in Ethiopia. Through his organisation, Sobek, he seemed to have shot most of the world's rapids. "I'm Jib." His chin did indeed have a confident look about it. "Now let me tell you." The 'you' appeared to be a tiny seventy-year-old American woman. "The real danger is getting down on in there. That's where the legs get broken. The rapids is easy. And then there's the climb right on out at the other end. Five hundred feet straight right on up to the top." The lady was unimpressed by the string of prepositions.

"Ah did the Choler-ado end Ahm dooin this one."

So we clambered down to the whirlpool – the Boiling Pot – past the grinning curio sellers. "Hey! Buy now, madamsir. You are being too, too tired after Sobek, isn't it?"

A steep path through spray forest and then we were on to mossy boulders. Only one of us slipped. Me, twice. Collapse of the agile mountain man pose.

Our three rafts dangled over the water, small against the black cliffs. The river, a mile wide up there, squeezed into 150 yards down here. It objected to the constraint. We were all trying not to look at the first rapid, delicately yet furiously turning in on itself. I tightened my lifejacket for the fifth time.

"Okay!" Jib bellowed at us a couple of feet away. "No-one has to flip if they just remember a few basic rules." A twist of his flat hand showed what flipping meant. "All you gotta do is hold on hard to the rope around the side. And go where the wave is. If there's a wave hanging over you on the right side, then you throw yourself on that side. That's the *high* side. You gotta go for the *high* side! Okay?"

The high side. He'd shouted it as if it held the key to the meaning of life. I glanced at the rapid. Maybe it did.

In our raft were a middle-aged dentist from a Namibian diamond mine, his silent, teeth-baring wife, a thin and earnest German ("What is bail please?"), two perfectly mannered teenage sons of a senior Zambian official whose mountainous wife we had left behind at the hotel ("I'd sink it"), us and Jib.

We were last to cast away, but first through the rapid. Whatever happened to queuing? Why us? . . . Dentist and I threw ourselves half out of the bows to become a bouncing, double-headed figurehead. The waves swept over us; we came up, twisted, went under again, rammed the gorge side and finally got flicked out into the calm.

"Bail!"

The German was picking up English fast.

The water, very cold, sent up streams of bubbles. We shivered in the gorge's shadow. Above us was the bridge. Little figures lined the railings. As we waited for the others to come through, I thought of the first time I had crossed here, nineteen years before. Two armed soldiers had stood either side of that white line, three feet apart, both black, silent and avoiding each other's eyes. The next time, in 1971, the soldiers had moved back out of sight. The young white Rhodesian I'd passed on the bridge had told me not to bother trying to get into Zambia. "Bleddy munts, man . . . told me I was illegal!"

I was luckier. An immigration officer in Botswana had given me a full-page visa with "VSO" stamped all the way across it. It didn't mean anything but it opened every border. I had made sure, too, that no Rhodesian stamp sullied my passport; instead I got one on the back of a piece of cornflakes packet. Now there was still tedious form-filling. But the hostile line had moved on, "down south", to the Limpopo. The mighty Zambesi had become a tourist's plaything.

The next two rapids were similar to the first. We were all joining in the atavistic yell: "Hit the high side!"

Jib soon cut us down.

"Okay, guys. Now, the Real Thing. *Yoohaa* . . . Number Four!"

We could hear it. It was round the bend. Dentist's wife's rictus smile showed that we all were.

"Second Gorge," Dentist said. "That's where that Canadian girl got shot . . . by the Terrs." He glanced nervously at the half-caste Zambians. But they were staring hard at Number Four.

Sucked in and spat out, I still don't know how we avoided being liquidised. But the terror wasn't enough for Dentist. He had to tell his tale of murder. I nodded. Why bring up yesterday's war? Wasn't this exciting enough for him?

Number Five had us falling into a very deep hole, riding vertically along a wave called the Rooster Tail and bending so far that bow almost touched stern. At least, that's what Jib told us we had done.

Dentist decided to look around for rare falcons instead of guerrilla ghosts. Sarah began to feel that the bath-dipping had not really been adequate preparation. The German appeared to have been reduced to a fearful mute. Dentist wife kept on grinning. The half-castes sat on the raft side as if waiting for cucumber sandwiches to be served. And Jib rolled his words around the gorge and gave us a geology lesson.

A klipspringer buck leapt up an invisible path on the cliff face. Most of the others weren't interested: they wanted their lunch. I remembered the comments book in the self-catering lodge where we had stayed the previous two nights in Zimbabwe. A narrow strip of chopped grass and scrub leading down to the Zambesi had been the subject of a long-running dispute. Forget the bushbuck, baboons, vervet monkeys and warthogs that could be seen there. Instead:

"Why no lawn?" (a Brit.)

"Go back to the UK for your bloody lawns." (an Aussie)

"A *lawn* equals *civilisation*." (another Brit.)

Lunch came out of sealed containers together with the cameras. Some were eager to cut carrots and avocados. Others stared at the next rapid. The American lady sat down very gingerly on her patch of rock ledge and said little. A group of English students – "Coal not Dole" on their T-shirts – talked politics. "British politics are a sham by comparison with South Africa. They mean something down there."

Dentist looked disapproving.

Nobody flipped. We were all disappointed (provided it had been somebody else's raft, of course). The end was the slow toil up Jib's 500 feet – "straight up". Local carriers climbed steadily past us with oars, rafts and boxes. No hesitation, no pauses for breath, sweat runnelling down their backs. From the top we watched the progress of aged America. An hour to push and pull her up like some truculent donkey. But at the end: "Ah tol' you'all Ah cud do it. Just gimme time. Okay . . . why don' we'all do that agin?"

The spectacular 300ft drop of the Victoria Falls. (*Shooting the Zambesi*)

MARY FANE

Janus and the Turks

Turkey is Janus-faced. One face turns east and the other west, and one is nice and the other, usually in uniform, nasty. The head turns in seconds, so there is always the feeling of slight uncertainty, of things going on that perhaps one would rather not know. This was illustrated forcefully at Izmir Airport, both coming and going. After laboriously queuing our way through Passports and finding the luggage, we had to face Customs. The official standing there could have come straight out of That Film, unsmiling, swarthy, armed. "Passports!" he snarled.

I disengaged them again from the bottom of my handbag. He peered suspiciously. "Where you go?"

Suddenly neither of us could remember, out of sheer terror, and I pointed feebly at the suitcase label. The Customs man squinted down at it.

"Ah Kusadasi! You say, Koo*shad*asi." We tried. An entrancing smile. "Veree good. You have nice time. Bye bye."

The homeward flight was exactly the reverse, first the smile, then the snarl. But we'll come to that later.

Then there were the sheep. On our drive to Kusadasi in the minibus, bowling along the dusty potholed roads, we must have seen thousands of them. Sheep in ones, twos, threes, in herds, in lorries and, I swear, one in a taxi.

"Tomorrow you see," said the driver enthusiastically. He was strong on sprinkling us with lemon cologne but weak on English. "All sheeps make pretty with flowers."

What a lovely custom, we thought. "Then . . ." and he made a very vivid slashing gesture across his throat. Oh. This, we later discovered, was the great Islamic celebration of Abraham and Isaac and is a sort of equivalent of Christmas, with the whole family gathered together.

ABOVE: The magnificent head of Apollo at his temple in Didyma. (*Janus and the Turks*)
BELOW: On safari in the Ngorongoro Crater in Tanzania, home of the much poached rhino. (*Off the Scale*)

We passed a gaily caparisoned procession led by a young boy in a scarlet cloak, riding a white horse. Numerous splendidly decorated carts and cars followed him. How exciting and how colourful. "Circumcision," said the driver cheerfully. Oh.

"Er . . . how?" coughed one of the male passengers delicately.

"Now, anestheric. For me, not. There was much blood. All relations singing and dancing round bed. Is great day for boy, great day." Gatwick seemed a long way off.

A relief, then, to find the hotel reassuringly Western. We did, in fact, stay at three different hotels in and around Kusadasi, not from choice but because of overbooking. All were extremely pleasant, with excellent swimming and watersports. The one in the town centre was perhaps a little noisy at night, an unhappy donkey and the muezzin adding an extra dimension of sound, and I would not recommend it to poor sleepers.

We approached our first meal with some trepidation but all one can really say is that Turkish food is delicious. What with cheese pies, stuffed aubergines, pilaff, shish kebab, subtly flavoured lamb, tender steaks, chicken in yummy sauces, marvellous fish, we didn't have an awful lot of room for puddings. There was *baklava* light as a cloud, honey cakes, milk puddings (and you have never had a milk pudding until you have had a Turkish one), things made with chocolate, and ice cream made in heaven.

Another doubtful plus, apart from the wine which was drinkable but forgettable, was Entertainment. In two of our hotels we dined to the strains of a genuine Palm Court Orchestra, belting out airs from Strauss and Weber and Lehar to loud German applause.

Kusadasi itself proved to be delightful, a lively bustling little port full of shoeshine boys, people carrying glasses of tea, and people selling things.

"Sir! Sir! May I ask you one question? Just one?"

"Yes?"

"Do you want to buy a carpet?" And we did, how we did. The shop windows, heaped with jewel colours, were irresistible temptation. Prices are far below London's, and the whole process of buying is sheer enchantment. Where else does the salesman sit cross legged on the floor while one sips tea? The fact that he wears designer jeans and Gucci shoes doesn't really matter.

Another good buy is leather. Beautifully designed and made dresses and suits can be had from about £80 or so, and indeed many of those on sale in British shops for at least double the price are made in Turkey. Jewellery is also cheap, and all cotton goods.

We were on half-board terms at our hotels, but eating out cost so little that it seemed a pity not to explore the restaurants. They are very varied and tend to specialise, some being renowned for their *mezes,* an apparently endless procession of fascinating *hors d'oeuvres*. The whole town turns out at night for its evening promenade, strolling at leisure between sellers of roasted corn, nuts, mussels, soft drinks, spun sugar and, of course, carpets.

Other delights of Kusadasi include the enormous market, so big that all the food in the world seems to be there. The country women come here to buy and sell, wearing brightly coloured baggy trousers and long scarves round their heads. The quality of vegetables, meats and cheeses seemed superb and prices incredibly low, and we were told that many of the cruise ships stock up here. We stocked up ourselves on honey, nuts and spices, and a pair of baggy trousers. Afterwards we went to Bird Island, which is joined to the mainland by a causeway. A fine old fort stands there, surrounded by trees and winding paths, and here we came across a tree in bandages. Every twig of every branch was covered with tiny strips of paper or cloth, carefully tied on. It was decidedly eerie in that little grove, with the cloth and paper fluttering, and we left rather quickly.

We could have taken a day trip across to the Greek island of Samos, but "Samos is terrible place, terrible", said a Dutch couple we met. On the other hand Istanbul sounded marvellous, according to a delightful pair from Leytonstone. "You wouldn't believe it, not even when you're looking at it. It's really beautiful, all the things in the museums. And the buildings, and the people. Four thousand shops in the Grand Bazaar, you could never get round them all." There were trips there too, but we decided August was not the best time.

But we went to Ephesus and saw the beautiful, strangely Indian looking, Diana of the Ephesians, and to the ancient towns of Priene, Metelus and Didyma, where Cyrus and Alexander and Tamerlane came and the teasing river Meander changed its course. Didyma was the most sacred oracle in all Asia Minor and what remains of the temple (to Apollo) is colossal. Janus turned up here as well. A woman in our group was forbidden to take her cine camera in to the site, and moreover was not allowed to leave it at the ticket office. So the poor lady had to remain outside. "A regulation."

We also went to the site of Aphrodisias, largely unexcavated, which will always be remembered, by me at any rate, for having the only museum with a cookery book, *The Aphrodisias Cook Book,* for sale.

Another worthwhile trip was to Permalukele, which is somewhat like Bath, being a hot mineral spring running into a Roman pool where one can swim amid the fallen pillars. The difference is that the spring is at the top of a hill and the water cascades gently down over a cliff, leaving behind a fantastic deposit of mineral salts, carved by the wind into glistening pools and miniature glaciers.

Turkish archaeological sites, incidentally, make no concessions to visitors, in contrast to the museums which seem exceptionally well planned. Tough walking shoes and a stiff upper lip are highly recommended, as guides think nothing of suddenly veering off across a field of thistles or expecting one to negotiate ancient courtyards littered with fallen masonry and potholes. But the scenery in this part of the Aegean coast is always a delight, with rocky hillsides and that strangely magic mixture of olive trees and cypresses.

The Turks are nice. We heard of one lady who injured her head in a fall. A taxi driver, summoned by her anxious daughter, took her to the local hospital, waited while she was attended to, and then drove her forty miles to Izmir for a brain scan for which he paid. "You are guest in my country," he said. Then there was the girl who cleaned our room.

"Madame, cigarette?" she said one day.

I gave her the packet, which had about ten left in it. Tears came into her eyes. "Oh madame!" and I was hugged and kissed like a long lost grandmother. We later found that my husband had left his wallet lying on the bed.

"Why you English not come more?" a taxi driver said to us. Why indeed? And as for Janus at the airport . . .

"Nice time?" asked a relaxed, smiling official. Flick.

"All suitcases to be open and looked!" he snarled, and the whole atmosphere changed, leaving many a holidaymaker vowing they would never come back. All the more room for us.

MARIAN BALL

OFF THE SCALE

We were one degree and fifty seconds south of the equator. We were five and a driver. Hot, impatient, fatigued, we had the dust of eight hours' travelling in our teeth. We wanted a cold beer and a cold shower. We hoped.

The beer was warm . . . "technical problem with the fridge". The towels were wet . . . "rainy season ma-am". We didn't complain. We were the "evaluation team", and this was Tanzania.

The situation was familiar to us. "If it vosn't like zis, ve vouldn't be here" had become almost a catchphrase as we wined, dined and dossed at around fourteen hotels and lodges between Dar-es-Salaam and Lake Victoria. Our mission was to evaluate these establishments in comparison with hotels of international standard, as expected by standard international tourists.

We had arrived in Tanzania from a sub-zero Geneva in January. The intensity of heat, the dripping humidity, the smell of vegetation, bodies and decay presented a sharp contrast. The team members – three Swiss, myself and an Italian – provided a variety of cultures. The Swiss could be considered in sweeping generalities. They were rigorously mechanistic in all they pursued, be it work, wine or women, and even in the spontaneously magical atmosphere of Serengeti they always wished to maintain a routine. Each carried a Swiss Army knife.

The Italian spoke Swahili and had a love of birds that enabled him to identify anything with wings and describe its song and sex life. As the token English person and the only female, I felt life on safari would be interesting.

In Dar, our base was "the best hotel in town", a weary establishment with shabby fittings, leaky toilets, greasy spoons, no water and no air-conditioning. It had been okay once, and some of the staff remembered, but had lost all heart and hope of ever regaining the days when every room had lightbulbs and there was water in the swimming pool.

It was here that we realised the project would take very little time, for the three major hotels in Dar suffered from identical problems: a good deal of corruption, a lack of trained personnel, and no spare parts. It was the latter that was held by Tanzanians to be entirely responsible for the decline of tourism. Everything was "out of order", including the two-year-old notice apologising for the "temporary inconvenience" whilst "rehabilitation" took place.

Kilimanjaro was to be our first major stop outside Dar. On the way, we called at the New Savoy, Morogoro, our first taste of an "out-of-town" hotel. We split up into our various disciplines, armed with extensive forms and complicated questionnaires. My job was to look at accommodation and laundry facilities. "What are the guest-room give-aways?" . . . Shower gel, sewing kit, safari hat? . . . I looked in vain for the soap, toilet paper, lightbulbs. Next question: "Cleaning methods, frequency, equipment used?" . . . Hmmm . . . kicking away a cockroach carcass from the floor, I gave up on the bedroom and headed for the laundry, wondering if my questions on the PH value of the detergent, and the rpm of the hydro-extractor, were not a little ambitious.

The laundry was a small room with a tap. The cold water and soda hand-wash, hand-wring and dry-on-the-grass method took three lines to document, and invalidated further questions on pressing techniques and dry cleaning. On our scale of one to ten, the New Savoy was off the scale.

At four miles high, we felt Kilimanjaro would be hard to miss. Shrouded in mist, and being evasive of its enormity, it loomed in the dusk over the Moshi Hotel – a once prestigious hostelry famed for afternoon tea, now alas also off the scale. It was clear something was badly wrong with its kitchens when our Swiss chef, evaluating food preparation, ordered boiled eggs for dinner. Giving them penalty points for being unable to produce a dippy yolk, he peeled off the shell. "Never mind, if it vosn't like zis, ve vouldn't be here."

Larger than we had ever imagined, Kilimanjaro was visible in the morning sun. Devoid of its misty hat, it revealed its snow-capped peak and forced itself to be included in every conversation. We had a quick sortie to its foothills and discussed "doing Kili" at the end of the project. I picked some violets and arranged them for pressing inside *Birds of East Africa*, a now much-thumbed volume as my ornithological knowledge increased. I could now identify hawks, weavers and barbets.

Before the sun set that evening we encountered our first mechanical breakdown when the Rover ground to a halt on one of those long dusty roads that disappear over the horizon in both directions. I resented the comments from the Swiss that British workmanship was responsible for our dilemma. As the toolbox was missing – sold by the driver in Morogoro – they gathered under the bonnet each wielding a Swiss Army knife, discussing which of the sixteen gadgets would save the day.

An approaching cloud of dust turned out to be the Minister of Communications in a VW Combi, who gave us all a ride to Mount Meru Hotel, his and our destination. It was here that we re-designed the scale, using the Mount Meru as an example of the best we were likely to find. Indeed, after the previous establishments there was an air of luxury here . . . the "Dodoma Rose", Tanzania's home brew, available cloudy, medium cloudy, or clear, was chilled before service.

After inspecting Arusha's three hotels, one of which boasted a disco with a rule "No Bull dancing" – men dancing together – we left for Meru game reserve for our first close encounter with African wildlife.

At the hippo pool, an authorised observation point, we left the vehicle. The creatures wallowed and yawned widely for the cameras. The Italian and I were at the water's edge when a snapping of twigs behind us revealed the dark and surly face of a buffalo. We ran back to the Rover.

My colleague slipped on a rock, hurting his ankle, which was badly swollen by the time he removed his shoe. My time in the Wigan Brownie pack had given me hours of practice in cold compress application, and, having seen *African Queen* several times. I was only too willing to tear up my dress to make bandages. Sadly I was wearing trousers, but improvised with wet leaves and a scarf until we got to a hospital where a plaster cast was applied. It was a gruesome place and we were happy the ankle was sprained not broken.

The next few weeks took us through Lake Manyara reserve, to the Ngorongoro Highlands, into the crater and off across the Serengeti Plain.

We continued to look at lodges. They were "different". Baboons in the bar, receptionists asleep at the desk, and a disappointment for the Swiss – no prostitutes. My study of animal life was not restricted to game.

Between work we were on safari. We looked hard for, but never found, the tree-climbing lions of Manyara, though we did see the huge buffalo and elephant herds, and a memorable sight: a horizon of soft pale pink taking to the air above the lake – flamingoes.

To see dawn over Ngorongoro Crater is to witness the perfect creation of a new day. The twelve-mile-wide, mist-filled caldera appears out of the darkness and the soft glow of the early morning sun gently warms the air. Fronds of mist steal quietly out of the crater until it clears to reveal the green and bustling home of gazelles, antelope, cheetah and the much poached rhino. The chill evening air makes the log fire in the lodge a welcome sight.

The wildebeest were producing young as we drove through Serengeti. They learned to walk and run with amazing speed, essential in their harsh environment. It was here, picnicking under an acacia and listening to the World Service – "the dollar almost parity with the pound" . . . "hailstones ruin strawberry crop in Kent" – that I looked around. For 360 degrees the land stretched to distant blue horizons, and was populated by thousands, no millions, of animals. I realised how very privileged we were to be there.

We left behind the whistling thorns for a 200km drive to the Mwanza Hotel on Lake Victoria, our last stop. Derelict but full, with smugglers trading in hushed voices in the grimy bar.

The Italian's cast was removed at a "private clinic", using a hacksaw, chisel, and pliers borrowed from a carpenter's toolbox (the plaster saw was "out of order"), and after a hot, tiring eight-hour drive we found ourselves back in Serengeti at Seronara Lodge. A notice in the lobby said, "The hotel is situated one degree and fifty seconds south of the equator". Our mission over, unwashed but with a warm beer, I repeated the line on a postcard home.

February 28th, "Just sitting one degree . . ."

DAVID ARMSTRONG

CHAIN GANG

End of term. Decide to go to Brittany for a week's cycling with colleague David and his son Simon. Planning meeting in lounge bar of Wynnstay hotel. David arrives wearing blue and white horizontal striped Breton sweater. Couple in corner snigger, but he is served. I have never seen him order Pernod before. Also, I believe that the 'd' is silent. Whilst at the bar David looks at the barmaid with that look of his: I hope he will behave responsibly whilst abroad.

FRIDAY.
Rail journey to Portsmouth uneventful. Simon is dressed in very fashionable clothes but seems quite a nice boy. He seems to have rather a lot of money for one week in France. (It would be nice if he bought a drink occasionally; he can certainly drink Scotch and Coke with ease.)

On the boat David waxes lyrical about Breton flowers. He also tells Simon and me that the roads are very well signposted and that every French driver is also a cyclist. Sounds good.

Prepare to find cabin for sleep. David insists on using French to stewardess who speaks perfect English. He appears unaware of delay he is causing to passengers behind him in queue.

SATURDAY.
Pavement café in St Malo for coffee and croissants. "This is France," declares David. Wave to Frenchman on cycle exactly like mine. Return to bikes to find mine stolen. Can provide *gendarmerie* with reasonable description of smiling waving thief.

Buy new bike on Access card. I now own a cheap red Gitane instead of an expensive black Raleigh Royale. Eventually leave St Malo having gone fifteen kilometres in wrong direction. Signposts in France less good than claimed by David. It is "because it's a port" he says. Simon scowls and mutters something to his father. He seems a fairly quiet boy except when stating the obvious with a fairly pronounced lisp.

On right road, going in right direction, when Simon rides his white Peugeot into hedge clippings whilst trying to get foot into toe-clip. Puncture. Further resent French bicycle thief in possession of new puncture kit.

Take turns carrying Simon's panniers as he wheels his bike to one of "numerous" cycle shops in Brittany. Have first serious row when no cycle shop has been sighted in two hours' walking.

Eat last of yesterday's salad sandwiches and perk up, agreeing that adversity welds friendship. Reach cycle shop in large town. Profound relief. New resolve of friendship sorely tested when we find cycle shop closed for public holiday.

Simon damages bowling shoe, big toe and two spokes when he lunges a kick at punctured cycle wheel. Decide to find B & B until tomorrow. David comments on pink Brittany cottages as fine gardeners' drizzle soaks us. I wonder when he will use his extensive French to find us a room.

SUNDAY.

Puncture repaired but still raining. Bretons appear liberally supplied with mackintoshes and umbrellas. We cycle off in shorts and T-shirts. Catch yesterday's *Sun* headline: one word, "PHEW", and picture of scantily-clad, well-endowed young lady disporting herself in English public place. Also, it's the end of the third day and we still have no idea of the Test match score. David's French continues to let us down badly. Nearly had fight today with man he was asking directions of: David started to tell him (unnecessarily I thought, in view of the rain) about Offa's Dyke. The man had been a seaman, had a smattering of English and thought that David was making a homosexual approach. Cycled away very fast.

MONDAY.

Bonhomie continues to be the rule in youth hostels: eight beds in a room and one coat hanger.

In the evening ribald songs from French school party followed by bonfire in the courtyard. German rucksack forms centrepiece of blaze. Hour later German boys return full of Kronenburg spirit and join French celebrations. French and German groups decamp with expressions of much love.

Silence.

Heinz is heard knocking Italian about room with acrimonious accusations about "Fascist Mussolini rucksack stealers". French warden acts as peacemaker. Snoring descends, mattress oblivion.

TUESDAY.

The day is hot. It is strangely enervating following David's gold

Viking with its half-inflated rear tyre for mile after mile. Also, he refuses to adjust his toe-clips properly; there is room for at least two feet in each of them. Simon has gone miles ahead and rides in the wrong gear always. Why aren't I ahead? I use the right gear, have inflated tyres and adjust my toe-clips, even whilst on the move.

Evening. Simon refuses to eat pizza as we ate pizza only two nights ago. I scowl. Simon claims that there are plenty of four-course set menus for forty francs. We scour St Brieuc before returning to *crêperie* for pizza. Simon scowls.

Night. Back at youth hotel Simon insists that he cannot undress without a light on (it is 1am). The three Dutchmen in our room feel that he can. I think they are probably right.

Simon and David finish undressing in the dark. Simon's money falls noisily to the floor; David bangs his head on the bunk above. I am settled in bed when Simon calls me from near slumber to shut the door. *Merde.*

WEDNESDAY.
I have broken off diplomatic relations with Germany on account of sharing a bunk with Hanoverian who has erotic dreams when he should be asleep.

Breakfast. Coffee at village café. David tries his French. He asks about the Brittany Orchid. An old man smiles. The others look at the space in front of their wine glasses. David describes with his fingers and exactly the same words as previously – but with an additional puckering of the brow and contorting of the Gallic syllables – the Brittany Orchid. The madame behind the bar shrugs and turns away.

As we leave the café a fat man appears from the alley beside it ushering before him a reluctant waif.

"Orchid," he says, "Orchid, Bretagne Orchid." We ride away. No-one has his feet in his toe clips.

Night. Tonight's youth hostel is worse. We are in a large tent. It is filled with mattresses. We three stare blankly as the flat-chested German girl removes her T-shirt for sleep.

David snores. Simon wakes me to ask me the time. As I fall asleep I hit out at my wife, Julia, in my dreams and fall off my mattress.

It is morning and the tent is empty.

THURSDAY.
I notice that I am the only one of the party servicing my cycle. They will doubtless regret their lack of maintenance when some part of their bike malfunctions.

Cycling to Binic. Unfortunately, whilst spinning my rear wheel for "true" this morning, I caught a spoke with my screwdriver and now have to find a cycle shop. My definitive cycling book issues grave warnings about "aggravated spoke failure" and speaks of "collapse of wheel without warning".

It seems hardly fair that I should encounter these problems when David's head nut is very loose and Simon's cones are a joke to any self-respecting cyclist.

Afternoon. David cycles in the middle of the road. Cars swerve and hoot. David waves to them and shouts back to me: "Not like England, eh?"

One fat, lumbering Citroën's progress is arrested by David's serpentine glide. David calls something about corn marigolds and gestures with his arm. The paint of the elderly blue Renault coming the other way welds itself to the stately grey of the big Citroën as it swings out to avoid David's flailing limb. A kilometre up the road the Citroën languishes. A pale Frenchman waits. David sails into the lay-by, his progress arrested by a juddering front brake. *"Ça va, Monsieur."*

Frenchman takes one step towards David; I try to recall the terms of the holiday insurance. David pulls his tattered map from his back pocket: *"Cartes, Monsieur . . . pour vous . . . direction?"*

The Frenchman snatches the map from David and, without a downward glance, drops it to the floor. What does the term "accident" cover in terms of insurance, I wonder? He points to his front wing with its newly acquired smudge of blue paint. David walks round to the front of the car, proffers his best Gallic shrug and recommends cycling with an *"Ah velo"*. Frenchman is silent as David remounts, feet on top of pedals, toe-clips scraping the road surface, and clanks away.

FRIDAY.
Spend day on beach having sand kicked in our faces by small French people. Heat is extreme and prospect of cycling back to St Malo fills me with gloom.

Evening. Pleasant youth hostel. Out for a drink with three attractive Belgian girls. Simon calls it "going out for drinks". All would-be middle class people have one drink and call it "going out for drinks"; drongoes like me go out "for a drink" and have several. Simon speaks to the girls as though he has recently learned the English language from a phrase book: "What/are/youth/hostels/like/in/Belgium?"

Also, his lisp has really become very tiresome. If he tells me about the "marvellous wevver" again, or seeks to berate David with one more stern "fadder", I will hit him. Quite hard.

SATURDAY.
Regret having hit Simon. It was when he came in from the girls' room this morning with that look of simpering, smug satisfaction and said that Belgian girls were "weally nice" that I did it. I don't think it would have happened but for his constant references to the girls as "the

Belgians", which makes them sound like something in the European Cup.

Afternoon. The lisp is now worse. Perhaps it will be better when the lip has ceased swelling. Both serve as constant reminders of my rash deed. He has started to use vague sexual innuendoes to suggest to his "fadder" (and provoke me) a catalogue of sexual delights experienced at the hands (or worse) of one (or more!) Flemish girls.

SUNDAY.

Fine weather. David, in high spirits, sights the legendary Brittany Orchid and applies his front brake. Simon bowls past him and ends up in unfashionable position amongst roadside gravel and, possibly, clump of Brittany Orchid.

Evening. Pleasant meal with David at cheap restaurant. He shows typical lack of remorse for son in youth hostel nursing sore knees. Am becoming increasingly depressed at thought of long cycle ride back to St Malo.

MONDAY.

Feel churlish and smug as I slip away unnoticed to inquire times of St Malo trains. Spend evening at youth hostel watching uncouth youths from Lewisham breaking windows. Am going to cancel my CND membership when I return to England. There must be at least one SS20 targeted on Lewisham.

TUESDAY.

Up early to sabotage cycle.

At point of departure for two-day ride to St Malo express mild annoyance at puncture. "I'll catch you up." Wave them off. Orange juice prior to amble to train station for eleven-thirty train.

Ten-thirty. Cannot inflate tyre, appear to have damaged valve during sabotage. Cycle does not push easily with full load on flat tyre. Slightly regret separation from (imperfect) French-speaking David and lisping, swollen-lipped son. In great heat and confusion scramble cycle into guard's van as train draws out of station.

Compose self. Say mantra. Special prayer of thanks for deliverance from two-day cycle ride before allowing smug smile to crease face.

Having made spiritual peace with self begin plotting evil deed. Approach next compartment of guard's van for removal of valve from unsuspecting fellow cyclist. Shocked at cunning deception of fellow travellers: gold Viking with rocking head stem and half-inflated rear tyre stands next to white Peugeot.

NOT MEMSAHIB

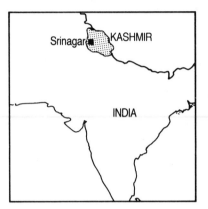

Every time I heard the word memsahib I wanted to take an ice-pick to the user. I'd gone on the Hindu trail clutching my libertarianism to my bosom, a cosy cocoon from which I could rationalise and contain the shrieks from the inferno – not that Dante, I'm sure, ever went to Calcutta. Very right-on. Very arm's-length. But keep your liberal sensibilities Gandhi-pure? Emerge unscathed? Forget it.

Sympathy, empathy, had long since given way to simmering hysteria, cringing shame and a seething, at times uncontrollable rage which was generalised in its target but oh so localised in its pain. It wasn't even a consolingly righteous anger at the pulverising poverty, the callousness of caste or the stalinisation of women – more a deep-seated disgust and hatred welling up from deep down and spewing out over all humanity, most of all myself . . . Well, OK, you try and make sense of the matchstick people of Madhya Pradesh, the execrable excrement of Bombay and Dehli, the obscene opulence of Jaipur jewellers, the blinding, vivid hues of Rajasthani women's skirts – and all of it sinking in one great ubiquitous quicksand of suffocating, strangulating bureaucracy.

I arrived in Srinagar, Kashmir's tourist paradise, demented and not exactly in holiday mood.

"J and K Palace" houseboat was where my companion and I were headed – on the bizarre recommendation of an English couple encountered on a camel in the Great Thar Desert. I asked one of the shikara boys to paddle us over – much to the incredulity and amusement of the whole Lake Dal Wild Bunch. Ten minutes later I could see their point. A forlorn and faded chicken shack that floated is what it looked like. Our arrival caused something of a tidal wave – hysterical joy and wild terror chasing hard on the heels of utter bewilderment. It took a good fifteen minutes of hard talking to convince Gulam, the youngest of three brothers and self-appointed front man, that he actually had paying guests on his hands. When the wonder of it had finally penetrated, he clasped us tearfully to his bosom and cucumber sandwiches appeared as if by magic. It was at this point that we entered the fantastical world of Rajarama through the looking-glass.

Coughing and spluttering as, with a flourish, he majestically whipped off the dust covers from forty years of unrequited Anglophilia, he ushered us into a faded English drawing-room, circa 1930, choked up with the solid, silent self-satisfied paraphernalia of the past. Here was one patch of water where the memsahib, evidently, still ruled the waves. And I was expected to fill the daunting doyenne's snug smug slippers. Terrific. Funnily enough, though, Gulam was never in danger of an ice-pick. Unlike the deeply distressing, scraping obsequiousness encountered along the road, his kow-towing to the Brits had been refined to an art form.

He was a chancer of the first order; a half-deaf alcoholic with the backside hanging off his trousers and the swagger of a screen idol. He had a languorous air about him, heavily tinged with the melodrama of the star-crossed. And, indeed, the gods did seem to have had it in for him. He was slowly drinking himself into a coma, an apparently irreversible process of disintegration triggered by the drowning of his beloved only son. Now he was the talk of the lake because he insisted on dressing up his little daughter as a boy. They could be seen everywhere together, he shooting his mouth off, she looking pained and wounded about the eyes – tattered, fractured Laurel and Hardy reflections shimmering in the shikara-splintered waters of the lake . . . But he had charisma – and he loved the camera. There but for the grace of God walked Valentino. I quickly learned to make my financial transactions with Ali, the long-suffering middle brother, arch-pragmatist and solitary beacon of reason, moderation and the good old Moghul work ethic.

Ali was desperately trying to make a little money. Not an exorbitant ambition, surely. But as hard as he would bale out water in futile but ever-giggling attempts to keep the operation afloat, either Gulam or Abdul, the eldest brother, would lurch towards a mirage (alcoholic or metaphysical) and up-end the lot. The Marx Brothers, it seemed, were alive, well, drinking and kicking in Kashmir.

Except that Abdul didn't drink. He didn't eat much either. And he wasn't exactly a wow at social intercourse. He spent most of his time crouching gloomily behind three big black cooking pots whence came, every night, a magnificent feast, deep-frozen since Independence. It was absolutely pointless – more, it was a downright insult – to ask him to cook anything Indian. "Rubbish," as Gulam would say when, with flattened ears and shifting feet, we tentatively suggested that a curry might be nice for a change. "What you like? Roast duck? Roast chicken? Apple pie?" And so it would inexorably come, course after course, vegetable after vegetable, jam roly-poly after spotted dick. A miracle.

Ali normally waited on us with his usual no-nonsense aplomb during the (duck) soup, whereupon, on a good night, Gulam, fresh from his fourth bottle of gut-rot would lurch in, sweeping mediocrity in front of him like Dorothy Lamour's skirts scattered men, and brandishing a dirty napkin over one arm and an expression of pained patronising subservience. We had no choice but to comply. They expected us to play the Raj duet and, after all, it was the least we could do. And so it was that we'd sit like relics in that creaking, lugubrious dining-room, under the extravagant gaze of the gaudy plastic flowers, primly playing culinary cricket with Lady Bracknell – while outside . . . the mighty, barbaric Himalayas as a backdrop and the primeval shrieks of a suspected child molester, burned to death and then thrown in the lake, echoing in our ears. It was unhinging, to say the least. But I wouldn't have offended Abdul for the world – and the world, for him, was his English cooking.

He was the nearest I reckon I'll ever get to one of Gurdjieff's remarkable men. A fine tortured soul. The nights were often fractured by his wailing. He was a failed Sufi mystic, a marked man – one fatal Shakespearian character flaw, the gossips on the lake would have it, having led to a lifetime of spiritual flagellation. His nocturnal crying was a fearsome, heart-rending lament which still haunts me . . .

It was usually thrown into grotesque relief, however, by the pantomime which preceded it – to wit, normally a ding–dong of cataclysmic proportions if Gulam had drunk one bottle too many. Indeed, the cook first impaled himself on my memory during one of these fraternal fracas. Gulam was running amok with a burning log that night, stopping frequently to plead for my approbation regarding fratricide or, at the very least, boat-burning – when a supercilious, black, sooty face peered round the doorway and, with plummy BBC vowels, invited him to desist as he was "disturbing" the guests. And all the while Ali sobbed, drowning the sofa in his tears . . .

But things began to look up for "J and K Palace" – as I noticed on my return from a trip to stern and seductive Ladakh. Rowing out from the jetty long after dusk, it felt like I was coming home. But what was this? I saw the lightbulbs first, beckoning promiscuously where before there'd only been dark, deep, time-pocked sockets. Then the ebb and flow of contented murmurings. I boarded the boat to find, to my horror, that the plastic flowers had been replaced by real ones. And there were current copies of the *Times of India* on the coffee table. I felt cheated, abandoned and, yes, usurped by the new guests. I couldn't help it. I'd taken the brothers to my heart and, like a lover, I was sensitive to the smallest slight, the smallest indication that my moon was on the wane.

But, oh God, maybe this was just the memsahib bug sitting up and biting me at last. Maybe I'd simply grown to like being top dog – a Brit in a country which, maddeningly, still looks up to its one-time

The 'J and K' Palace houseboat at Srinigar and its proprietors – Ali, Gulum and Abdul – waiting for the British to return. (*Not Memsahib*)

overload, however mediocre s/he was back home. From Simla to Bangalore the miracle of the nobodies into somebodies.

At any rate, I needn't have worried. I was greeted like a prodigal daughter. They're hanging on to the runaway rickshaw until the Return of the Memsahibs, you see. Abdul, in particular, is riding shotgun, in the firm conviction that the "London Government" is poised to regain the handlebars any moment now. And then we'll be back to the grand old days of bear-bagging in the mountains, gin slings on the veranda and telegrams across the lake. That's why he's keeping his English cooking on the boil and his white turban in the trunk. You never quite know when the call for crême caramel might come again.

Until then he'll have to make do with stragglers like me. I'm not exactly *Jewel in the Crown* material, he knows – but we can all pretend. There's no harm in that . . . Is there?

Mountain architecture in fortress Hajjah. (*Getting High in the Yemen*)

FRANCIS R. GARDNER

GETTING HIGH IN THE YEMEN

Question: how can you see London, Paris and New York simultaneously while sitting in a remote corner of the Arabian Peninsula? Answer: adopt the national pastime of North Yemen and devote the entire afternoon to chewing the narcotic *qat* leaf. Our host, his eyes dreamy and his cheeks bulging with the drug, rocks with laughter at his own joke.

We had landed that morning to find ourselves catapulted into a medieval Manhatten, a confusing world of centuries–old mud skyscrapers and lavish exteriors that make a mockery of the Middle Eastern practice of living behind blank façades. Resting in a secluded courtyard we watch a veiled face peer out from behind a half-opened shutter high up on a crumbling wall. A basket lowers itself to the ground from a distant rooftop. A train of three camels, loaded down with bundles of *qat*, squeezes through a tiny alleyway and lurches past the massive studded door of a mosque.

This atmosphere of the unreal is compounded by the costumes: a shaft of sunlight catches the billowing crimson robes of two completely veiled women as they emerge from a garden; a turbaned old man pauses in a doorway, his gnarled hands fingering the hilt of his dagger. This, we tell ourselves, is the Old Arabia, the Arabia that has already vanished from most Arab cities, to be replaced by tenement blocks, glass-fronted banks and supermarkets.

Round the corner roars a motorcycle driven by a seven-year-old with his two brothers on the back. In true Yemeni style every inch of surface on the machine has been decorated: there are panels of assorted mirrors, arrays of lights, swaying ostrich feathers, a horn that plays *Silent Night* and a radio that competes with the horn for sheer volume and distortion. This, we realise, is part of the New Arabia that has swept through Yemen since the mid-1970s, bringing television, motorcycles and bottled water to every village.

Sanaa, the capital, is full of surprises. From out of a mosque springs an eager young man, his eyes flashing beneath his pure white turban. "Does God exist?" he demands, pointing up into the sky. "Of course." "And did Muhammad exist?" "Beyond question." "And is

Muhammad the Prophet of God?" "Yes." He looks disappointed and retreats back inside the mosque. Later, the sight of a Yemen Air Force MiG–17 jet in a backstreet does not seem out of place. Complete with camouflage markings and undercarriage intact, it is neatly sandwiched between two buildings, partially blocking the entrance to a busy café.

The road from Sanaa to the Red Sea coast is an adventure in itself. With consummate skill the driver spins the bus round hairpin bends as we career through some of the wildest landscapes in Arabia. Plunging valleys bracket the road, sometimes disrupted by the vivid green of terraced crops, sometimes bordered by sheer drops of hundreds of feet. Spiralling down towards the coast, faces break out in perspiration as the temperature soars. Papaya groves and banana trees appear where before the road was lined with granite.

At sea level the heat becomes intense. The local architecture has shifted from flat roofs to conical thatch huts that would look more at home in Africa across the water. Within the space of an afternoon the change in scenery has been so dramatic that when we pass a road sign bearing simply an exclamation mark we feel that this applies to the whole of Yemen and not just to the bend in the road.

Heading south towards the coastal village of Khokha, we stop to eat at a wayside stall. A dark-skinned boy kneels down to put his arm into a clay oven in the ground and pulls out a smoking bundle wrapped in banana leaves. It is knuckle of goat, baking in hot ashes, and surprisingly good.

As in most countries, you change down a gear when on the coast. Here pelicans float between palm groves like obsolete airships, men sit cross-legged as they caulk their boats, and little stirs save for the flurry of elbows and lines as the day's catch of shark is brought in.

The town of Harad comes as an unpleasant shock. Being only a stone's throw from the Saudi border, the prices are exorbitant and we find ourselves forced into the cheapest hotel at twenty pounds a room. A thick layer of dust covers the soiled mattresses, the remains of discarded food fester behind the beds and the nearby lavatory is in a perpetual state of flood. We eat poorly that night and return to a shower room that is alive with cockroaches and a fan that ceases to function as the electricity is cut off. Bathed in sweat and troubled by scuttlings in the night, we sleep fitfully.

The following morning I try to convince the taxi drivers that a road which is marked on the official "tourist" map must exist. As the temperature tops a hundred degrees a dozen voices chant advice at me while oil-blackened fingers tug at my sleeve. "No, my friend, you must go back to Sanaa!" "You must go back to Hodeida." "Come this way and I will show you." "May God help you!"

We reach the mountaintop town of Hajjah in the cool of the evening after passing the burned-out hulk of an armoured car, a souvenir from the Civil War of the 1960s. Our first impression is that the inhabitants are pleasantly insane. Two venerable old men wander into the café, draw their daggers and execute a quaint little dance around our table. We applaud and one comes over to show us a coin in his hand; he then passes his other hand over it and the coin disappears completely. We look on perplexed as, feigning great solemnity, he blows his nose into his hand and out pops the coin from his nostril.

It is *qat*, of course, that sends the Yemenis slightly off the rails. Looking and tasting like a privet hedge, it is cultivated legally, sold in sprigs costing about five pounds each and chewed all afternoon by the vast majority of adult Yemenis. Only the tenderest leaves are plucked, and then they are crushed into a ball inside the cheek where they are sucked continually, producing a long and imaginative "high". "It makes me think I am driving an aeroplane," taxi drivers are fond of telling you as they hurtle past the wreckage of other vehicles that never made it.

At Saada, in the wild and barren north, we are awoken one morning by the crackle of gunfire. During the civil war it was from here that the Royalist rebels marched on the capital and, although ultimately defeated by the Republicans from the south, they were never wiped out. Almost every male, from ten-year-old to wizened shepherd, totes a machine-gun, loaded and cocked. Today it is the Eed Al Adha – an Islamic festival – and the gunfire is peaceful.

We drive north with Yemeni friends to indulge in a little weekend sport. A Yemeni shooting range has to be seen to be believed. Just off the road, in a natural bowl in the mountains, tribesmen cluster together on prominent boulders and blaze off in all directions while their children swim naked in a nearby stream, the bullets whining over their heads. Our friends open fire at a small crag and an irate farmer comes charging towards us, screaming insults. The bullets, he says, are ricocheting all around his farm.

Returning from Marib on our final excursion, we are stuck with a maniac driver who does not know the way. He plucks at his leaves of *qat*, he takes a swig of water, he selects a cigarette, a match, a cassette, he adjusts the wing mirror, combs his hair and spits out of the window – he will do anything, in fact, rather than look at the road while he is driving. At last we pull up at the military checkpoint outside the capital. The soldiers are searching the vehicles. "What for?" I ask. "Weapons," replies our driver with his pistol resting pertly on the dashboard.

The following morning we are on the way to the airport when it occurs to me that, like our taxi driver, Yemen seems uncertain of which course to follow. On the tarmac, glistening in the monsoon rain of August, Soviet-built troop helicopters are parked side by side with American-built jet fighters. In the departure lounge heavily-veiled wives queue behind their men, clutching jewel boxes; forty minutes later, as we swing out over the Red Sea coast, these paragons of modesty emerge from the toilets dressed for a night on the town. Skintight lurex trousers, fluorescent T-shirts and cascades of flashing jewellery. I look for smiles on the faces of their husbands but I find instead that familiar glazed look and a trace of foliage around the lips. For them, London has begun thirty thousand feet up in the air.

ANGUS MACAULAY

DOWN MEXICO WAY

Real travellers, if they travel by Mexican rail, travel first class. Fools, authors, dogs, pigs, chickens, goslings and real Mexicans go by second class. I went 1,000 miles with the goslings for about five pounds. Well, dumbclucks and their pesos are soon parted, aren't they?

It all started on a sunny day in El Paso, Texas. General Santa Ana, a past President of Mexico, once said that if he owned Texas and Hell, he would rent out Texas and move to Hell. Since he actually *sold* Texas to the USA and was shot trying to escape to Venezuela with the proceeds, he must have been serious about it. Standing in the main Plaza, melting quietly in the heat, I knew what he meant. I had thought of catching a bus to the border, but there were too many strange people around. One man in particular kept muttering, "Don't rock the boat, man, don't be rocking the boat." He then showed what he meant by rocking the bench that I was sitting on. It occurred to me then that I could do worse than walk to the border, navigating south by the sun. That way I wouldn't have to speak to anyone.

This caused no problems, except that I couldn't buy any sensible food for the journey. The walk to the border was about a mile, down a hot wide dusty street. There were no groceries or supermarkets, only pawnshops and dodgy-looking finance companies offering a walk-in loan service. Every fifty yards a man called, "Taxi?". The border is a bridge that costs five cents to cross. I paid and walked halfway over. "You goin' over there?" asked the man who had suddenly appeared behind me, eyeing my backpack. "They'll shake ya. They'll shake ya for sure. Some people just don't care." And he was gone.

From the border I walked a mile to the railway station. The street was narrow and dusty, and lined with cut-price dentists and blood-banks. Every twenty-five yards I expected, on general principles, to be knifed. Every fifty yards a man emerged from the shadows, saying "Taxi?". There were no sleepers left. There were no first-class seats left. I waited three hours for the second-class ticket office to open, and queued another hour for a ticket. The train was due to leave in two hours, and the waiting room looked like part of the movement of the twelve tribes. Many times that afternoon, I considered retracing my steps and spending the rest of my trip in a tent by the sea, possibly in Bournemouth. Because, as I reasoned, it is often more difficult to admit to yourself that you're wrong and retrace your steps. *"Cojones, gringo,"* said my better self, and spat.

By some minor miracle, we and all our luggage found space on the train. Life in Mexico would not continue without several of these minor miracles every day. I wound up in the middle of a family of uncertain size. The father was a small man who kept leaping in and out of the window with fresh bags and boxes. When all was in, he rearranged his family's and everyone else's luggage to his own satisfaction. This included mine. He then offered me a seat on a large bag of shoes, an unexpected bonus. It did not occur to me till late that night just how many brand new pairs of shoes this family must have. About thirty-six cubic feet, as I remember. They were amused to find a gringo on the train but, besides laughing at everything I did, they were very kind to me. I was offered peaches, *tacos, burritos, gorditos* . . . all of which I refused. Like a true Briton, I remained obsessed with my bowels. (Well, what if I get the runs amid all this . . .?)

Most of North Mexico appeared to be desert. It also smelled bad, usually burning rubbish or cement works. But it was the smell of the *tortillas* (flat maize pancakes, the staple of all Mexican meals) that really got up my sensitive gringo nostrils. Is maize flour really that alien? As night fell, everyone jockeyed subtly for positions of least agony to sleep in. Since sleep wasn't really on the cards, I thought about the shoes, and a line from Bob Dylan kept running through my head: "The soles of my feet, I swear they're burning". No-one seemed annoyed by the two goslings that whistled with panic every time the train jolted. I also tried to count the number of times the goslings whistled.

By some strange chance I was awake at dawn. It was worth being awake just to see the beauty of the desert before the sun came up. You can appreciate the desolation without getting too desolated by the climate. By ten o'clock we were 400 miles from the border and it was time for the Customs Inspector to get off. He had been wandering up and down the train all night imposing strange surcharges on people with too much luggage. This is where the variable size of the family all round me came in handy. When one of their outposts spotted him, bags were rearranged and ownership shifted. But the finest moment came as the Inspector and the family got off together. A huge music box, as long as my leg, appeared from under the seat, wrapped in a cloth, and disappeared out on to a waiting cart. It struck me that the family might have done this sort of thing before.

From this point on I had a seat, but the journey was less eventful, and passed in a sort of blur. Cowboys got on and off; the land grew fertile; I saw a pig try to mount a cow; I slept. At last, Mexico City. As soon as I got off the train, an official seemed to think I looked suspicious. This was merely because I was dirty, unshaven and slightly vacant from surviving thirty-six hours on three oranges and six Cokes. But my papers were in impeccable order, and he couldn't touch me.

SARAH POPE

MUSICAL SOJOURN ITALIAN-STYLE

Italy! Music! What more can life offer? I was thrilled to be offered a place in the strings of the London Chamber Orchestra for their forth-coming Italian tour.

January 10, 1985, began inauspi-ciously, with Italy reporting the coldest weather on record and a block of flats exploding in Putney at 7.05am, as the orchestra set out for the airport.

Flight 459 was delayed two hours, for fog, at Heathrow, and diverted to "the other" airport in Milan.

The orchestra of fifteen waited for the charter-bus to re-direct itself to the new airport. We spent an hour sitting on the borrowed, wicker music hamper (marked "London Philharmonic Orchestra"), five at a time, wondering if we'd be late for the afternoon rehearsal in La Spezia. Having passed through Customs, we were beyond the reach of airport life-support systems. We broached the duty-frees. Card tables were improvised from violin cases. There were no brass players, so it was a muted group.

When the bus arrived, we had plenty of time for the two-and-a-half-hour journey to La Spezia. We helped load the double bass and music hamper; and Tom, the manager, began doing sums in millions of lire on his solar calculator to determine the daily subsistence allowance.

It was to be a short tour – three concerts in three days – but the itiner-ary was hardly a masterpiece of planning. Day One would take us to north-west Italy, and La Spezia. Day Two would take us across the width of the country to Castelfranco, in the north-east; Day Three would take us back to Novara, near Milan, to the north-west again.

This kind of schedule keeps musicians out of the bars, but reckons without natural hazards such as weather and duty-frees.

The scenery was spectacular, and not a bit reminiscent of the Old Masters. To me, Italy will always be a cold climate. It was my first visit, and the Apennine snowfield had reclaimed the land, excepting only one lane of the motorway. The only facility on our bus was a temperature gauge which registered a steady four degrees below freez-ing. The heating system made no impression. After three hours of traffic jam it seemed possible that we would be late for the rehearsal. The "heavies" passed round the duty-frees in a burst of camaraderie. Rehearsals on tour are as unpopular as bus journeys.

The French conductor sprang to life in his fur coat, begging, "Please to not drink – we have concert". He was met with jeering. Angélique, the liaison girl-to-speak-Italian, looked depressed.

After four hours behind the same *routier* there was a murmur of rebellion. The beer-drinkers were demanding a pee-stop – or, at least, another empty bottle. Vincent, the thin-skinned Old-Timer who had come out of retirement for the fun of one last tour, looked dreadfully blue-lipped. He had run out of personal Beecham stories.

Tom, the manager, stopped calculating and began to double-glaze the coach with Sellotape. We tried to wedge the double-bass in the draught.

Maestro Pierre stopped interfering with Angélique and began to swear at the uncharacteristically patient driver. The maestro offered to drive faster, himself. A violinist restrained him with superficial bruising.

The bass player then threatened the driver, in English, and ordered him to stop at the next services. The driver appeared to understand. The services resembled base camp from *Scott of the Antarctic,* but they were still serving *espresso*. When Britain succumbs to the ice-age, the tea will freeze over at once. We can always learn gastronomy from the Continentals.

The Heavies, to the maestro's alarm, were also able to stock up on firewater.

We did get to La Spezia that night – at 11.30pm, local time, instead of 4pm. It had taken thirteen-and-a-half hours to get there in time to miss the concert. We still hadn't found the hall.

"Who's got the A-to-Z of La Spezia?" called the 'cellos. Certainly not the equable driver. He shrugged, and manoeuvred through the snowfield marked "Town Centre" until it began to look familiar. The same pedestrian offered the same advice a second time round. Suddenly we recognised the Lord Mayor outside the Town Hall.

The orchestra disembarked for a snowball fight, while maestro, manager and Angélique struck up a grim-faced financial meeting in the line of fire. Summer or winter, the Italians take music very seriously. It suddenly became clear why Italian is the esperanto of musicians.

After the meeting we were informed that the audience had waited for us from nine until eleven, and would not be satisfied with their money back. The mayor insisted that the orchestra stay another day to give the concert. He intended to impound our passports. We would certainly not be paid until then. Never mind tomorrow's audience in Castelfranco. We could foresee an endless series of furious mayors as we reached each concert a day late.

At 2am we were escorted to our hotel, after the bosses had agreed reluctantly to meet the next morning. We didn't get much sleep. The hotel was very cold, and disappointed members of the audience telephoned members of the orchestra in their rooms to complain. No – they didn't want a refund. What about the music?

In the morning we were up before the mayor and made a break for Castelfranco. The management promised a new, warm bus in Parma, lots of motorway stops and overtime payment. The orchestra grumbled. Another seven hours on the bus.

Day Two resembled Day One. Parma came and went with no change of bus. Tom did endless calculations: "If an orchestra is paid one million lire for three days, and four people didn't have the spaghetti, how much does everybody owe each other?" The problems were never solved because the bus kept entering spectacular Apennine tunnels, blanking out the calculator's solar memory.

Suddenly, old-timer Vince, leader of the violas, delivered the ultimatum. He stood up and the Sellotape double-glazing stuck to his head. Further enraged, he announced that he was going home immediately, and would never play again for this ridiculous two-bit outfit. He demanded an airport stop immediately.

The bridge-players looked up encouragingly. The management suggested a pit-stop to discuss it.

The motorway services were not coping with the weather. The airy building offered a slow but interested canteen service. The staff were pleased to see new faces, but the food was cold before it reached the checkout. The washbasins were frozen, and an alarming notice, translated for us, belied the welcome we received: "Distrust abusive retailers of various articles".

By the end of the checkout queue, Vincent had extracted promises of a bonus payment, a new bus and no more touring. But he looked so unwell that we had to do something. He looked quite ready to audition for that Great Symphony in the Sky.

We put our lire together and, ignoring the warning, bought a fur-lined sleeping bag in the service shop. We got Vince back in the bus, and into the bag, without much trouble. He seemed almost content, smoking his pipe through the zip. The rest of us continued to complain. At least Vince had escaped hypothermia.

We were late for the rehearsal in Castelfranco, and the maestro demanded overtime for the Tchaikovsky 'Serenade'. We played our first concert, at last, in the marble hall of the fairytale castle. No time to eat – or drink. The audience wanted encores and autographs. The mayor of La Spezia was on the telephone.

Next morning we intended to boycott the heatless bus. We had a leisurely breakfast. Meanwhile the problem was resolving itself outside.

Our stoic driver went out to start the engine, and found that the diesel had frozen. Resourcefully, he tried lighting a small fire under the engine . . .

Within the hour a modern, luxury coach and new driver appeared. We waved sadly to our dispossessed hero, who had survived without his bus. We loaded the bass, music and Vince, and made our way back across Italy, harassing Tom with problems for his calculator, like, "How many miles is 573 kilometres to Milan?", "Do you know the square root of Mahler 9?" and "What is the meaning of Life?"

We made it to Novara in time for the rehearsal. More encores, autographs and a civic reception. The players crawled to bed at 3am. The mayor of La Spezia telephoned to say he would stop us leaving Milan airport next day.

In the morning, our airport was closed again. At 6am we were driven, protesting, to the "other" airport. Apparently, the mayor could not keep up with us. We got the last flight from the other airport, before that, too, closed.

We left the peacemaking to Princess Diana, who was to visit La Spezia a few months later.

DICK HUGHES

ABROAD IN BALLYBUNION

We are on the Atlantic coast of Ireland at a place with the curious name of Ballybunion. The wind roars in across the sea and over the clifftop, a steady, enormous volume of air that batters at the rock and drives the breakers before it, ripping the foam from their tops and hurling it up the beach. In all this sound and fury a small party of ringed plovers run and bob at the water's edge. A hundred yards further on a flock of oystercatchers ignore the elements and stand motionless on a patch of sand.

Chris has been quiet all day but now, as we walk, she comes back to me. I suppose that most people are quiet from time to time but just the same I worry. What has she been thinking about? We walk along the beach exhilarated by the wind and with salt and sand on our shoes. I wanted to walk in bare feet but it's far too cold. The impulse to take off shoes and socks on the beach is often attributed to childhood memories, a kind of universal nostalgia, but is it not something more deep and primitive? Few of us are unmoved by the sight or memory of the sea and it's surely no coincidence that sailors usually retire to a place inland where they are not constantly reminded of the endless turbulent distance that led them to take the sea for their profession in the first place. Several grey miles away a tiny red freighter seems to stand still, and the Loop Head lighthouse flashes periodically beyond it. A cormorant skims the wavetops on stiff wings, intermittently visible like the lighthouse.

The town itself is closed and empty. The summer trippers have gone, the seafront and clifftop hotels, the bed and breakfast places, the bingo hall and dance hall are closed and even the private houses are shut and curtained. So it will be until spring.

Somewhere over the sea is America. I try to orient myself by the pale afternoon sun. At school the quiet maths master who taught us general studies once a week – to broaden our horizons – had once explained Great Circle routes. Music, navigation, astronomy: it must have been because of his knowledge of subjects that appeared eccentric or recondite to his narrower colleagues that he was delegated to what must have appeared an unrewarding task, but that afternoon I heard an echo of his quiet, courteous voice as I looked longingly in the direction of the North American continent. As I looked, the fantasy of a single-handed crossing formed in my mind, but even as I saw it in my mind's eye – weeks of being alone, huge waves, unseen freighters in the night, icebergs off the Grand Banks – the contrail of a high flying jet emerged above the inland cloud, a long, white streak heading west.

We kicked the sand off our shoes and got back into the car. One of the pleasures of driving in Ireland is the emptiness of the roads, though the potholes are deep and frequent. It has taken a few days for me to begin to assimilate this landscape, though it is landscape and its distances that have always informed my dreams. By a curious paradox it is the technology that makes any foreign place accessible within hours that mocks the dream which makes them so desirable. I remember asking Chris once if she had ever been to Boston. Yes, of course she had. Two or three times. Went down there on the bus from Canada to see some friends. In that casual reply was part of the answer to the constant, nagging question which reasserted itself on the beach that afternoon. If being far away is so casual and ordinary to others, why is it so important to me? Partly because I never have, I suppose.

Parts of the inland country here remind me of Northern France. It is relatively flat and treeless. There are water towers like ungainly mushrooms every few miles, and some stretches, field after field, are undivided by hedges. On the more mountainous coast, however, and especially along the peninsula, there are dozens of corbelled neolithic huts like stone beehives which even after three thousand years or more are sometimes still used by the farmers. Inland are numbers of egregious new bungalows with scalloped edged blinds at the windows and often a cement mixer in the drive, indicating perhaps that the proud owners of these tasteless constructions have not yet finished laying the patio. If they last the same time then maybe these buildings, too, will become monuments to the progress of domestic architecture.

In each small town there are numerous small bars, often just a part of a shop or some other local business. ("O'Brien's Bar, Taxi Service and Valuations.") The Guinness is rich and full, quite unlike the stuff they serve back home. Each pint is like a three-course meal. Some of the shops might have been designed as part of a period film set, their windows filled with Fifties-style ladies' overcoats, dusty sausages, galoshes, dried-up bottles of Indian ink and yellowing boxes of calf weaning powder. We stop at midday for some of the marvellous Guinness. Already some of the customers are well gone in drink. Their eyes are not quite in focus in their seamed faces and they are arguing loudly. The landlord is a young man who greets us politely and tells us that he himself is a teetotaller and that his passion in life is the game of hurling. He opens the door of the back kitchen where an old lady in black nods by the stove, and shows us his hurling stick. At the far end of the bar the argument rose in a crescendo and somebody thumped the bar with his fist. Our host indicated his regulars with a contemptuous nod of the head.

"Do you know what they are?" he asked. "They're the drunken paddies that you've heard about, that's what they are." I almost laughed but there was genuine anger in his voice. "Do you see that one there?" He pointed to a red-eyed gnome of a man with a flat cap whose head was nodding dangerously near to the top of his glass. "He sold the farm that was left him this ten years ago and now he'll have to sell the other. His wife and children live on tea and bread. It's the same with the others. That's why they'll not entertain the changes in the law of divorce. As soon as they were able their wives would get rid of them and then what would they do?" It was a sobering thought. We drank up, thanked him for his company and left with our parcel of groceries. We were heading for our camp site, a point of rock sticking out into the Atlantic with a tent-sized patch of grass only yards from the breakers. One of the snippets of information we had gleaned in the bar was the weather forecast. Pressure was going down and the wind was already rising.

From a short distance away the green flysheet was almost invisible against the grass. With the downwind zip open we struggled to cook over the primus. As the wind increased the blue flame fought but eventually produced a warm mess of convenience food and a cup of coffee each. By then the sun was setting in a wild blaze at the end of an infinite pathway of light, and then we were in our sleeping bags with the tent booming and flapping around us like a mad parachute. The noise was incredible but did not quite hide the noise of the sea. Every moment I expected the tent to give one final vicious crack and whirl away into the sky.

Chris moved closer to me in her sleeping bag, as nearly asleep as is possible in this maelstrom of sound. I lay awake planning what to do if the tent flew. It occurred to me that this soft and verdant country can be bleak and even savage. Yet it has bred a reputation for gentle and ec- centric people. An old English couple I knew once toured this West coast by car and stayed overnight at an hotel where they were kept awake until the small hours by local lads on motorbikes roaring up and down outside. The next morning they went to the local Garda to com- plain. Do you think it's reasonable, they asked, for people to roar along the road all night on loud motorbikes? The sergeant hooked his thumbs into his braces and considered for a moment. "Well, I expect it'll be all right," he said at last, "as long as it's just the two of you."

In the middle of the night we finally beat a retreat to the car and dozed until morning. It was the last day and we had to head east. As we drove and finally lost sight of the sea, the sense of wonder I had felt on this rare and unexpected holiday finally related itself to a realistic sense of scale. It was the map that did it. From where we were to where we live (in a cottage under a hill in an ancient corner of England that American tourists would regard with proper admiration) was only about three hundred miles in a straight line. And yet the evidence of what we had done was in a bag on the back seat behind us. We had to bring our passports. We had been Abroad.

MARLENE WHYTE

LIFTING THE CURTAIN

Russia comes as no surprise. After a three-and-a-half hour flight we make a three-and-a-half hour journey through Customs.

En route to our Moscow hotel, rows of thin leafless trees cast ghastly cowering shadows against gaunt buildings. In the morning, our Edith Piaf lookalike Intourist guide intones, in an accent as lovely to hear as the curlicued Cyrillic calligraphy is to see, that Moscow is growing more beautiful. We are travelling through grey suburbs with raised eyebrows.

"It's worse than Mallaig," groans my eleven-year-old son, Martin.

Golden domes on the cluster of cathedrals in the Kremlin's grounds suddenly bring some truth to the guide's claim. So, too, does St Basil's, set at one end of Red Square. It is a child's concoction. A confection of architecture. Ivan the Terrible ordered its architects to be blinded to prevent them from designing something better for someone else.

A stillness and quietness settles on Red Square as the guard is changed at the Lenin mausoleum. Three straight-backed soldiers, with arms and legs rhythmically swinging in different planes, slowly and precisely goose-step to the doors of the tomb. They arrive as the Kremlin clock strikes a new hour in the life of the nation. One quick, interlocking movement puts two new guards on duty and takes two off. They are escorted back to barracks at exactly the same metronomic pace. People start breathing again.

Across the square is a large, government department store. Like most Russian buildings it's very hot inside. It's drab, functional and, where fish is being sold, reeking. Our children can't leave fast enough.

We reboard our bus and visit the university environs, where we hear singing coming from a small church. A Russian Orthodox service, smelling of incense, is under way with deep chanting, exotic icons, flickering candles. Kandinsky colour and thronging people. Outside an old lady crosses herself and a young man gobs.

To the left, youths and boys practise dry ski jumping. Red skis flash horizontally through trees some thirty metres away.

Fledgling soldiers are everywhere. They're like frisky puppies. One is playing with a Rubics cube. They constantly wink at Anitra, my pretty, blonde, thirteen-year-old daughter, and smoke. There's a considerable quantity of aromatic smoke wafting around Russia.

We're bossed back to our bus. We mustn't be late for dinner and the folk evening scolds our guide, Tanya.

I am eager for dancing. We get balalaikas and singing. I day-dream about Ukrainian dancers. On comes a bull-necked Bolshoi bass. I sigh. He sings. Magic. His mighty voice doesn't need amplification but he gets it all the same. My son curls himself protectively into a small ball and rams his fingers in his ears. Had he been sitting nearer that voice, it would have sliced through him and killed him.

Next day the Exhibition of Economic Achievement in the USSR is on the agenda, unfortunately. The vast, gorgeous pavilions house little of interest to foreign tourists, unless they are into old space technology, hydroelectric systems and blast furnaces.

Our children head straight back for the hotel, using a thirty-storey high representation of a rocket blast-off as a landmark. Thank God for the Russian penchant for big monuments.

A woman's voice warbles out of a tree near a booth selling bits and bobs. Cheap-looking ballpoints are on sale for £3.50 each. There's a booklet with a coloured youth on the front being held in a stranglehold by a man in uniform. The uniformed man is a British bobby.

For the equivalent of five pence each we gad about on the Metro all afternoon. Everything goes on fast forward from the foyer. We watch, then copy. The escalator drops away at speed. It's like being on top of a waterfall and pouring over the edge. The depth is such that people on the up escalator look as though they are leaning backwards.

I count the lights on the way down. Approximately twenty-one set at four-metre intervals.

At the bottom is an ornately decorated station grotto, bearing a strong resemblance to a wedding cake. Each station comes as a lovely surprise. Red marble, black labradorite, onyx, stainless steel, oak, walnut, shimmering chandeliers and so on, are used with feeling in their construction.

Some passengers stare intently at us – not in a critical way, just expressing interest.

Tanya manages to round us up for the Leningrad train. The berths are narrow and space severely limited. It's a close encounter of an intimate kind for strangers sharing a compartment. The sexes are mixed.

There is a savagely smelly lavatory for the entire carriage at one end, and a coal-stoked boiler at the other. By morning the heating is on full blast and birdsong is being relayed through compartment radios. We wake, wondering where in the world we are. Hot, sweet liquid, pretending to be tea, is served from a samovar.

We are taken to our hotel, not knowing which one beforehand, for breakfast. We have slices of cheese, brown and white bread, butter (EEC?), jam, thick white gunk in a glass, real tea, sweet pastries and salted semolina.

The window of this hotel room frames a Lowry view, with trams and trolley buses, chimney stacks with pencil lines of smoke, and sundry bridges across the river Niva. Small wonder that Leningrad's sister city is Manchester.

We count three-hundred-and-thirty paces from our room to the main lift. Female floor attendants, called *dezhurnayas,* are stationed near all lifts. They have the right to break down hotel doors if they suspect hanky-panky. Our huge *dezhurnaya* sports a high, bleached, bouffant hair-do like a giant haystack. She would look wonderful wielding a battering ram.

Bussing around we get the impression that Leningrad is graciously composed of noble buildings, waterways and monuments. Our guide says *"Reeva Neeva"* frequently. She is proudly possessive of everything Russian. During stops, hubby stampedes all over the place taking photographs. No-one minds.

Honesty, patience, gentleness and courtesy are always in evidence. On the packed trams people pass their fare towards the self-service ticket machine and wait for a ticket to come back. Jammed passengers who won't or can't pass on are made to suffer the worst violence we encounter, a resentful stare.

We notice that elderly people are always given a seat.

That evening we go to the Kirov Theatre to see a ballet. I am making a pilgrimage.

"Read the numbers on your tickets," snaps the usherette in English, when we go to the wrong place. I examine the scraps of paper that pass for tickets. They're written unintelligently in tortured spaghetti.

We are settled eventually and are dazzled by the setting and appalled by the seating. Back of the box, round at the side. I can see sod all.

I encounter a recurring dream the next day in a frightful lavatory between the Peter and Paul Fortress and the Artillery Museum. In the dream I'm sitting on a WC when the walls melt away, leaving me exposed in a room full of staring people. Here there are four public pans and many broken panes, effectively making open windows. Coffee makes me desperate. I throw caution to the wind and have a public pee. No-one stares.

It's worth visiting the amazingly horrid Artillery Museum on three counts. One, for the fabulous, fantastic seventeenth-century war chariot which appears to be Dali's 3D version of "The Hay Wain". Two, for the beautiful cannons and three, for the helpful darlings on duty in the cloakroom who told us such a lot about their museum. At least I think that's what they were doing.

Martin and I gave up an afternoon's sightseeing for a round-table discussion with ordinary Russian people. I tell him that Russian society is becoming more open by allowing this. The people don't materialise. We have a knee-tremblingly handsome professor instead. He's evasive about the foul treatment of dissidents. Perhaps they are part of the price paid for the absence of most negative aspects of capitalist life.

This two-hour session is called "The Bored Meeting" by Martin.

It's another day and we visit Nevsky Prospekt, the main street. My husband buys a map of Leningrad. Most Russian maps incorporate distortions to confuse a potential enemy. Spot the deliberate mistake.

A guttural German woman with blocked glottals barks at her companion. People avert their eyes. Germans have to be tolerated here out of economic necessity.

Friday afternoon has arrived already so we are herded into the Hermitage. It's too much. I goggle to saturation point, and then some more, and then cannot react to anything.

So home. England comes as no surprise. It takes a quarter of an hour to collect our luggage and clear customs. We are directed to the wrong train by British Rail personnel. Anitra has her face slapped by a strange girl.

VINTAGE SUMMER

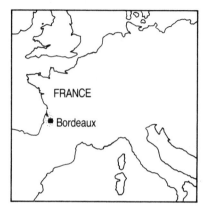

I arrived at the small Bordeaux vineyard well equipped for cold rain, with three pairs of woolly socks, wellies and winter gloves. It was funny how, after our terrible English summer, I couldn't imagine how anywhere could possibly be hot. But it was. Endlessly. They hadn't felt rain for three months. The barefoot, T-shirted French looked brown and relaxed. Mobilettes buzzed by. All that sun gave them an enviable ease. Rows of red-wine vines curved over the humpy landscape. The harvest would be good, the sugar content high. Sun on the sprawling Cinderella pumpkins and lazily unweeded tomatoes. Untidyness, neglect and a light layer of dirt. Cultivated, slovenly charm which makes me feel so comfortable.

The two rooms we were to live in were dim chambers with lumpy beds sloping to their middles. On the mantelpiece, bits of found wood were dragons amongst a collection of broken clocks. We had acquired apples and bowls of walnuts to crack by the fire. Rats scratched overhead and Granny and Grandpa were shrill from behind their partition. Sometimes we saw her eye peeping through, and she might shout: "Do you want an apple?" Once she came to look at our art pinned on the walls. Art done by candlelight. A lot of abstract tending towards the grape. Bunches forever before your eyes.

We ate in the farmhouse kitchen. The especially long table beneath crossed guns on the chimney breast. French up one end, English down the other, and Spaniards midway. Most of the English were vegetarians. Pascale, wife and cook, was pleased to rise to this peculiar challenge and the men mocked English masculinity. How could they be men if they didn't eat raw, red meat? Pornographic pictures were brought out of a murky corner to test manly response. Gently bespectacled Richard managed to eat his mouthful of tomato salad gracefully while musing over what, exactly, that scantily clad woman was doing with her tennis racket.

We attacked the meals with vigour, oohing and aahing over bite-sized chunks of garlic in the salad, the puff and moisture in the

omelettes, the power and purity of the home-grown claret of a year
which some of us had picked, the special flavour of the meat, grilled
over vine prunings. Then our stomachs revolted, craving wholefood.
Knotted up with constipation I dreaded Pascale's roving eye, making
sure that all our plates were full, and commanding *"Mangez, mangez!"*
I would have preferred a quick cheese sandwich and time to myself.
The treat, after a week, was drinking new wine. This sweet fermenting juice gustily pumped the contents through our digestive tracts.

We breakfasted cradling big bowls of milky coffee. Pierre had been
up for hours watching and testing the wine. He joined us to knock
back, in a gulp, a glass of the 1983. A tractor towed us out to the field,
our secateurs and baskets dew-damp, sticky from yesterday's pick.

Working down either side of a row, rhythmically thrusting secateurs in amongst the leaves, dextrously avoiding fingers. A
novice grapepicker with black scars on her hands, cuts stained with
juice and dirt. Heads bent low and in the first, early morning hour our
hair was dulled with leaf wet. Sometimes we noticed the beautiful
autumnal stains on the foliage as we snipped past. Or the classic shape
of the bunch ripe for dangling over an open mouth.

Blue bunches plopped into baskets. *"Pannier! Pannier!"* to call the
hod. We emptied into the plastic bin strapped to his back. On top of a
ladder he stooped and the grapes poured over his head into the over-
flowing trailer. We jumped the squashy pile down – the nearest we got
to treading them.

Singing Spaniards picked flowers for their hats and drank long
squirts of wine pressed from a hairy pigskin. Quick, working with the
minimum of movement, laughing. They brought me a bird's nest,
quietly enjoying my maternal exclamations over the softly-lined
little home.

Sometimes I hated the work and tore at the leaves. Then a moment
of tenderness, gently lifting a sagging, hundred-year-old vine. Should
the plants be warned, prepared before I plucked their fruit? Better with
unhurried care and gentleness, brooding sadly over plundered rows.
A scattering of ripped leaves on the sand.

Soon all will be done by machine. It towered over the vines and us.
Roaring over rows. Shaking and sucking off the grapes with a great
blast of leaves blown out behind. I once saw it working at night,
streaming headlights searching and disturbing. Then the spirit of the
vendage will be lost, held tenuously now in places like St Emilion. A
fancy dress, tourist display of robed priests extols the virtue of wine
from ancient turrets, while the well-heeled, high-heeled bourgeoisie
get drunk and trip over cobblestones.

Two large scouring basins fed by a gushing spring served as the village laundry. We rushed there after work, field-muddy. An icy plunge
startled our weariness away. As the swirling water settled, time to

stare into cool depths and watch a leaf float by. Unnoticed by young couples who came dallying, hand in hand, fetching water for the table.

Pierre remained in the cellar for most of the night, attentive to the temperature of the wine. Pumping the overheated juice out of the vat and through a barrel to cool it. I went to see him; to learn. He wasn't the callously drunken husband I thought he was, coming into dinner dazed and slurred. Overworked, he complained that his soup was cold. He was drunk on the fumes in his workplace. His dog went everywhere with him, to bark if he fell into the wine.

Working and living so closely, tensions bubbled up. The pickers moaned about the hod: "Look at him dawdling and chatting. How dare he complain that we're picking too slowly?" The hod whispered about a certain pair: "It's embarrassing that they're so slow. They're cutting air, missing the grapes altogether."

One disaster-struck day, Pierre fell and broke his arm; a picker poisoned himself from eating too many grapes sprayed with copper sulphate; a bee stung another and Pascale brought out the antidote – a lizard drowned in a bottle of *eau de vie* to dab on the swelling. She herself had been a victim that morning when Mimim, the cat, had leapt on her from the dresser leaving deep, long scratches. At dinner the French complained, the Spaniards shouted and the English argued. Embroilment made us aggressive and easily insulted. Anne cried when the puppy played with her foot. She was afraid of dogs. I stormed at the sugary woolliness of their comfort and said that if I had my way I'd tie her up in a room with eight dogs.

Afterwards I walked out into the vines. It was still with cricket sound, the air heady and thick with fermenting fruit. Corn crackled, stirred by a little breeze. The moon was full.

Two nights later I was out again, going across to the apple trees to collect white-when-you-bite windfalls. There was a slice off the moon. I stared up at it awhile, feeling her grip evaporate and the relief that feelings would now get back to normal.

On the last day, crouching among the leaves, I was hit on the head by a large, squashy grape bunch and then the air was filled with flying grapes. Heads popped up, from picking, to aim. Girls were thrown into the half-full trailer. People chased each other with handfuls to catch and ritually smear cheeks with purple stain. The tractor was garlanded and the last load danced home. We prepared ourselves for the feast. Elaborate food and the best wines, older bottles opened each time. Plums soaked in *eau de vie,* guitars, bullfighter's fire in the Spaniards' eyes, dancing on the table and later, perhaps, romance; breathing the fervid air under stripped vines.

CAROLINE DILKE

A FLYING VISIT TO INDIA AND NEPAL

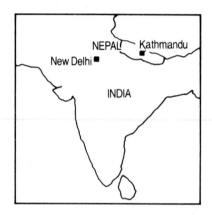

From the seventh floor of the Taj Palace you see kites swaying across the sky over Delhi; and they fly close up around the hotel, chestnut feathered like aerial cockroaches.

Across the wide road, faint in the haze like a stage set, a village of tattered, grubby tents has a dung fire always burning. A graceful matchstick carries a waterpot, and ants bark.

Downstairs, the marble lobby covers two acres and has three interior marquees with a florid design of peacocks' tails. Chrysanthemums in brass pots stand on tables beside deep turquoise armchairs. In each of the marble-tiled elevators Hindi muzak softly whistles, and outside the main doors a distinguished, moustachioed figure summons taxis and accepts tips.

We'd arrived at Delhi airport at 5am to find a motor coach waiting; and as we entered it each passenger received a garland of slightly faded marigolds. The gangway was very narrow and a stout American caught and ripped his trousers on each projecting seat arm, saying "Jee-sus" each time under his breath.

In the dawn there were bicycle rickshaws stirring, and an old man walked stiffly in a tweed jacket and white ankle-length lunghi. The sun came up in a mist like a sleepy eye opening.

There wasn't time to get our bearings, then slowly explore the foreign city at our own pace. On a guided tour you see a lot of sights in a short time, but the penalty you pay is feeling passive. That didn't seem to matter on the first day. We drove along avenues of tree to the tomb of the Emperor Hamayun, a beautiful and graceful brown building which is architecturally the forerunner of the Taj Mahal.

I was surprised by the green open spaces of New Delhi. The city seems to have more trees than people. A typical landscape has a mosque or a temple somewhere in the distance, and in the foreground two women sitting languorously in the grass. Somewhere else the grass is being mown by men with sickles or, more grandly, by a white humped ox pulling a machine. Tiny striped squirrels quarter the ground discreetly, and people pop up from nowhere: shoe cleaners, fortune tellers, children, confidence tricksters, and earnest young men with a great respect for England.

Before our departure we'd received a passenger list giving a name and a town for each person on the tour, like the page at the start of a whodunnit. Now faces and biographies were added to the names. We ate with them at breakfast and at dinner, and as we began to make friends we pushed tables together to make a more amusing party.

A guided tour creates its own life wherever it goes. As our coach stopped beside a monument it would be surrounded by hawkers and some of the party would embark, giggling, on a mercantile flirtation. Within seconds we'd see beggars approach. Then a figure carrying a cloth and a primitive musical instrument would race towards us. He'd unwrap the cloth to uncover a flat, round basket. The lid would come off, the man would settle himself cross-legged, a groggy cobra would waver towards the sun. And we'd hear the sound that followed us in our journey across India: a nasal, bagpipe-like jangling.

As for beggars, here's something strange. If you give them money you can forget them, but if you don't they stay with you for ever. There's a certain leper in a sheepskin cap I dream about often.

At the fringes of our programme, things happened stealthily as if a truer India stalked us.

We'd journey by coach a hundred miles to the next city as avid, astonished pairs of eyes. In a landscape of red earth and low trees, camels pulled ploughs at the behest of biblical human figures; a flock of green parrots fluttered in the leaves of sugar cane; houses were of mud with intricate, ancient decorations; vultures congregated round a dead dog. We'd see dancing bears, and village potters; and the Sikh driver ruthlessly swept cyclists, cows and herdsmen into the ditch.

Or we'd swim in the blue waters of the hotel pool and always, it seemed, wherever Western women disrobed, there'd be a scowling figure on a rooftop somewhere.

Or we'd escape the rest of the party and walk down a side street and lose immediately the beggars, hawkers and starers. People housekeeping, shopping and transporting goods would pay us no attention and we'd wander for hours in a fascinated daze. Then without consciously looking for it we'd find a shop where the sympathetic owner would seat us and offer tea, and show us treasures and be disdainful of our attempts to bargain. He'd tell us how to spot a forgery, and sell us silver ornaments by weight.

On our tour we were led through pop-up picures of Mughal architecture. Most of the palaces and mosques were dead – deserted and stripped bare of furnishings – and we saw delicate shells of what had been halls of private audience or living quarters, built of marble and mirror and intricately worked sandstone. In contrast, a modern Hindu temple was garish and lively. No postcard or picture book could have prepared us for the messy offerings and bright, florid paintings, the people wandering about throwing flowers at gods dressed in silver and red and set like dolls in a shop window. We were shocked by our own ignorance.

But the mosques and temples and palaces became a blur. The efficiency with which we were woken in good time, breakfasted, bussed to an airport, then loaded into a coach for yet another tour, allowed us to see too much. Then we'd relax by chatting or shopping. We seldom had energy to go back to the monument or museum, to see it and think about it for ourselves.

One building I did take the trouble to see properly.

I hadn't expected the Taj Mahal to be three dimensional. It was solid, yet as light as a meringue, and the shadow of a vulture fled across its great white dome. Inside, the marble walls were grubby with fondling by many hands. There were inlays of semi-precious stones, exquisite folded leaves and petals, berries and stamens. You could go in with a botany book and identify all the plants.

I went again in the evening, hoping to see the Taj glow pink as night fell. Crowds swarmed over the building and peopled its gardens. There were men in dark clothes, women in bright colours, fiancés photographing fiancées, college chums lying on the grass in casual, Greyfriars attitudes.

A moon rose, and the white building turned to creamy yellow, then pinky yellow, then grey. A voice over a loudspeaker announced closing time. Lights moved across the darkening lawns, and people thronged indolently between the cypresses and the artificial lakes. The creamy building faded with the daylight, the arched windows became dark, and one light below made shadows move across the lower walls.

I walked back a mile to the hotel along a street that was warm, dusty and deeply dark except for the bobbing lights of cycles and scooters. A rickshaw driver followed me doggedly, though I said I preferred to walk. "It's not poss-a-bul," he kept calling plaintively; then fifty yards from the gate of the hotel he turned and pedalled off with a despairing cry.

In two weeks we saw five great cities: Delhi, Jaipur, Agra, Varanasi and Kathmandu. We also visited Khajuraho to see the temples there, which are set in green landscape and are covered in erotic sculptures. From a distance they're like intricately carved termite mounds. Close up, the fine sandstone shows wrinkles, and teardrops, and the transparency of flimsy garments.

At Jaipur we stayed in a maharaja's palace decorated in cream and terracotta. We had tea on a veranda, served with excruciating slowness by gaunt individuals in slightly lopsided orange turbans with an organza crest like a cock's comb and a dangling scarf at the back.

Perhaps they were the gardeners and polo pony grooms of the maharaja, now pressed into service as waiters.

In Varanasi two of us defected from a guided tour to explore the holy city on our own.

In the main thoroughfare, between the cycle rickshaws and blaring scooters, corpses wrapped in red or white cotton were borne above the crowds. On the pavement people sold padlocks, or lottery tickets, or fruit, or twigs to clean teeth.

In a back street a pregnant goat ate a pile of dead flowers and dust; exhausted dogs slept on rubbish; householders swept dirt from one side of the street to the other. In the silk district each shop had a platform covered in white cotton on which the merchant sat, and his assistant threw down length after length of gold-encrusted fabric with a calculated and passionate flourish. In the district of curds each doorway housed a skillet of damp cheese. In the street of brass were gleaming buckets and pots. A house had red palm prints – suttee marks – on its walls. Dark doorways led to courtyards and temples. Pilgrims in white clothes walked solemnly past shrines, bound for the river.

A dark, small man with a monkey's face attached himself to us, and whenever we thought we'd lost him his alter ego would appear, a taller man in white pyjamas who was first seen on a bicycle, but then must have parked it somewhere. These two each explained, in reasonable tones edged with panic, "I am a guide. You see, that is my job," and offered to show us silk factories belonging to their uncles.

We had come to Varanasi to see dawn on the Ganges. We were called at 4.30am and rode through the squalor of the city, to take a flat-bottomed boat and float out onto the sulphurous, muddy river.

On the west bank people worshipped the rising sun. They seemed unconcerned that in front of the sun were boat loads of staring tourists. Brahmin priests sat under tatty, mushroom-like umbrellas. A circle of women chanted on a high platform. Energetic *dhobis* stood in the sedately swirling water and flung clothes onto stones, then spread them on the muddy bank to dry. Everywhere along the river's margins people washed in the water, immersed themselves, cleaned teeth, prayed, filled brass pots. Bulky black corpses of buffaloes moved in the river, and the body of a boy floated face downwards.

Beside the cremation ghats an acrid, choking smell floated out. A man shovelled ashes into a basket and tipped them into the river, where they swirled around the boats in bobbing black strings.

Later that morning we took an aeroplane to Kathmandu. Some people left India with relief. Nepal was prettier, and cooler, and the poor lived in houses and were warmly clothed. It was disorientating to find ourselves in a sort of Indian Switzerland, where hills were terraced for rice and the people had Mongolian features, and there were astonishing Buddhist *stupas* with glaring eyes. But the streets of

Kathmandu were just as ill-swept as those of Varanasi.

"I can forgive the poverty," said one of our party. "It's the dirt I can't forgive."

By this time the fury of shopping had come over all of us. Things were so cheap, and so beautifully made. Everywhere we went, we'd discuss what we'd bought and what we'd paid for it.

We bought, for £50, a sight of the Himalayas to carry home. We flew for an hour in a clear blue sky along the jagged frieze of mountains, taking turns to visit the cockpit and photograph Mount Everest.

Then we returned to Delhi to stay in the Taj Palace hotel for one more night before flying to London. The vast marble lobby welcomed us like home, though now there was a sexologists' congress there. Our window looked out on the same tattered shanty town we'd seen a lifetime ago.

Caroline Dilke was the winner of the 1984/85 *Sunday Times* Travel Writing competition. Her contribution is not a competition entry but a special report, commissioned by *The Sunday Times*, describing her prize journey to India and Nepal.

MALCOLM BROOKS*

PROPOSITIONS IN PERU

If you are blonde and looking for marriage, this is the place. Mind you, maybe not all the proposals will suit you. A four-foot-eight-inch, black-haired, fat, toothless Indian may not be everybody's idea of the perfect husband. But the fact remains that nowhere does a girl get propositioned (I'm sure some of the proposals were nearer propositions) more than in Peru. In all I had seven serious proposals and many more propositions – so many that I seriously considered dyeing my hair brown.

What brought me to a land so full of marital prospects? Well, it certainly wasn't to find a husband. After all I'm only seventeen, and although I'm not against the idea of wedded bliss I certainly can't see myself cooking *yukka* (Indian potatoes) over an open fire in the middle of the jungle for the rest of my days, and I certainly can't see myself having baby after baby throughout my now shortened life (forty-five is old here) and giving birth so casually. One woman had a baby in front of our eyes on a night train from Puno to Arequipa. There was very little help and not much fuss; the whole thing was over in twenty minutes.

So I didn't come to find a partner. Neither am I one of the more fortunate ones with money to enable me to while away three months in South America on a whim. I'm part of Operation Raleigh – you know, the boat thing, sailing round the world full of youngsters of all nationalities, all looking as though they are having a great time. Well let me tell you, it's bloody hard work. We were on a land-based project in the Amazon jungle, and if you can imagine digging holes for bridge foundations, cleaning out the lavatory pits and living for two months on *yukka,* rice, paw paw and beans which need soaking overnight and boiling for months to remove the poison, you may realise what I mean by hard work.

It's amazing how you can adapt, though. Before I left I had grown to love the little village of Rafael Balunde. In Peru deprivation really

*Malcolm Brooks compiled this report from the diaries of Deborah Stafford, venturer for Operation Raleigh in Peru.

means something. It's true there are some very rich, but the divide between them and the poor is much greater than anything I've ever seen.
There are enormous grand houses with cars and servants, and close by
shacks and shanty towns of unbelievable poverty. To be well off in
terms of the poor is to have two rooms in your shack and clothes to
wear. Beggars and thieves abound, and at that level who can attach
morality to survival?

We were assigned to the village to build bridges and store houses,
and give help to the natives generally. Access was through the jungle,
which was dark and almost impenetrable on either side of the very
muddy path. The village had been in existence for only four years and
there were some flooding problems. Operation Raleigh were also
operating three other projects – one at Tamba Parta in the rain forest,
which was mainly concerned with wildlife preservation; one at Huares
in the mountains, working with Indians; and one at Pacalppa, building
hovercraft ramps. I'm pleased to say the Rio Mayo project at Rafael
Balunde was the most successful, though it is easy to see how the
difficulties of terrain, climate and politics can easily foul up well-made
plans.

Three of my seven serious proposals came from the village, and
perhaps they were the most sincere. We got along well with the
Indians and learnt enough Spanish to communicate reasonably well. I
formed a particularly close relationship with Maria, who had two
adorable pretty children – Daisy, aged nine months, and Olga, aged
three. Her husband worked the maize field most of the day so I never
saw him; but Maria used to come to the clinic. We had a doctor there
called Ali, short for Alison, and I used to help her pulling teeth and
stitching wounds. Anyway, Maria always brought me three eggs –
very rare in the jungle, though there seemed to be chickens
everywhere. Maria had a lovely personality, bright and cheerful. She
was tiny and beautiful with lovely features and rich black glossy hair,
and her children had taken after her. I did quite a bit of teaching at the
school as well as helping in the clinic. The children were delighted
with jigsaws, colouring books, balloons and toys and we were amazed
how much they enjoyed themselves.

In the village there was a store owned by a woman called Rosa. She
was fairly old – about forty-two – and looked after a girl of thirteen
who had been orphaned. One day the girl came to the clinic complaining of sickness; she was three months pregnant. Rosa was absolutely
delighted and immediately started knitting. I asked who the father was
but nobody knew or even cared.

It was not all work. Occasionally we got some beer from Rosa's and
had a party playing stupid games and ended up romping in the muddy
river (carefully avoiding the piranhas).

A trip down to the nearest town, Moya Bamba, and a stay in a hotel was a great luxury – though it was an hour's trek through the jungle to the river, then three hours by *pequi pequi,* a long, very low river boat with a two-mile-an-hour top speed, and then a further hour to the town.

Perhaps the low point of my stay in the village was when I caught a touch of malaria. That, coupled with extremely sore festering mosquito bites, put me out of action for a week or so. I remember lying in my bunk at three in the morning with the huge insects zooming round and attacking me, thinking why on earth have I come to this god-forsaken place! Great – we built the bridges and the top brass and the British Ambassador came to open them. Lousy – we had to cook for 360 people. (But what a meal – coleslaw, stewed steak, potatoes, sweetcorn, rice, carrots, onions and corned beef. Apart from the rice it was super.)

We left the village on Monday – which Monday I don't know, as we had been in the jungle about two months and I'd lost track of time. My friend Claire came down with dysentery and had to be flown to hospital, but I was ready for the next part, the tourist bit. This started with a bus trip across the Andes. They were magnificent but the bus was a mess. It broke down three times for four hours at a time – brakes, springs and everything. Eventually it was changed and we finally arrived in Lima on Friday. Three days on a bus is no joke.

Time for some shopping and more proposals of marriage. One I really fancied. His name was Andy (or near enough), and he sold beads and things in the shopping street of Lima. He was taller than other Indians and good looking, although a bit of a hippy. Anyway, I turned him down. Claire joined me after her stint at the hospital (she seemed okay and raring to go again). We went to the Liverpool pub, which has pictures of the Beatles and plays their music all night.

We were now free to explore Peru for a couple of weeks and, to be honest, Claire and I did so much travelling in such a short time that much of it is a blur. I remember visiting Lake Titicaca, near Huares. Very beautiful, surrounded by huge snow-covered mountains. Nearby was the tombstones of Yungay where 40,000 had died in a volcanic eruption.

I was proposed to twice at least in Lima and had a few very scary moments being pursued by an Indian in a van. I nearly won a free flight (anywhere in Peru) as a bingo prize on my plane ride to Cuzco but was pipped at the deciding draw (the chap who won didn't propose to me; I was quite miffed). We couldn't miss the famous Inca ruins of Macchu Picchu but the five-hour train ride there and back was torture; we had to stand all the way. Another train journey of about eleven hours took us to Puno, which I thought was a horrid dirty town. We were warned that there was a ninety per cent chance of being robbed on this train, but we were lucky. I received another proposal on the reed island of Lake Titicaca but I didn't fancy his moustache. I got quite good at smiling and pretending ignorance. I sank into the reeds up to my knees and everybody thought it hilarious.

A big party in Lima signalled the end of what had been a unique experience and brought together all the friends we'd made. The thought of a journey home of fifty-five hours didn't bother me as it had when I was setting off for Peru three months earlier. Slowly the sadness of leaving the friends I had made, and Maria and all the other people in the village, changed into a longing to get home and I was absolutely delighted to see my mum and everybody when I arrived at Heathrow.